The New York Bartender's Guide

The New York Bartender's Guide

SALLY ANN BERK
GENERAL EDITOR

PHOTOGRAPHS BY GEORGE G. WIESER, JR.

BLACK DOG & LEVENTHAL PUBLISHERS
NEW YORK

Published by

Black Dog & Leventhal Publishers Inc.
151 W. 19th Street
New York, New York 10011

Distributed by

Workman Publishing Company
708 Broadway
New York, New York 10003

Manufactured in Hong Kong

ISBN: 1-884822-13-4

b c d e f g h

CONTENTS

INTRODUCTION

New York is the Empire State Building. It's the Statue of Liberty and the Chrysler Building. These are classics with style and perfection. Cocktails are Martinis and Gimlets, Margaritas and Manhattans. These drinks are also timeless masterpieces. They are quintessential luxuries and demand proper and consistent execution. The New York Bartender's Guide gives you the tools to make the perfect drink, brimming with more than 1,300 alcoholic and non-alcoholic recipes for traditional and up-to-the-moment concoctions, old stand-bys, and popular new drinks.

The New York Bartender's Guide contains all the drink recipes you will ever need plus time-tested tips from famous New York bartenders. Why New York? Because, after all, if you can't find it in New York, it probably doesn't exist! Here is some of the collected wisdom of our favorite bartenders—good advice for anyone wanting to learn about bartending, entertaining, or just creating a good drink.

FAVORITE DRINKS

Nicholas Mellas, bartender for 26 years, Gallagher's Steak House: *"My all-time favorite drink to make is a classic dry Martini with beautiful, extraordinary olives. Martinis have been drunk forever."*

Billy Steel, bartender for 15 years, '21' Club, Hudson River Club, Mesa Grill: *"The most poured drink at '21' was anything on the rocks, mostly Scotch. My favorite drink to make there was a classic Martini, with a little more vermouth than usual. At '21' they are into making drinks the way they should be made."*

Dale De Groff, bartender for 20 years, Head Bartender, The Rainbow Room, The Rainbow Promenade Restaurant/Bar: *"Looking out from the 65th floor over New York, people can't resist ordering Manhattans and Martinis."*

Peter Mellett, bartender for 15 years, Au Bar, Mesa Grill: *"I have watched the old standards fade from popularity, ordered only by folks of a certain age, only to be brought back into vogue. I saw a resurgence of the Martini as early as the late eighties, along with variations of it such as the Cosmopolitan, made famous at Odeon, in New York City."*

ON BARTENDING AT HOME

Peter Mellett: *"There is a big difference between mixing drinks at home and doing it at work. But in both instances people love to watch a bartender in action."*

Dale De Groff: *"Behind the bar we keep a juicer and have eliminated mixes. It is so important to have only fresh juices in your drinks, and at home this is easy."*

John Nathan, bartender for 10 years, Phoebe's: *"I've had to use all sorts of makeshift shakers at people's homes. Everyone loves drinks shaken and up but no one has a proper shaker. It's important to have a good shaker at home."*

TIPS AND TRENDS

Dale De Groff: *"As Head Bartender at The Rainbow Room I listed house drinks from famous old New York bar spots, and also included more modern classics. We got so much press for this list that I believe it was responsible for the 'retro' cocktail craze."*

John Nathan: *"The best tip I can give as a bartender is that you must make contact with your client immediately."*

Peter Mellett: *"All the up drinks are fun to make, Margaritas, Martinis, Gibsons, etc. It's interesting to note that if one person is drinking them, most of the bar will follow suit. They look fun to drink."*

Sarah Fearon, bartender for five years, Hi-Life Bar and Grill: *"Every party needs a host to make sure things flow well. As a bartender you have to host a killer party every night. The first step to making this experience incredible is inviting your clients to feel welcome."*

BAR ETIQUETTE AND ODDITIES

Billy Steel: *"Bartenders at '21' would come in wearing a suit and tie, carrying a briefcase with their bartending tools in it. They don't let you behind the bar there until you have trained for about five months, no matter what your background. This is real old-school, where bartending is a respected art."*

Nicholas Mellas: *"One of the most memorable things that happened during my time bartending was when Joe Namath,* *while eating at a table in the restaurant, came to the bar and started talking to some kids that were eating with their parents. He started to play football with the kids with the rolls on the table. They were tossing the rolls around the room, but no one minded too much because it was Joe Namath. All of a sudden he left the restaurant, came back with a football he had bought, signed it and gave it to the kids – he's a real gracious guy."*

John Nathan: *"I have found that the most effective way to sell a drink or beer special is to put it up on the board above the bar. No matter what we write, our specials sell. The power of suggestion is phenomenal."*

Billy Steel: *"The strangest thing I had to do as a bartender was at my first job, in this Mafioso bar called Paul's Lounge. I used to act as the middle man for bookies and the bar clientele. They would place the bets and make the payoffs through me. Bartending really goes beyond pouring a drink."*

John Nathan: *"Bartending in New York also poses its own challenge. I have an ongoing purse-snatching problem. So on top of all the regular elements, I keep an eye open for this guy who takes bags from around the bar. It's gotten to the point where he'll walk in, I'll sense him, and he'll wave to me as if to say 'Oops, you caught me this time, better leave now.' He dashes out only to return at another time."*

SETTING UP YOUR HOME BAR

Sally Ann Berk, amateur bartender: *"When I first came to New York City, I lived in a studio apartment not much larger than a good-sized walk-in closet. In the kitchen area there was barely enough room for food, plates, and other necessities, let alone a well-stocked bar. I still wanted to entertain, and found improvisation to be the answer to the space problem.*

Underneath the one window in the apartment was a large hole in the wall that had been cut out for a wall-unit air conditioner. I used that hole for a liquor cabinet/wine cellar. It was perfect."

THE BASICS FOR A SMALL BAR

Here are the "bar essentials" for a complete small bar. Nothing too fancy. Improvise and tailor your bar to the tastes of your friends and guests.

BEER, WINE AND SPIRITS

Beer, Lager (refrigerate)

Blended whiskey or Rye

Bourbon

Brandy

Gin

Pernod

Red wine, Cabernet Sauvignon and/or dry French

Rum, light

Scotch

Sherry, dry

Tequila, white

Triple Sec

Vermouth, dry and sweet

Vodka (keep in freezer)

White wine, dry French or California Chardonnay (refrigerate)

MIXERS (KEEP REFRIGERATED, USE FRESH FRUIT JUICES)

Cola

Cranberry juice

Diet soda

Ginger ale

Grapefruit juice

Lemon juice

Lemon-lime soda

Lime juice

Orange juice

Sparkling water

Tomato juice

Tonic water

GARNISHES AND CONDIMENTS

Angostura bitters

Bar sugar

Black pepper

Cocktail olives

Grenadine

Lemons

Limes

Maraschino cherries

Oranges

Tabasco sauce

Worcestershire sauce

GLASSWARE

Brandy snifter

Champagne flute

Cocktail glass

Highball glass

Old-Fashioned glass

Pilsner glass

Wine goblet

BARTENDING TOOLS

Bar spoon

Blender

Bottle opener

Citrus reamer

Corkscrew

Jigger

Measuring cup

Measuring spoons

Mixing glass

Paring knife

Standard shaker

Strainer

THE BASICS FOR A FULL HOME BAR

If you have enough room for a full bar, add the following components to those mentioned above. For mixers and ice, you may want to purchase a small refrigerator and keep it next to your liquor cabinet or bar. It is extremely convenient and saves time and space when you are entertaining.

BEER, WINE AND SPIRITS

Aguardiente

Ale (keep in refrigerator)

Amaretto

Amer Picon

Apple brandy

Aquavit

Armagnac

Benedictine

Brut Champagne

Calvados

Campari

Canadian whisky

Chartreuse, green and yellow

Cognac

Cointreau

Crème de Bananes

Crème de Cacao, light and dark

Crème de Cassis

Crème de Menthe, white and green

Crème de Noyaux

Curaçao, blue and white

Drambuie

Dubonnet, blanc and rouge

Eau de Framboise

Flavored vodkas (citrus, Cherry Heering, pepper, currant; keep in the freezer)

Galliano

Grand Marnier

Grappa

Irish Cream liqueur

Irish whiskey

Jagermeister

Kirschwasser

Lillet

Madeira

Maraschino liqueur

Peppermint Schnapps

Pernod

Pimm's No. 1

Poire

Port (ruby, tawny, and vintage)

Porter

Punt e Mes

Rock and Rye

Rum, Anejo, dark, Demerara, and gold

Sake

Sherry, fino and cream

Single malt Scotch

Silver tequila

Slivovitz

Sloe gin

Southern Comfort

Stout

Tequila, gold and silver

White Sambuca

Wishniak

MIXERS (KEEP REFRIGERATED)

Apple cider

Beef bouillon

Bitter lemon soda

Clamato juice

Coconut cream

Coffee

Ginger beer

Guava nectar

Half-and-Half

Peach nectar

Pineapple juice

Spring water, bottled

GARNISHES AND CONDIMENTS

Allspice

Apples

Bananas

Celery

Cinnamon, ground

Cinnamon sticks

Cocktail onions

Coriander

Cucumber

Eggs*

Honey

Horseradish

Margarita salt

Mint, fresh

Nutmeg, ground

Orange bitters

Orgeat (Almond) syrup

Passion fruit syrup

Peaches

Peychaud's Bitters

Pickled jalapeño peppers

Pineapple

Raspberry syrup

Raspberries

Rose's Lime Juice

Semi-sweet chocolate

Strawberries

Sugar cubes

Sugar syrup

Tamarind syrup

White pepper

Whole cloves

*PUBLISHER'S NOTE: Please use caution when using raw eggs in any of the recipes included in this book. Raw eggs have been known to cause salmonella poisoning.

GLASSWARE

Beer mug

Irish Coffee glass

Margarita glass

Pousse Café

Punch cup

Red wine glass

Sherry glass

Shot glass

Sour glass

White wine glass

BARTENDING TOOLS

Champagne stopper

Glass pitcher

Ice bucket

Ice tongs

Muddler or mortar and pestle

Punch bowl

A NOTE ON INGREDIENTS

Making a great cocktail depends not only on your technique but on using quality ingredients. It may be tempting to save a few dollars on a cheaper brand of gin, but your Martini will suffer for it. Using reconstituted lemon juice may be easier than squeezing fresh, but the taste of fresh juice is far superior. When bartending for guests, you must offer them the best.

You will notice that many of the recipes in this book call for fresh juice. A small electric citrus reamer makes squeezing citrus fruits a cinch and can be purchased for under $25 almost anywhere. If you must use prepared juices, buy "all natural," made without added sugar or syrups. Read the labels. Even cranberry juice cocktail can be found in most supermarkets prepared with grape juices for sweeteners instead of sugar or high-fructose corn syrup. Buy juices in glass bottles. If you buy citrus juices, go for the ones in the dairy case marked "not from concentrate."

When a recipe calls for spices, use freshly ground ones. Keep whole nutmeg and cinnamon sticks in your kitchen. You can use a nutmeg grater for both. Freshly ground pepper makes a Bloody Mary perfect, and a Margarita tastes much better when the glass is rimmed with the proper coarse salt.

Finding some of the more exotic ingredients may prove a challenge, but it is worth it. If you live in an urban area, you can find ingredients such as tamarind syrup and guava nectar at many Caribbean or Mexican grocery stores. Many natural food and specialty gourmet stores also carry hard-to-find components. Use mail-order gourmet catalogues, or call friends who may have access to more variety and would have them mailed to you. If you don't find what you're looking for, your grocer or liquor store manager will probably be happy to special order something for you.

GLOSSARY OF DRINK TERMS

Apéritif Traditionally, a drink served before a meal to stimulate the appetite such as a fortified or aromatized wine in a vermouth style. These include Byrrh, Dubonnet, Lillet, Campari, Pernod, Amer Picon, and St. Raphael. The term apéritif now refers more to the time the drink is served than what it consists of.

Aromatized Wine This includes vermouth (Italian and French types), and the quinined or other apéritif wines of various countries, whose alcohol content is 15 to 20 percent.

Bitters A flavor enhancer made from berries, roots, and herbs, usually used to provide a smoothness to biting whiskey. (See also section on Beers for Bitter)

Brandy A spirit aged in wood, obtained from a fermented mash of fruit or the distillation of wine.

Cobbler A tall drink served in a collins or highball glass, filled with crushed ice, wine or liquor, and garnished with fresh fruit and mint sprigs. The traditional cobbler is made with sherry, pineapple syrup, and fresh fruit garnishes.

Collins A tall glass filled with ice, sugar, a spirit, citrus juice, and club soda or seltzer.

Cooler Usually served in a tall glass such as a collins or highball, consisting of a carbonated beverage such as ginger ale or club soda, a wine or spirit, and a lime or orange rind cut in a continuous spiral, hooking over the rim of the glass.

Daisy An oversize cocktail such as a Margarita, made with proportionally more alcohol, sweetened with fruit syrup, and served over crushed ice.

Dry A term used for wine, liquor, or a cocktail to indicate a lack of sweetness. For example, a dry Martini is one with very little vermouth, which is the fortified wine that adds sweetness to the spirit.

Falernum A syrup from the Caribbean made of mixed fruits, sugar cane, and spices, used to sweeten mixed drinks.

Fix A drink mixed in the serving glass, may be another name for a highball. Always served over a lot of ice.

Fizz A drink named for the siphon bottle that added "fizz" to a recipe of sugar, citrus juice, and, traditionally, gin.

Flip A cold, creamy drink made with eggs, sugar, citrus juice, and a spirit. It got its name in Colonial times, when a hot flip iron was used to mull the ingredients in the drink.

Fortified Wine It includes Sherry, Port, Madeira, Marsala, etc.

The alcohol content is between 14 and 24 percent.

Grog A rum-based drink originally served to sailors. The contemporary version consists of rum, fruit, and sugar.

Julep Made with crushed ice, usually Kentucky bourbon, sugar, and mint leaves.

Liqueur A beverage naturally processed or manufactured by adding a flavoring to a distilled spirit. The flavor accents include, but are not limited to, almond, strawberry, orange, coffee, hazelnut, mint, and chocolate.

Mist Spirits added to a full glass of crushed ice.

Mull Drinks where the ingredients are heated for thorough blending.

Neat Term for serving a spirit straight, in a glass without any ice or mixers.

Negus A hot, sweet wine drink traditionally made with Sherry or Port.

On the rocks Term denoting wine or spirits poured over ice cubes.

Pousse-Café Made from several liqueurs and cordials, each having a different weight and color so when poured one on top of another, they layer and "float."

Rickey A drink consisting of lime or lemon juice, mixed with gin or some other spirit and club soda, usually with no added sweetener.

Shooter A mixed drink or shot of some kind of spirit, swallowed in one gulp.

Sling A tall drink usually served cold, made with spirits, lemon juice, and sugar, and topped off with club soda.

Sour A short drink made with lime or lemon juice, sugar, and spirits.

Spirit A beverage made from the distillation of a liquid containing alcohol. The alcohol content of the original liquid matters very little, as the distillation process separates all the alcohol out from the liquid. Congeners, flavor compounds, may also be separated from the original liquid along with the alcohol. The congeners provide the spirit with its distinct characteristics.

Swizzle This was originally a tall rum beverage filled with cracked ice and stirred with a long spoon, twig, or stirring instrument until the glass was frosty. These days, any tall drink made with spirits and crushed ice and stirred with a rod until frosty is called a "swizzle."

Toddy Originally this was a hot mixture of spirits, sugar, and spices like cloves and cinnamon, lemon peel, and water, served in a tall glass. Today it may be served cold, with any combination of spirits, spices, and ice.

Variety A term used to classify a type of grape used in the production of wine. Varieties is the term for types of grapes whose juice or wine is blended together. The term varietal wine means one grape variety.

Whisky A spirit aged in wood, produced from the distillation of a fermented mash of grain. Examples are Canadian whisky, Irish whiskey, Scotch whisky, Rye whisky, and Bourbon whiskey.

A NOTE ON THE RECIPES

Many of these cocktails are served "straight up" in a cocktail glass. You may prepare them "on the rocks" if you prefer. Simply follow the recipe, then strain over ice cubes into an Old-Fashioned glass.

These recipes make generous cocktails. If you want a short cocktail, halve the recipe, split the drink with a friend, or save the rest in the refrigerator.

Many people adore gin, but many do not. The gin drinks in this book are varied and interesting, but you may substitute vodka in almost any of the gin recipes. They will be different, but delicious, although the special gin flavor will be lost.

If you crave a Mint Julep but are out of bourbon, try substituting another whisky in its place. You may try this with other whisky recipes. Rye is a decent substitute for bourbon; Canadian whisky is also a good substitute for blended or American whiskey. Experiment, but keep in mind that the whiskey called for in the recipe is the preferred and recommended one unless others are mentioned. There is really no acceptable replacement for Scotch.

Tequila is also in a class by itself, although some of the tequila drinks will work as rum drinks, and vice-versa. Again, experiment, invent your own specialties. Bartending is an evolving art form.

GLASS ICON KEY

Almost every drink recipe has an icon next to it denoting the proper glassware to use. The alcoholic drink icons are blue, the non-alcoholic drink icons are green.

The following is a key to the glassware specified by the icons.

Balloon wine glass

Beer mug

Brandy snifter

Champagne flute

Cocktail glass

Coffee mug

Collins glass

Double Old-Fashioned glass

Highball glass

Old-Fashioned glass

Parfait glass

Pitcher

Pony

Pousse Café

Red wine glass

Sherry glass

Shot glass

Sour glass

MEASUREMENTS

Spirits

OLD BOTTLE SIZE	OLD U.S. MEASURE	NEW U.S.. MEASURE	METRIC MEASURE
Miniature	1.6 oz.	1.7 oz.	50 ml.
Half pint	8.0 oz.	6.8 oz.	200 ml.
Pint	16.0 oz.	16.9 oz.	500 ml.
Fifth	25.6 oz.	25.4 oz.	750 ml.
Quart	32.0 oz.	33.8 oz.	1 liter
Half gallon	64.0 oz.	59.2 oz.	1.75 liter

Wine

NAME	U.S. MEASURE	METRIC MEASURE
Split	6.3 oz.	187 ml.
Tenth	12.7 oz.	373 ml.
Fifth	25.4 oz.	750 ml.
Quart	33.8 oz.	1 liter
Magnum	50.7 oz.	1.5 liters
Double magnum	101.4 oz.	3 liters

Bar Measurement

1 dash	$1/32$ ounce
1 teaspoon	$1/8$ ounce
1 tablespoon	$3/8$ ounce
1 pony	1 ounce
1 jigger	$1 1/2$ ounces
1 wine glass	4 ounces
1 split	6 ounces
1 cup	8 ounces

CALORIE COUNT (APPROXIMATE AMOUNTS)

ALCOHOLIC BEVERAGE	AMOUNT	CALORIES (KCAL)
Beer		
Regular	12 fl. oz.	146
Light	12 fl. oz.	100
Cider, fermented	1 fl. oz.	12

DISTILLED SPIRIT	AMOUNT	CALORIES (KCAL)
Gin, Rum, Vodka, Whiskey		
(80 proof)	1½ fl. oz.	96
(86 proof)	1½ fl. oz.	104
(90 proof)	1½ fl. oz.	109
(94 proof)	1½ fl. oz.	115
(100 proof)	1½ fl. oz.	123

LIQUEUR	AMOUNT	CALORIES (KCAL)
Brandy, Cognac	1½ fl. oz.	75
Coffee liqueur (Kahlua)	1½ fl. oz.	176
Crème de menthe	1½ fl. oz.	186
Curaçao	½ fl. oz.	60

WINE	AMOUNT	CALORIES (KCAL)
Champagne (Sparkling wine)	4 fl. oz.	90
Sherry, dry	2 fl. oz.	84
Table, red	3½ fl. oz.	74
Table, rosé	3½ fl. oz.	73
Table, white	3½ fl. oz.	70
Vermouth, dry	1 fl. oz.	33
Vermouth, sweet	1 fl. oz.	44

MIXERS	AMOUNT	CALORIES (KCAL)
Club soda	12 fl. oz.	0
Cola	12 fl. oz.	144
Cranberry juice	3 fl. oz.	54
Diet cola	12 fl oz.	0
Fresh lemon juice	1 fl. oz.	8
Fresh lime juice	1 fl. oz.	8
Fresh orange juice	2 fl. oz.	28
Ginger ale	12 fl.	124
Heavy cream	1 tbs.	53
Pineapple juice, unsweetened	2 fl. oz.	34
Tomato juice	2 fl. oz.	12
Tonic water	12 fl. oz.	113

A GUIDE TO WINE

Wine is quickly becoming more popular in many drinking establishments as well as at home. People have moved away from jug wines and white wine spritzers, and are experimenting with a full variety of reds, whites, rosés, and sparkling wines from various countries. The world's most popular wines are produced in France, Italy, Spain, Portugal, Germany, the United States (especially California, New York, Oregon, Washington, and Texas), Argentina, Chile, Australia, and New Zealand.

RED WINE (from Judson Grill)

Wine is not as confusing as it may appear. Many have abandoned the old rule that white must be drunk with fish and red with meat. Use your imagination! If you come across a spicy red wine that complements a salmon dish, go ahead and drink it. Focus on the characteristics of a particular region and variety of grape, and get creative. A simple rule to follow is this: light wines go best with subtler, more delicate foods; full-bodied wines go best with spicier, more robust foods. Learn for yourself how your palate responds to a dry or a sweet wine.

White wine should be served at about 55° F; rosé wines and Beaujolais red wines at about 60°F. The key is to avoid chilling a wine to the point where its flavors become masked. Red wines should be served at room temperature and their flavors are enhanced when you remove the cork and let the wine stand in the bottle or in glasses before drinking. This permits it to "breathe." When wine is aerated, its tannic or astringent flavors will soften and mellow. Generally, the older and better the wine, the more important "breathing" becomes.

The following is an explanation of how various countries categorize their wines. The most common classifications are by region and by grape variety, though wine classifications differ from country to country.

FRENCH WINES

The French wines here are grouped according to appellation which refers to the town name or place of origin. The main regions are: Bordeaux, Loire, Rhône, Burgundy, Alsace, and Champagne. The best wines are classified by *Appellations d'Origine Contrôllées*, which is a term used by the French government to guarantee the origin and quality of the wine.

Bordeaux

Red Bordeaux Bordeaux is a 260,000-acre wine producing area that yields millions of bottles each year.

The Bordeaux wine-maker blends Cabernet Sauvignon, Merlot, Cabernet Franc, Malbec, and Petit Verdot grapes into combinations that will yield the best vintage blend.

SELECTED POPULAR REGIONS:

Médoc/ Haut Médoc	St. Emilion
Pomerol	Graves
Margaux	

White Bordeaux Made primarily from the Sauvignon Blanc grape.

SELECTED POPULAR REGIONS:

Graves	Sauternes/Barsac
Entre-Deux-Mers	

Loire

The majority of these wines made from the Chenin Blanc and Sauvignon Blanc grape are white, though some are rosé, red, or sparkling.

SELECTED POPULAR REGIONS:

Sancerre	Pouilly-Fumé
Vouvray	Coteaux Du Layon
Muscadet	Chinon

Rhône Valley

Famous for full-flavored reds, typically bigger and heavier. These wines contain up to thirteen different types of grapes, the Syrah grape being the most common.

SELECTED POPULAR REGIONS:

Côte Rotie	Hermitage
Cornas	Châteauneuf-du-Pape
Condrieu	St. Joseph
Côtes du Rhône	

Burgundy

Red Burgundy The main grapes used to produce these wines are Pinot Noir and Gamay.

SELECTED POPULAR REGIONS:

Côte de Nuits	Beaujolais
Gevrey-Chambertin	Volnay
Chambolle Musigny	Mâconnais
Côte de Beaune	

White Burgundy Made mostly from Chardonnay and Aligoté grapes.

SELECTED POPULAR REGIONS:

Chablis	Meursault
Montrachet	Aloxe Corton
Côte de Nuits	Mâconnais

Alsace

These wines are made primarily from the Riesling grape and the Gewürztraminer grape. They are similar to German-style wines, but drier.

Champagne

Wine makers of this region blends three grapes, Chardonnay, Pinot Noir, and Pinot Meunier. Champagne ages in the bottle along with yeast cells to help develop its complex, toasty character and carbonation. Its yeasty body and relative dryness vary from producer to producer. When the wine is properly chilled, the Champagne bubbles should be very active and tiny. "Brut" Champagne is very, very dry; "Extra dry" is a bit sweeter; "Dry" or "Sec" is medium-sweet; and "Demi-sec" is sweet.

Non-Vintage Brut A blend of wines made in two or more years.

Vintage Brut Made in an occasional outstanding vintage, aged five or more years.

Rosé Champagne The pink tint comes from a small portion of red juice added at the time of fermentation. Rosés are usually richer and more flavorful than other Champagnes.

ITALIAN WINES

Italian wines are named either for the grape variety used or for the towns near where the grapes are grown. The categorizations below are first by region; then, within each region, are town and varietal.

Piedmont

The most widely planted grapes in this region are the Nebbiolo and the Barbera. The wines are labeled by varietal and then by place, as in as Barbera d'Alba, Barbera d'Asti, Nebbiolo d'Alba, etc.

Barolo This red wine is made mostly from the Nebbiolo variety. All Barolos must spend at least two years in barrels of chestnut or oak.

Barbaresco Produced from the Nebbiolo vines, but variations in the soil of this area create different wines.

Tuscany

Chianti The region is subdivided into seven districts, and the wine is made from several grape varieties. The principle grape is the Sangiovese; then comes the Canaiolo Nero; the white Trebbiano Tuscano; and Malvasia del Chianti.

Types of Chianti include a wine light in body and in color, made for early consumption (Chianti); a wine of better quality whose tannins soften after about a year of aging (Chianti Vecchio); a high-quality wine with a higher alcohol content, which takes longer to mellow (Chianti Classico); and Chianti Riserva, released after an additional two years in the barrel.

Brunello di Montalcino A red varietal wine made exclusively from a clone of the Sangiovese grape, locally called Brunello.

Vino Nobile de Montepulciano This wine uses the same grapes as Chianti but requires a two-year minimum oak aging. If the wine is labeled Riserva, there is a three to four-year aging minimum.

Veneto

Valpolicella

Soave

Italian White Wines (various regions)

Trentino

Alto Adige

Friuli

GERMAN WINES

The Riesling grape accounts for 20 percent of total plantings. The Müeller-Thurgau grape is the biggest producer, and constitutes 27 percent of Germany's grapes. This particular grape ripens earlier than others, producing light-bodied, highly aromatic wines. The Silvaner grape makes up 11 percent of total plantings. The Gewürztraminer makes a very spicy wine. The Ruländer, or Pinot of Burgundy, produces wines with intense flavor and full aroma.

German wines range from very dry to very sweet and are rated on their bottles along a six-level "ripeness" scale. Kabinett wines are the driest, and Eiswein, whose grapes are harvested after a deep frost and frozen, are the sweetest.

SPANISH WINES

The most important wine-producing regions of Spain are Rioja and Valdepeñas.

Rioja

This region has three wine-growing districts. The Rioja Alta produces wines with high acidity. The Rioja Alavesa produces fruity wines. The Rioja Baja is the hottest district and produces wines high in alcohol. Wines from Rioja are traditionally blends of the harvest of all three districts.

The red grapes of Rioja are the Tempranillo, Garnacha Tinta (Grenache), Graciano, and Mazuelo. The main white wine grape is the Viura, which is blended with Garnacha Blanca and Malvasia.

Valdepeñas

This central region produces wines less delicate than the wines of the north, and are popular as carafe wines in Madrid. The popular red grape is the Cencibel, and the white is the Airen.

Sherry

Spain is known for its Sherries which are fortified wines. Jerez has been famous for its Sherry production throughout the centuries of the driest to the sweetest wines.

PORTUGUESE WINES

Portugal produces mainly Port and table wines.

Port

Vintage Port This fortified wine has a deep ruby color.

Ruby and Tawny Ports These are blended wines. Ruby Port has a bright ruby color. Tawny Port is paler and usually drier.

Late Bottled Vintage (LBV) LBV is a Tawny Port from a single good year that remains in a cask and is not blended.

Table Wines

Colares dry white wine

Bucelas dry red wine

Vinho Verde white, red, or rosé always light.

Madeira

A Portuguese island in the Atlantic off the North African coast gives Madeira its name. Madeira wines range from very dry to very sweet.

UNITED STATES WINES

The most popular wine-producing regions in America are California, the Northwest, and New York. There are, however, some lesser well-known wine-makers in Texas, Idaho, New Mexico, and Virginia, among other places. The basic identifier of American wines is the type of grape. Grape types are very important in the classification of American wines.

Red Wines

Pinot Noir The finest Pinot Noirs are light in color. Oregon is fast-becoming known for its Pinot Noirs. This grape is the American version of a Red Burgundy.

Merlot This wine has an oaky richness because of its oak-barrel fermentation proceess.

Cabernet Sauvignon These wines have the same basic characteristics as Red Bordeaux from France, because they are made from the same primary grape.

Zinfandel Similar to the French Rhône wines. It is a versatile food wine.

White Wines

Sauvignon Blanc Made from the same grapes as White Bordeaux from France.

Chardonnay This wine may be made in a medium-bodied style, or a buttery, oak-enhanced style. The difference in characteristic is due to fermentation techniques. It is made from the same grape as the French White Burgundy.

Gewürztraminer This is a slightly sweet and spicy wine.

Rosé wines Wines containing any red coloring are classified as red wines. The coloring comes from the grape skins during fermentation. Wines only come in white and red — and red wines vary from pink rosés to deep inky reds.

Sparkling Wines

These wines are made like French Champagne, but cannot legally be called Champagne. California sparkling wines have more of a fruit accent than French Champagnes.

ARGENTINIAN WINES

The three principle wine regions of Argentina are Mendoza, San Juan, and Río Negro. The varietals used for red table wines are the Criolla, Malbec, Cabernet Sauvignon, Barbera, Petite Sirah, Pinot Noir, Tempranilla, Merlot, Sangiovese, and Lambrusco. White table wines use the Criolla, Sémillon, Sauvignon Blanc, Pinot Blanc, Riesling, Chardonnay, and Trebbiano. Fortified and dessert wines are made from Malvasia, Muscat of Alexandria, and Pedro Ximenez. The most widely produced wines of the region are made from a blend of Criolla, Malbec, and Barbera grapes.

CHILEAN WINES

The three principle wine-producing regions are divided among the Chilean provinces as follows:

Atacama and Coquimbo The wines from this northern area are mainly sweet, fortified types with a high alcohol content.

Aconcagua to Talca These central provinces produce the best table wines of Chile.

Maule to Bío Bío These southern provinces produce the bulk of the country's wine.

The red wine producers use mostly the Cabernet Sauvignon, Malbec, Cabernet Franc, Merlot, Pinot Noir, and Petit Verdot grapes. The white varieties most used are the Sauvignon Blanc, Sémillon, Pinot Blanc, Chardonnay, Trebbiano, Riesling, and a specifically Chilean variety, Loca Blanca.

AUSTRALIAN WINES

Australian wines are produced in South Australia, New South Wales, Victoria, Western Australia, and Tasmania. Many varieties of grapes are grown, but if a wine is varietally labeled, there must be a minimum of 80 percent of the named grape in the wine.

Shiraz is the most widely planted grape for the production of red table and fortified wines. Cabernet Sauvignon, Merlot, and Pinot Noirs are also used for red wine production. The white wine varieties include: Sémillon, Chardonnay, Rhine Riesling, Sultana and Muscat Gordo Blanco, Traminer, Doradillo, Palomino, and Pedro Ximenez.

NEW ZEALAND WINES

New Zealand is composed of two large islands, North Island and South Island. The biggest wine-growing areas are Marlborough on South Island, and Poverty and Hawkes Bays on North Island. White grape varieties account for more than 80 percent of the total grape plantings in New Zealand. In addition, there are Riesling-Sylvaner, Chardonnay, Gewürztraminer, Savignon Blanc, and Rhine Riesling. Red varietals include Pinot Noir, Cabernet Sauvignon, Pinotage (a hybrid of Pinot Noir and Cinsaut), and Shiraz.

BEER

Beer comes in many flavors and styles, from domestic and imported producers as well as an increasing number of micro-breweries. Beer is a fermented beverage made from malted barleys and other starchy cereals, which gets its bitter flavor from hops. During fermentation the yeast sinks to the bottom; therefore, beer is known as a bottom-fermentation brew. Beer is a generic term for all malt beverages. The various types of beer are as follows:

Ale Sharp and strong with a fruity characteristic, it is more bitter than beer. Ale is a top-fermentation brew because it is fermented at a higher temperature, causing the yeast to rise to the top.

Bitter Usually more acidic and bronze-colored, it is a well-hopped ale.

Bock Beer or Bockbier This is a brew of heavy beer, sweeter and darker than regular beer.

Dry Beer This beer is cold-filtered, leaving no aftertaste.

Lager This is a light-bodied, bright, clear, sparkling beer brewed from malt, hops, water—and in some cases

BEER (from Pete's Tavern)

made from cereals such as cracked rice or corn grits. The brew is fermented, lagered (stored) for aging, and carbonated. All American beers are of the lager type.

Malt Liquor This is a malt beverage that is brewed like beer but usually has a higher alcohol content. The color is pale and light.

Pilsner A term used for light colored beers. They are all bright, light, and lagered.

Porter This is a variation of stout, but is lower in alcohol, with a bittersweet taste and a dark color.

Stout A very dark ale that is slightly bitter and malty. Roasted barley is added to flavor and color the brew.

Drink recipes are organized alphabetically by name and are cross-referenced by ingredient in the index. Amounts are listed in parts and then parenthetically in ounces, for easy proportion adjustment. Icons appear next to each recipe designating the proper glassware for each drink. Blue icons denote alcoholic drinks, green icons denote non-alcoholic drinks.

ABBEY

3 parts gin (1½ oz.)
3 parts Lillet (1½ oz.)
2 parts orange juice (1 oz.)
2 dashes orange bitters
Maraschino cherry or orange peel

Pour all ingredients except cherry or peel into cocktail shaker. Strain over cracked ice. Garnish with cherry or orange peel.

ACAPULCO

4 parts light rum (2 oz.)
1 part Cointreau or triple sec (½ oz.)
1 part fresh lime juice (½ oz.)
bar sugar (1 tsp. or ⅛ oz.)
1 egg white
1 sprig fresh mint

Combine rum, Cointreau, lime juice, sugar and egg white into a cocktail shaker half filled with ice cubes. Shake well. Strain into a glass almost filled with ice cubes. Garnish with mint.

ACAPULCO CLAM DIGGER

3 parts Tequila (1½ oz.)
6 parts tomato juice (3 oz.)
6 parts clam juice (3 oz.)
Horseradish (¾ tbsp.)
Tabasco sauce to taste
Worcestershire sauce to taste
Splash of fresh lemon juice
Slice of lemon or lime
Note: Clamato juice (6 oz.) may be substituted for the tomato and clam juices.

Mix all ingredients in glass with cracked ice. Garnish with slice of lemon or lime

ADONIS

6 parts dry sherry (3 oz.)
2 parts sweet vermouth (1 oz.)
Dash orange bitters
Orange peel

Mix sherry, vermouth and bitters in cocktail shaker with ice. Strain into chilled glass. Twist orange peel over glass and drop.

AFFINITY

2 parts dry vermouth (1 oz.)
2 parts sweet vermouth (1 oz.)
2 parts scotch (1 oz.)
3 – 6 dashes Angostura bitters

Stir all ingredients together in a mixing glass and strain into chilled cocktail glass.

AFTER DINNER COCKTAIL

2 parts apricot brandy (1 oz.)
2 parts triple sec or Cointreau (1 oz.)
Juice of one lime
Slice of lime

Pour brandy, triple sec and lime juice into a cocktail shaker. Strain into cocktail glass and garnish with lime slice.

A.J.

3 parts applejack or Calvados (1½ oz.)
2 parts grapefruit juice (1 oz.)

Mix ingredients in cocktail shaker and strain into chilled cocktail glass.

ALABAMA SLAMMER

2 parts amaretto (1 oz.)
2 parts Southern Comfort (1 oz.)
1 part sloe gin (½ oz.)
Splash of fresh lemon juice

Stir all ingredients except lemon juice in a highball glass over ice. Add the lemon juice.

ALABAMA SLAMMER

ALASKA

4 parts gin (2 oz.)
1 part green Chartreuse (½ oz.)
3 dashes orange bitters
Lemon twist

Stir all of the ingredients except the lemon twist in a mixing glass with ice. Strain into chilled cocktail glass and garnish with lemon twist.

ALBERMARLE FIZZ

4 parts gin (2 oz.)
1 part fresh lemon juice (½ oz.)
Raspberry syrup (1 tsp.)
Dash of Framboise
Sparkling water

Mix all ingredients, but sparkling water, with cracked ice in a cocktail shaker. Strain into a highball glass over ice cubes and fill the glass with sparkling water.

ALEXANDER

2 parts gin (1 oz.)
2 parts crème de cacao (1 oz.)
2 parts half-and-half (1 oz.)
Nutmeg to taste (freshly ground)

Combine all ingredients, except the nutmeg, with crushed ice in a cocktail shaker and mix well. Strain into a chilled cocktail glass and sprinkle with freshly ground nutmeg.

30

ALEXANDER'S SISTER

3 parts gin (1½ oz.)
2 parts crème de menthe (white or green) (1 oz.)
2 parts half-and-half (1 oz.)
Nutmeg to taste (freshly ground)

Combine all ingredients, except the nutmeg, with crushed ice in a cocktail shaker and mix well. Strain into a chilled cocktail glass and sprinkle with freshly ground nutmeg.

ALGONQUIN

3 parts American blended whiskey (1½ oz.)
1 part dry vermouth (½ oz.)
2 parts pineapple juice (1 oz.)

In a cocktail shaker, combine all ingredients with ice cubes and shake well. Strain into a chilled cocktail glass.

ALGONQUIN BLOODY MARY

4 parts vodka (2 oz.)
8 parts tomato juice (4 oz.)
Salt to taste
Pepper to taste (freshly ground)
Juice of half a lime
Worcestershire sauce (1½ tsp.)
6 – 8 dashes Tabasco sauce
1 lime wedge

Combine all ingredients, except the lime wedge, in a cocktail shaker filled with ice. Shake quickly (about 9 to 10 times, as not to cause the tomato juice to separate). Strain into a highball glass over ice. Drop in the lime wedge.

ALHAMBRA ROYALE

3 parts cognac (1½ oz.)
Hot chocolate (1 cup)
1 wide slice of orange peel
Whipped cream (optional)

Fill mug nearly to the brim with hot chocolate. Twist the orange peel over the mug and drop in. Warm cognac in a ladle over hot water, ignite, and pour carefully while still flaming, into the mug. Stir. Top with a dollop of whipped cream if you wish.

ALLEGHENY

3 parts bourbon (1½ oz.)
2 parts dry vermouth (1 oz.)
Blackberry-flavored brandy (1 tbsp.)
Lemon juice (2 tsp.)
Lemon twist

Shake all ingredients but lemon peel with ice in cocktail shaker. Strain into chilled cocktail glass. Garnish with lemon twist.

ALLEN COCKTAIL

3 parts gin (1½ oz.)
1 part maraschino cherry liqueur (½ oz.)
Lemon juice (1½ tsp.)

Combine ingredients in cocktail shaker and shake well with ice. Strain into cocktail glass.

ALLIES

2 parts gin (1 oz.)
2 parts dry vermouth (1 oz.)
Kummel or Jagermeister (¾ tsp.)

Stir all ingredients with cracked ice in a cocktail shaker. Pour into chilled old-fashioned glass.

ALMOND COCKTAIL

4 parts gin (2 oz.)
2 parts dry vermouth (1 oz.)
1 part peach brandy (½ oz.)
Kirsch (1 tsp.)
1 part sugar syrup (½ oz.)
6 almond slivers

Warm gin in a mixing glass. Add peach brandy, sugar syrup and almond slivers. Chill mixture. Pour into chilled old-fashioned glass filled with ice cubes. Add remaining ingredients and stir well.

ALLEGHENY

ALOHA

3 parts rum cream liqueur
(1½ oz.)
2 parts dark rum (1 oz.)
1 part fresh lime juice (½ oz.)
4 parts pineapple juice (2 oz.)
4 parts fresh orange juice (2 oz.)
2 parts coconut syrup (1 oz.)
Small scoop vanilla ice cream
Pineapple spear

Mix all ingredients except pineapple
spear in blender with cracked ice. Be
careful not to over mix or mixture will
be runny. Pour into chilled hurricane
glass and garnish with pineapple
spear.

AMARETTO AND
CREAM

4 parts amaretto (2 oz.)
4 parts light cream or half-and-half
(2 oz.)

Combine ingredients with cracked ice
in a cocktail shaker and shake well.
Strain into chilled cocktail glass.

32

AMARETTO COFFEE

1 cup hot coffee (8 oz.)
3 parts amaretto (1½ oz.)
Whipped cream (optional)
Ground coriander

Pour amaretto into hot coffee and stir. Top with whipped cream if you like and sprinkle with ground coriander.

AMARETTO MIST

4 parts amaretto (2 oz.)
Lemon twist

Pack an old-fashioned glass with crushed ice. Pour the amaretto into the glass and garnish with lemon twist.

AMARETTO SOUR

4 parts amaretto (2 oz.)
2 parts fresh lemon juice (1 oz.)
Orange slice

Shake amaretto and lemon juice well in a cocktail shaker. Strain into chilled sour glass. Garnish with orange slice.

AMARETTO STINGER

4 parts amaretto (2 oz.)
2 parts white crème de menthe (1 oz.)

Shake ingredients well in cocktail shaker. Strain over cracked ice into chilled cocktail glass.

AMBROSIA

3 parts brandy (1½ oz.)
3 parts apple brandy (1½ oz.)
Raspberry syrup (½ tsp.)
Chilled champagne or sparkling wine
Fresh raspberries

Pour both brandies and syrup into a cocktail shaker with cracked ice. Shake well. Strain into chilled white wine glass. Top off with champagne. Drop in a few raspberries.

AMERICAN BEAUTY

3 parts brandy (1½ oz.)
2 parts dry vermouth (1 oz.)
2 parts fresh orange juice (1 oz.)
2 – 3 dashes grenadine
2 – 3 dashes white crème de menthe
1 part port (1 oz.)

Shake all ingredients, except the port, in a cocktail shaker with cracked ice. Strain into chilled cocktail glass. Float the port on top.

AMERICAN FLYER

3 parts light rum (1½ oz.)
Fresh lime juice (1 tbsp.)
Sugar syrup (½ tsp.)
Champagne or sparkling wine

Combine the rum, lime juice and sugar syrup in a cocktail shaker with cracked ice. Shake well. Strain into a chilled white wine glass and top off with champagne.

AMERICAN ROSE

3 parts brandy (1½ oz.)
Grenadine (1 tsp.)
½ fresh peach, peeled and mashed
Pernod (½ tsp.)
Champagne or sparkling wine
Small wedge of fresh peach

Mix all ingredients, except the champagne and peach slice, in a cocktail shaker. Pour the mixture into a chilled white wine glass. Top off with champagne and stir gently. Garnish with peach wedge.

AMERICANO

3 parts sweet vermouth (1½ oz.)
3 parts Campari (1½ oz.)
Sparkling water
Lemon peel

Pour vermouth and Campari into a chilled highball glass over ice cubes. Fill with sparkling water and stir. Garnish with lemon peel.

AMARETTO SOUR

AMER PICON COCKTAIL

4 parts Amer Picon (2 oz.)
2 parts fresh lime juice (1 oz.)
Grenadine (1 tsp.)

Pour all ingredients into cocktail shaker with cracked ice and shake well. Strain into chilled cocktail glass.

ANATOLE COFFEE

1 part cognac (½ oz.)
1 part coffee liqueur (½ oz.)
1 part Frangelico (½ oz.)
12 parts iced coffee (6 oz.)
Whipped cream
Chocolate shavings

Mix all ingredients, except whipped cream and chocolate shavings, with a little cracked ice in a blender. Pour into chilled white wine glass. Top with whipped cream and sprinkle with chocolate shavings.

ANCHORS AWEIGH

3 parts bourbon (1½ oz.)
Triple sec (2 tsp.)
Peach brandy (2 tsp.)
Cherry liqueur (2 tsp.)
Half-and-half (2 tbsp.)

Mix all ingredients with cracked ice in cocktail shaker or blender. Pour into a chilled old-fashioned glass.

ANDALUSIA

4 parts dry sherry (2 oz.)
2 parts brandy (1 oz.)
2 parts light rum (1 oz.)
Angostura bitters (¼ tsp.)

Combine all ingredients in a mixing glass with ice cubes. Stir well. Strain into chilled cocktail glass.

ANGEL FACE

3 parts gin (1½ oz.)
1 part apricot brandy (½ oz.)
1 parts apple brandy (½ oz.)

Combine all ingredients and shake well in cocktail shaker with cracked ice. Strain into chilled cocktail glass.

ANGEL'S DELIGHT

½ part grenadine (¼ oz.)
½ part triple sec (¼ oz.)
½ part sloe gin (¼ oz.)
½ part half-and half (¼ oz.)

Pour ingredients into glass in order given, carefully so each each floats on top of the previous one without mixing.

ANGEL'S KISS

½ part white crème de cacao
(¼ oz.)
½ part sloe gin (¼ oz.)
½ part brandy (¼ oz.)
½ part half-and-half (¼ oz.)

Pour ingredients into glass in order given, carefully so each floats on top of the previous one without mixing.

ANGEL'S TIT

½ part white crème de cacao
(¼ oz.)
½ part maraschino cherry liqueur
(¼ oz.)
½ part half-and-half (¼ oz.)
Maraschino cherry

Pour ingredients into glass in order given, carefully so each layer floats on top of the previous one with mixing. Chill for ½ hour before serving. Top with cherry.

ANGLER'S COCKTAIL

4 parts gin (2 oz.)
3 dashes Angostura bitters
3 dashes orange bitters
3 dashes grenadine

Shake all ingredients in cocktail shaker with cracked ice. Strain over ice cubes into chilled old-fashioned glass.

ANKLE BREAKER

4 parts 151-proof rum (2 oz.)
2 parts cherry brandy (1 oz.)
2 parts fresh lime juice (1 oz.)
Sugar syrup (1 tsp.) (optional)

Combine all ingredients with cracked ice in a cocktail shaker. Shake well. Strain into chilled old-fashioned glass.

ANNABELLE SPECIAL

4 parts Benedictine (2 oz.)
½ part dry vermouth (¼ oz.)
½ part fresh lime juice (¼ oz.)

Stir all ingredients in a mixing glass with cracked ice. Strain into chilled cocktail glass.

PLEASE NOTE: Blue icons represent alcoholic drinks. Green icons represent non-alcoholic drinks.

ANNA'S BANANA

4 parts vodka (2 oz.)
2 parts fresh lime juice (1 oz.)
½ small banana, peeled and sliced thin
Honey (1 tsp.) (almond syrup may
also be used)
Slice of lime

Combine all ingredients, except for
lime slice, in a blender with 4 ounces
of cracked ice. Blend at medium speed
for 10 –15 seconds. Pour into chilled
white wine glass and garnish with
lime.

ANTIBES

4 parts gin (2 oz.)
1½ parts Benedictine (¾ oz.)
5 parts grapefruit juice (2½ oz.)
Orange slice

Pour all ingredients, except orange
slice, in a mixing glass with cracked
ice. Stir well. Pour into chilled old-
fashioned glass and garnish with
orange slice.

APERITIVO

4 parts gin (2 oz.)
3 parts white Sambuca (1½ oz.)
3 – 5 dashes orange bitters

Pour all ingredients in a mixing glass
with cracked ice and stir well. Strain
into a chilled cocktail glass.

APPETIZER

6 parts red aperitif wine
(such as Dubonnet) (3 oz.)
Juice of 1 orange, freshly squeezed

Mix wine and juice with cracked ice in
a mixing glass. Strain into chilled
cocktail glass.

APPLE ANNIE
FRUIT PUNCH

Apple brandy (1 quart or 1 liter)
6 parts raspberry liqueur (3 oz.)
20 parts fresh orange juice (10 oz. or
1½ cups)
16 parts fresh grapefruit juice (8 oz. or
1 cup)
4 parts fresh lemon juice (2 oz.)

Ginger ale (1 quart or 1 liter)
Sparkling water or lemon-lime soda
(1 quart or 1 liter)
1 orange, sliced thin
1 apple, sliced thin
1 lemon, sliced thin
12 –15 fresh raspberries

Combine applejack, raspberry liqueur
and fruit juices in a large punch bowl.
Stir well. Add one large block of ice.
Garnish with fresh fruit. Add the sodas
just before serving and stir again.
Serves 20.

APPLE BLOSSOM

4 parts brandy (2 oz.)
3 parts apple juice (1½ oz.)
Fresh lemon juice (1 tsp.)
Lemon slice

Combine all ingredients in mixing
glass except for lemon slice. Stir well.
Pour into chilled old-fashioned glass
over ice cubes. Garnish with lemon
slice.

APPLE BLOW FIZZ

6 parts apple brandy or
applejack (3 oz.)
Sugar syrup (1 tsp.)
Fresh lemon juice (½ tsp.)
1 egg white
Sparkling water

Combine all ingredients, except
sparkling water, in cocktail shaker
with cracked ice. Shake well. Strain
into chilled highball glass over ice
cubes. Fill with sparkling water.

APPLE BRANDY
COCKTAIL

4 parts apple brandy (2 oz.)
Grenadine (1 tsp.)
Lemon juice (1 tsp.)

Combine ingredients with cracked ice
in cocktail shaker and shake well.
Strain into chilled cocktail glass.

APPLE BRANDY COOLER

4 parts brandy (2 oz.)
2 parts light rum (1 oz.)
2 parts dark rum (1 oz.)
8 parts apple juice (4 oz.)
Sugar syrup (1 tsp.)
1 part fresh lime juice (½ oz.)
Slice of lime

Mix all ingredients, except dark rum
and lime slice, with cracked ice in a
cocktail shaker and shake well. Pour
into chilled collins glass. Float dark
rum on top and garnish with lime
slice.

APPLE BRANDY HIGHBALL

4 parts apple brandy (2 oz.)
Sparkling water
Lemon twist

Pour brandy over ice cubes in
highball glass. Fill with sparkling
water. Add twist of lemon. Stir well.

APPLE CART

2 parts apple brandy (1 oz.)
1½ parts Cointreau (¾ oz.)
1 part fresh lemon juice (½ oz.)

Pour all ingredients into mixing glass
and stir well. Pour into chilled old-
fashioned glass over ice cubes.

APPLE DAIQUIRI

4 parts light rum (2 oz.)
1½ parts Calvados (¾ oz.)
1 part lemon juice (½ oz)
Sugar syrup (1 tsp.) (use more or less,
depending on desired sweetness)
Apple slice

Combine all ingredients, except apple
wedge, in a cocktail shaker with
cracked ice. Shake well. Strain into
chilled cocktail glass. Garnish with
apple slice.

APPLE DUBONNET

4 parts apple brandy (2 oz.)
3 parts Dubonnet rouge (1½ oz.)
Lemon slice

Mix all ingredients, except lemon
slice, in cocktail shaker with cracked
ice. Shake well. Strain into chilled
old-fashioned glass. Garnish with
lemon slice.

APPLE FIZZ

4 parts apple brandy (2 oz.)
8 parts apple juice (4 oz.)
Fresh lime juice (½ tsp.)
Sparkling water
Lime slice

Pour all liquid ingredient into chilled
highball glass filled with ice cubes.
Stir gently and garnish with lime.

APPLE FRAZZLE

8 parts apple juice (4 oz.)
Sugar syrup (1 tsp.)
Fresh lemon juice (½ tsp.)
Sparkling water

Combine all ingredients, except
sparkling water, in cocktail shaker
with cracked ice. Shake well. Strain
into chilled highball glass over ice
cubes. Fill with sparkling water.

APPLE PIE

4 parts light rum (2 oz.)
1½ parts apple brandy (¾ oz.)
1 part sweet vermouth (½ oz.)
Lemon juice (1 tsp.)
Dash apricot brandy
Dash grenadine

Combine all ingredients with cracked
ice in cocktail shaker and shake well.
Strain into chilled cocktail glass.
(Note: You may also use a blender for
this drink. Blend for about 10 seconds
on medium.)

APPLE RUM RICKEY

2 parts apple brandy (1 oz.)
1 part light rum (½ oz.)
Sparkling water
Twist of lime

In a cocktail shaker, combine the rum
and brandy with cracked ice. Shake
well. Strain over ice cubes into a
chilled highball glass. Top off with
sparkling water and lime twist.

APPLE SWIZZLE

4 parts apple brandy (2 oz.)
3 parts light rum (1½ oz.)
1 part fresh lime juice (1 oz.)
Sugar syrup (1 tsp.)
2 – 3 dashes Angostura bitters

Mix all ingredients with cracked ice in
mixing glass. Pour into chilled old
fashioned glass.

APPLEJACK COLLINS

4 parts applejack or apple
brandy (2 oz.)
2 parts fresh lemon juice (1 oz.)
Bar sugar (½ tsp.)
3 – 5 dashes orange bitters
Sparkling water
Lemon slice

Pour all ingredients, except sparkling
water and lemon slice, into a blender
with cracked ice. Blend at medium for
about 10 seconds. Pour into a chilled
collins glass and top off with sparkling
water. Stir gently. Garnish with lemon
slice.

APPLEJACK DAISY

4 parts applejack or apple
brandy (2 oz.)
2 parts fresh lime juice (1 oz.)
Bar sugar (½ tsp.)
Grenadine (½ tsp.)
Lemon slice
Maraschino cherry

Combine all ingredients, except lemon
slice and cherry, in a cocktail shaker
with cracked ice. Shake well. Strain
into chilled cocktail glass. Garnish
with fruit.

APPLEJACK MANHATTAN

4 parts applejack or apple
brandy (2 oz.)
1 part sweet vermouth (½ oz.)
Dash orange bitters
Maraschino cherry

Mix liquid ingredients with cracked
ice in a mixing glass. Strain into a
chilled cocktail glass. Garnish with
bitters and cherry.

APPLEJACK SOUR

4 parts applejack or apple
brandy (2 oz.)
2 parts fresh lemon juice (1 oz.)
Bar sugar (½ tsp.)
Lemon slice

Combine all ingredients, except lemon
slice, in a cocktail shaker with cracked
ice. Shake well. Strain into chilled
cocktail glass. Garnish with lemon
slice

APRICOT COCKTAIL

2 parts apricot brandy (1 oz.)
Vodka or neutral spirits (1 tbsp.)
Fresh lemon juice (1 tbsp.)
Fresh orange juice (1 tbsp.)

Combine all ingredients with cracked
ice in a cocktail shaker. Shake well.
Strain into chilled cocktail glass.

APRICOT FIZZ

4 parts apricot brandy (2 oz.)
2 parts fresh lemon juice (1 oz.)
Sugar syrup (1 tsp.)
Sparkling water
Lemon peel

Combine all ingredients, except
sparkling water and lemon peel, with
cracked ice in a mixing glass. Stir
well. Strain over ice cubes into a
chilled highball glass. Top off with
sparkling water and stir again. Twist
lemon peel over glass and drop in.

APRICOT LADY

3 parts light rum (1½ oz.)
2 parts apricot brandy (1 oz.)
Triple sec (½ tsp.)
Fresh lime juice (1 tbsp.)
1 egg white
Orange slice

Combine all ingredients, except orange slice, with cracked ice in a cocktail shaker and shake well. Strain over ice cubes into a chilled old-fashioned glass. Garnish with orange slice.

APRICOT SHAKE

6 parts apricot nectar (3 oz.)
4 parts pineapple juice (2 oz.)
2 parts fresh lime juice (1 oz)
2 parts cherry syrup (1 oz.)

Combine all ingredients with cracked ice in a blender. Blend until slushy and pour into chilled collins glass.

APRICOT SOUR

4 parts apricot brandy (2 oz.)
2 parts fresh lemon juice (1 oz.)
Bar sugar (½ tsp.)
Lemon slice

Combine all ingredients, except lemon slice, in a cocktail shaker with cracked ice. Shake well. Strain into chilled cocktail glass. Garnish with lemon slice.

APRICOT SPARKLER

4 parts apricot nectar (2 oz.)
2 parts fresh lemon juice (1 oz.)
Sparkling water
Lemon peel

Combine all ingredients, except sparkling water, with cracked ice in a mixing glass. Stir well. Strain over ice cubes into a chilled highball glass. Top off with sparkling water and stir again. Twist lemon peel over glass and drop in.

AQUEDUCT COCKTAIL

4 parts vodka (2 oz.)
White Curaçao (1½ tsp.)
Apricot brandy (1 tsp.)
Fresh lime juice (1 tsp.)
Fresh lemon juice (1 tsp.)
Lemon twist

Combine all ingredients, except lemon twist, with cracked ice in a cocktail shaker. Shake well. Strain into chilled cocktail glass and garnish with lemon twist.

ARAWAK CUP

4 parts dark rum (2 oz.)
1 part pineapple juice (½ oz.)
1 part passion fruit syrup (½ oz.)
1 part fresh lime juice (½ oz.)
Orgeat (almond) syrup (1 tsp.)
Pineapple spear

Combine all ingredients, except pineapple spear, with cracked ice in a cocktail shaker. Shake well. Strain into chilled cocktail glass. Garnish with pineapple spear.

ARTILLERY COCKTAIL

4 parts gin (2 oz.)
1 part sweet vermouth (½ oz.)

Combine gin and vermouth in cocktail shaker with cracked ice. Mix well. Strain into chilled cocktail glass.

ARTILLERY PUNCH

Bourbon or rye (1 quart or 32 oz.)
Red wine (1 quart or 32 oz.)
Dark rum (1 pint or 16 oz.)
Apricot brandy (1 cup or 8 oz.)
Gin (1 cup or 8 oz.)
Strong black tea (1 quart or 32 oz.)
Fresh orange juice (1 pint or 16 oz.)
8 parts fresh lemon juice (4 oz.)
8 parts fresh lime juice (4 oz.)
Bar sugar (¼ cup)
1 lemon, sliced thin
1 lime, sliced thin

Mix all ingredients, except for fruit slices, and chill in refrigerator for at least one hour. When ready to serve, pour over block of ice in large punch bowl. Garnish with lemon and lime slices. Serves 30 to 35.

ARUBA

4 parts gin (2 oz.)
1 part white Curaçao (½ oz.)
2 parts fresh lemon juice (1 oz.)
½ egg white
Orgeat (almond) syrup (1 tsp.)

Combine all ingredients with cracked ice in a cocktail shaker. Shake well. Strain into chilled cocktail glass.

AVIATION

4 parts gin (2 oz.)
1 part fresh lemon juice (½ oz.)
Maraschino liqueur (½ tsp.)
Apricot brandy (½ tsp.)

Combine all ingredients with cracked ice in a cocktail shaker. Shake well. Strain into chilled cocktail glass.

AZTEC PUNCH

White tequila (2 quarts or 64 oz.)
Grapefruit juice (2 quarts or 64 oz.)
8 parts white Curaçao (½ cup or 4 oz.)
Cold strong black tea (1 quart or 32 oz.)
8 parts fresh lemon juice (1 cup or 4 oz.)
Orgeat (almond) syrup (¾ cup or 6 oz.)
1 part orange bitters (½ oz.)
Ground cinnamon (2 tsp.)

Mix all ingredients well in large punch bowl with block of ice. Serves 40.

B

BABBIE'S SPECIAL COCKTAIL

4 parts apricot brandy (2 oz.)
2 parts half-and-half (1 oz.)
Gin (1 tsp.)

Combine ingredients with cracked ice in a cocktail shaker. Shake well. Strain into chilled cocktail glass.

BABY BELLINI

Chilled sparkling cider
4 parts peach nectar (2 oz.)
2 parts fresh lemon juice (1 oz.)

Pour the fruit juices into a chilled champagne flute. Stir well. Add cider to the rim. Stir again gently.

BACHELOR'S BAIT

4 parts gin (2 oz.)
3 dashes orange bitters
Grenadine (¾ tsp.)
1 egg white

Combine all ingredients in a cocktail shaker with cracked ice. Shake well. Strain into chilled cocktail glass.

BAHAMA MAMA

2 parts dark rum (1 oz.)
2 parts white rum (1 oz.)
2 parts gold rum (1 oz.)
2 parts coconut liqueur (1 oz.)
4 parts fresh orange juice (2 oz.)
4 parts pineapple juice (2 oz.)
1 part fresh lemon juice (½ oz.)
2 dashes grenadine
Maraschino cherry
Orange slice

Combine all liquid ingredients with ice cubes in a cocktail shaker. Shake well. Pour into chilled collins glass and garnish with fruit.

BAIRN

4 parts scotch (2 oz.)
2 parts Cointreau (1 oz.)
3 – 5 dashes orange bitters

Mix all ingredients in a cocktail shaker with cracked ice. Shake well. Strain into chilled cocktail glass.

BALI HAI

4 parts light rum (2 oz.)
2 parts Aguardiente (1 oz.)
4 parts fresh lemon juice (2 oz.)
4 parts fresh lime juice (2 oz.)
Orgeat (almond) syrup (1 tsp.)
Grenadine (1 tsp.)
Champagne or sparkling wine

Combine all ingredients, except champagne, with cracked ice in a cocktail shaker. Shake well. Pour into chilled collins glass. Top off with cold champagne.

BALLYLICKEY BELT

4 parts Irish whiskey (2 oz.)
Honey (¾ tsp.)
Cold sparkling water
Lemon peel

In the bottom of a chilled old-fashioned glass, muddle the honey with a little water until it dissolves. Add the whiskey and ice cubes. Fill with sparkling water and stir gently. Twist the lemon peel over the glass and drop in.

BALMORAL COCKTAIL

4 parts scotch (2 oz.)
1 part Dubonnet rouge (½ oz.)
1 part Dubonnet blanc (½ oz.)
3 dashes Angostura bitters

Combine all ingredients in mixing glass with ice cubes. Stir well. Strain into chilled cocktail glass.

BALTIMORE BRACER

3 parts brandy (1½ oz.)
2 parts anisette or Pernod
(1 oz.)
1 egg white

Combine all ingredients in cocktail shaker with cracked ice. Shake vigorously. Strain into chilled cocktail glass.

BALTIMORE EGGNOG

4 parts brandy (2 oz.)
2 parts dark rum (1 oz.)
2 parts madeira wine (1 oz.)
12 parts Half-and-half (¾ cup or 6 oz.)
1 whole egg
Bar sugar (1 tsp.)
Freshly ground nutmeg

Combine all ingredients, except nutmeg, with cracked ice in a blender. Blend at medium for about 10 seconds. Pour into chilled collins glass and sprinkle with nutmeg.

BAMBOO COCKTAIL

4 parts dry sherry (2 oz.)
1 part dry vermouth (½ oz.)
Dash orange bitters

Stir all ingredients with ice cubes in chilled cocktail glass.

BANANA DAIQUIRI

4 parts light rum (2 oz.)
1 part triple sec (½ oz.)
1 part fresh lime juice (½ oz.)
1 part half-and-half (½ oz.)
Bar sugar (1 tsp.)
¼ sliced banana
Lime slice

Put all ingredients, except for lime slice, into a blender with about ½ cup cracked ice. Blend at low speed until smooth. Pour into chilled balloon wine glass and garnish with slice of lime.

BANANA ITALIANO

3 parts Galliano (1½ oz.)
2 parts crème de bananes (1 oz.)
2 parts half-and-half (1 oz.)

Combine all ingredients in a blender with cracked ice. Blend until smooth. Strain into chilled cocktail glass.

BANANA MILK SHAKE

4 parts light rum (2 oz.)
2 parts banana liqueur (1 oz.)
4 parts half-and-half (2 oz.)
Dash grenadine
Banana slice
Freshly ground nutmeg

Combine liquid ingredients in cocktail shaker with cracked ice. Shake well. Strain into chilled cocktail glass, garnish with banana and sprinkle nutmeg on top.

BANANA RUM FRAPPE

2 parts light rum (1 oz.)
1 part banana liqueur (½ oz.)
1 part fresh orange juice (½ oz.)
Banana slice

Combine all ingredients, except banana, in a blender with cracked ice. Blend at high speed for about ten seconds or until smooth.

BANFF COCKTAIL

4 parts Canadian whiskey
(2 oz.)
1 part Grand Marnier (½ oz.)
1 part kirschwasser (½ oz.)
Dash Angostura bitters

Combine ingredients with cracked ice in a cocktail shaker. Shake well. Strain into chilled cocktail glass.

BANSHEE

4 parts crème de bananes
(2 oz.)
2 parts white crème de cacao (1 oz.)
1 part half-and-half (1 oz.)

Combine all ingredients with cracked ice in a shaker. Shake well. Strain into chilled cocktail glass.

BARBADOS PLANTER'S PUNCH

6 parts gold rum (3 oz.)
2 parts fresh lime juice (1 oz.)
Bar sugar (½ tsp.)
Dash orange bitters
Sparkling water
Banana slice
Orange slice
Maraschino cherry
Freshly grated nutmeg

Combine all ingredients, except the fruit and nutmeg, with cracked ice in a cocktail shaker. Shake well. Pour into chilled collins glass. Garnish with the fruit and the nutmeg.

BARBARELLA

4 parts Cointreau (2 oz.)
2 parts white Sambuca (1 oz.)

Combine ingredients in cocktail shaker with cracked ice and shake well. Strain into chilled old-fashioned glass.

BARBARY COAST

2 parts light rum (1 oz.)
1 part gin (½ oz.)
1 part scotch (½ oz.)
1 part white crème de cacao (½ oz.)
1 part half-and-half (½ oz.)

Shake all ingredients together with cracked ice in a cocktail shaker. Strain into chilled cocktail glass.

BARNUM

4 parts gin (2 oz.)
1 part apricot brandy (½ oz.)
3 – 5 dashes Angostura bitters
3 – 5 dashes lemon juice

Combine all ingredients in a cocktail shaker with cracked ice. Shake well. Strain into chilled cocktail glass.

BARTON SPECIAL

4 parts apple brandy or Calvados (2 oz.)
2 parts gin (1 oz.)
2 parts scotch (1 oz.)
Lemon peel

Combine all ingredients, except for lemon peel, in a cocktail shaker with cracked ice. Shake well. Strain over ice cubes into chilled old-fashioned glass. Twist lemon peel over drink and drop in.

BATIDA DE PIÑA

6 parts light rum (3 oz.)
Fresh crushed pineapple (⅔ cup)
(if you must use canned pineapple, use the kind that's packed in natural juice)
Bar sugar (½ tsp.)
Sprig of fresh mint

Combine all ingredients, except mint, in a blender with cracked ice. Blend at high speed until smooth but not watery. Pour into chilled double old-fashioned glass. Garnish with mint sprig.

BAYARD FIZZ

4 parts gin (2 oz.)
Maraschino liqueur (1 tbsp.)
Fresh lime juice (1 tbsp.)
Raspberry syrup (1 tsp.)
Sparkling water
Fresh raspberries

Combine all ingredients, except the water and raspberries, in a cocktail shaker with ice cubes. Shake well. Strain over ice cubes into chilled highball glass. Top off with sparkling water and drop in a few fresh raspberries.

BEACHBUM

4 parts light rum (2 oz.)
1½ parts triple sec (¾ oz.)
1½ parts fresh lime juice (¾ oz.)
Dash of grenadine

Rim a chilled cocktail glass with
sugar by rubbing with a lime wedge
and dipping into sugar. Combine all
ingredients in cocktail shaker and
shake well. Strain into the glass.

BEACHCOMBER

10 parts guava nectar (5 oz.)
2 parts raspberry syrup (1 oz.)
4 parts fresh lime juice (2 oz.)

Combine all ingredients with cracked
ice in a cocktail shaker. Shake well
and pour into chilled collins glass.

BEACHCOMBER'S GOLD

4 parts light rum (2 oz.)
1 part dry vermouth (½ oz.)
1 part sweet vermouth (½ oz.)

Combine ingredients with cracked ice
in cocktail shaker. Shake well. Strain
into chilled cocktail glass filled with
crushed ice.

BEADLESTONE

4 parts scotch (2 oz.)
3 parts dry vermouth (1½ oz.)

Stir ingredients with ice cubes in a
mixing glass and strain into chilled
cocktail glass.

BEAUTY SPOT

4 parts gin (2 oz.)
1 part dry vermouth (½ oz.)
1 part sweet vermouth (½ oz.)
Fresh orange juice (2 tsp.)
2 dashes of grenadine

Drizzle grenadine in bottom of chilled
cocktail glass. Combine other
ingredients in a cocktail shaker with
cracked ice and shake well. Strain into
glass.

BEER BUSTER

Bottle of ice-cold beer
4 parts frozen 100-proof vodka (2 oz.)
Tabasco sauce to taste

Pour all ingredients into frosted beer
mug and stir gently.

BEE'S KISS

4 parts white rum (2 oz.)
Honey (1 tsp.)
Half-and-half (1 tsp.)

Combine all ingredients with cracked
ice and shake vigorously in cocktail
shaker. Strain over ice cubes in chilled
cocktail glass.

BEE'S KNEES

BEE'S KNEES

4 parts gold rum (2 oz.)
1 part fresh orange juice
(½ oz.)
1 part fresh lime juice (½ oz.)
Bar sugar (½ tsp.)
3 – 5 dashes white Curaçao
Orange peel

Combine all ingredients, except the
orange peel, in a cocktail shaker with
cracked ice. Shake well. Strain into
chilled cocktail glass and garnish with
orange peel.

BELLINI

Chilled champagne (Sparkling
wine is acceptable in a pinch)
4 parts peach nectar (2 oz.)
1 part fresh lemon juice (½ oz.)

Pour the fruit juices into a chilled
champagne flute. Stir well. Add
champagne to the rim. Stir again
gently.

BELMONT

4 parts gin (2 oz.)
1 part raspberry syrup (½ oz.)
1½ parts half-and-half (¾ oz.)

Stir all ingredients with cracked ice in
a mixing glass. Strain into chilled
cocktail glass.

45

BELLINI (from Cipriani)

BELMONT STAKES

4 parts vodka (2 oz.)
2 parts gold rum (1 oz.)
1 part strawberry liqueur (½ oz.)
1 part fresh lime juice (½ oz.)
Grenadine (1 tsp.)
Lime wedge
Orange slice

Combine all liquid ingredients in a
cocktail shaker with cracked ice and
shake well. Strain into chilled cocktail
glass and garnish with fruit.

BENNETT

4 parts gin (2 oz.)
1 part fresh lime juice (½ oz.)
Bar sugar (½ tsp.)
3 dashes Angostura bitters

Combine all ingredients in a cocktail
shaker with cracked ice. Shake well.
Strain into chilled cocktail glass.

PLEASE NOTE: Blue icons represent
alcoholic drinks. Green icons represent
non-alcoholic drinks.

BENTLEY COCKTAIL

4 parts apple brandy or
Calvados (2 oz.)
2 parts Dubonnet rouge (1 oz.)
Lemon twist

Stir liquid ingredients with cracked ice
in a mixing glass. Strain into chilled
cocktail glass and garnish with lemon
twist.

BERMUDA BOUQUET

4 parts gin (2 oz.)
2 parts apricot brandy (1 oz.)
1 part fresh lemon juice (½ oz.)
1 part fresh orange juice (½ oz.)
Bar sugar (1 tsp.)
Grenadine (1 tsp.)
Cointreau (1 tsp.)
Orange twist

Combine all ingredients in cocktail
shaker, except orange twist, with ice
cubes and shake well. Pour into
chilled highball glass. Add more ice if
necessary. Garnish with orange twist.

BERMUDA HIGHBALL

3 parts gin (1½ oz.)
2 parts brandy (1 oz.)
2 parts dry vermouth (1 oz.)
Sparkling water
Lemon peel

Pour liquors into chilled highball glass over ice cubes. Stir well. Fill with sparkling water. Add twist of lemon peel and stir again gently.

BERMUDA ROSE

4 parts gin (2 oz.)
Fresh lime juice (1 tbsp.)
Apricot brandy (2 tsp.)
Grenadine (2 tsp.)

Shake all ingredients with cracked ice in cocktail shaker. Strain over ice cubes in chilled old-fashioned glass.

BERTA'S SPECIAL

4 parts tequila (2 oz.)
Honey (1 tsp.)
1 egg white
5 – 7 dashes orange bitters
Juice of one lime
Sparkling water
Lime slice

Combine all ingredients, except lime slice and sparkling water, in a cocktail shaker. Shake vigorously. Pour over into a chilled collins glass filled with ice cubes and top off with sparkling water. Garnish with lime slice.

BETSY ROSS

3 parts brandy (1½ oz.)
3 parts port (1½ oz.)
Bar sugar (½ tsp.)
1 egg yolk
3 – 5 dashes triple sec
3 – 5 dashes Angostura bitters
Freshly ground nutmeg

Combine all ingredients, except nutmeg, in a cocktail shaker with cracked ice. Shake vigorously. Strain into chilled cocktail glass. Sprinkle with nutmeg.

BETWEEN THE SHEETS

4 parts brandy or cognac (2 oz.)
3 parts light rum (1½ oz.)
1 part white Curaçao (½ oz.)
1 part fresh lemon juice (½ oz.)

Combine all ingredients in shaker with cracked ice and shake well. Strain into chilled cocktail glass.

BEVERLY HILLS

4 parts triple sec (2 oz.)
2 parts cognac (1 oz.)
1 part coffee liqueur (½ oz.)

Combine all ingredients in cocktail shaker with cracked ice. Shake well. Strain into chilled cocktail glass.

BIFFY COCKTAIL

4 parts gin (2 oz.)
2 parts Swedish punch (1 oz.)
2 parts fresh lemon juice (1 oz.)

Combine all ingredients in cocktail shaker and shake well. Strain into chilled old-fashioned glass.

BIG APPLE

4 parts apple brandy (2 oz.)
1 part amaretto (½ oz.)
6 parts apple juice (3 oz.)
Apple sauce (1 tbsp.)
Ground cinnamon

Combine all ingredients, except cinnamon, in a blender with ice. Blend at medium speed until smooth. Pour into a chilled parfait glass and sprinkle with cinnamon.

BIJOU COCKTAIL

3 parts gin (1½ oz.)
2 parts green Chartreuse (1 oz.)
2 parts sweet vermouth (1 oz.)
Dash orange bitters
Lemon peel (optional)
Maraschino cherry (optional)

Stir liquid ingredients in mixing glass with cracked ice. Strain into chilled cocktail glass. Garnish with lemon peel and/or cherry.

BIG APPLE

BILLY TAYLOR

4 parts gin (2 oz.)
3 parts fresh lime juice (1½ oz.)
Bar sugar (½ tsp.)
Sparkling water

Combine all ingredients, except water, in cocktail shaker with cracked ice. Shake well. Strain over ice cubes into chilled collins glass. Fill with sparkling water and gently stir.

BIRD OF PARADISE COOLER

4 parts gin (2 oz.)
2 parts fresh lemon juice (1 oz.)
Bar sugar (1 tsp.)
Grenadine (1 tsp.)
1 egg white
Sparkling water

Combine all ingredients, except sparkling water, in a cocktail shaker with cracked ice. Shake vigorously. Strain over ice cubes into chilled highball glass. Fill with sparkling water and stir gently.

BLACK DOG

BISCAYNE COCKTAIL

4 parts gin (2 oz.)
2 parts light rum (1 oz.)
2 parts forbidden fruit (1 oz.)
2 parts fresh lime juice (1 oz.)
Lime slice

Combine all liquid ingredients with cracked ice in a cocktail shaker. Shake well. Strain into chilled cocktail glass and garnish with lime slice.

BISHOP

4 parts fresh orange juice (2 oz.)
4 parts fresh lemon juice (2 oz.)
Bar sugar (1 tsp.)
Cabernet Sauvignon or other full-bodied red wine
Orange slice
Lemon Slice

Stir juices and sugar together in a mixing glass. Strain over ice cubes into chilled highball glass. Fill with red wine. Stir again and garnish with citrus slices.

BITE OF THE APPLE

10 parts apple juice (5 oz.)
2 parts fresh lime juice (1 oz.)
1 part orgeat (almond) syrup (½ oz.)
Unsweetened apple sauce (1 tbsp.)
Ground cinnamon

Combine all ingredients, except cinnamon, in a blender with ice. Blend at medium speed until smooth. Pour into a chilled pilsner glass and sprinkle cinnamon on top.

BITTERSWEET COCKTAIL

3 parts dry vermouth (1½ oz.)
3 parts sweet vermouth (1½ oz.)
3 dashes Angostura bitters
3 dashes orange bitters
Orange twist

Combine all ingredients, except cracked ice, in a cocktail shaker and shake well. Strain over ice cubes into a chilled old-fashioned glass. Garnish with orange twist.

BLACK AND TAN

Chilled ginger ale
Chilled ginger beer
Lime wedge

Pour equal parts of each beverage into
a chilled pilsner glass. Do not stir.
Garnish with lime wedge.

BLACK DEVIL

4 parts light rum (2 oz.)
1 part dry vermouth (½ oz.)
Pitted black olive

Stir rum and vermouth in mixing
glass with cracked ice. Strain into
chilled cocktail glass and drop in the
olive.

BLACK DOG

6 parts bourbon (3 oz.)
2 parts dry vermouth (1 oz.)
1 part blackberry brandy (½ oz.)

Combine all ingredients in mixing
glass with cracked ice. Stir well and
strain into old-fashioned glass over ice
cubes.

BLACK HAWK

4 parts blended whiskey
(2 oz.)
2 parts sloe gin (1 oz.)

Stir ingredients in a mixing glass with
cracked ice. Strain into chilled
cocktail glass.

BLACK JACK

4 parts brandy (2 oz.)
1 part kirschwasser (½ oz.)
3 parts cold black coffee (1½ oz.)
Lemon twist

Stir liquid ingredients with cracked ice
in mixing glass. Strain over ice cubes
into chilled old-fashioned glass.
Garnish with lemon twist.

BLACK MAGIC

4 parts vodka (2 oz.)
2 parts coffee liqueur (1 oz.)
1– 2 dashes fresh lemon juice

Stir all ingredients in a mixing glass.
Strain into a chilled old-fashioned
glass over ice cubes.

BLACK MARIA

4 parts coffee liqueur (2 oz.)
4 parts light rum (2 oz.)
8 parts cold black coffee (4 oz.)
Bar sugar (1 tsp.)

Stir ingredients in a large brandy
snifter. Add cracked ice.

BLACK RUSSIAN

4 parts vodka (2 oz.)
2 parts coffee liqueur (1 oz.)

Pour into chilled old fashioned glass
over ice cubes. Stir.

BLACK STRIPE

6 parts dark rum (3 oz.)
Molasses (2 tsp.)
8 parts boiling water (½ cup or 4 oz.)
Lemon twist
Cinnamon stick
Freshly ground nutmeg

Dissolve molasses in the mug with a
little boiling water. Add cinnamon
stick and lemon twist and the
remaining boiling water. Float rum on
top and flame for a few seconds. Stir to
extinguish flames. Sprinkle nutmeg
on top.

BLACK JACK

51

BLACKTHORN

4 parts Irish whiskey (2 oz.)
3 parts dry vermouth (1½ oz.)
3 – 5 dashes of Pernod
3 – 5 dashes of Angostura bitters

Stir all ingredients in a mixing glass
with cracked ice. Pour into a chilled
old-fashioned glass.

BLACK VELVET

Chilled champagne or
Sparkling wine (½ pint)
Chilled stout or dark porter (½ pint)

Slowly pour both ingredients at the
same time into a chilled highball
glass. Do not stir.

BLANCHE

2 parts anisette or Pernod
(1 oz.)
2 parts Cointreau (1 oz.)
1 parts white Curaçao (½ oz.)

Combine all ingredients in cocktail
shaker with cracked ice and shake
well. Strain into chilled cocktail glass.

BLENDED COMFORT

4 parts bourbon (2 oz.)
2 parts Southern Comfort (1 oz.)
1 part dry vermouth (½ oz.)
2 parts fresh lemon juice (1 oz.)
Bar sugar (½ tsp.)
Fresh peach slices

Combine all ingredients, except peach slices, in a blender with cracked ice. Blend at low speed until smooth. Pour into a chilled collins glass over ice cubes. Garnish with peach slices.

BLINKER

4 parts rye (2 oz.)
5 parts grapefruit juice (2½ oz.)
Grenadine (1tsp.)

Combine all ingredients with cracked ice in a cocktail shaker. Shake well and strain into chilled cocktail glass.

BLIZZARD

6 parts bourbon (3 oz.)
2 parts cranberry juice (1 oz.)
Fresh lemon juice (1 tbsp.)
Bar sugar (1 tbsp.)

Shake all ingredients with cracked ice in a cocktail shaker. Pour into chilled highball glass.

BLOOD AND SAND

2 parts scotch (1 oz.)
1 part kirschwasser (½ oz.)
1 part sweet vermouth (½ oz.)
1 part fresh orange juice (½ oz.)

Shake all ingredients with cracked ice in a cocktail shaker. Strain into chilled cocktail glass.

BLOODHOUND

4 parts gin (2 oz.)
2 parts dry vermouth (1 oz.)
2 parts sweet vermouth (1 oz.)
3 fresh strawberries, halved and stems removed

Combine all ingredients in a blender with cracked ice. Mix at low speed until smooth but not watery. Pour into chilled cocktail glass.

BLOODY BREW

4 parts vodka (2 oz.)
6 parts beer (3 oz.)
8 parts tomato juice (½ cup or 4 oz.)
Salt to taste
Dill pickle spear

Mix all ingredients, except pickle, in chilled highball glass with ice. Garnish with pickle.

BLOODY BULL

4 parts vodka (2 oz.)
8 parts tomato juice (4 oz.)
8 parts chilled beef bouillon (4 oz.)
1 part lime juice (½ oz.)
Tabasco sauce to taste
Freshly ground pepper to taste
Lime wedge

Combine all ingredients, except pepper and lime wedge, with cracked ice in a cocktail shaker and shake well. Strain over ice cubes into chilled highball glass. Grind pepper over drink and garnish with lime wedge.

BLOODY MARY

4 parts vodka (2 oz.)
12 parts tomato juice (6 oz.)
Fresh lemon juice (½ tsp.)
Worcestershire sauce (½ tsp.)
Horseradish (½ tsp.)
Tabasco sauce to taste
Freshly ground pepper to taste
Salt to taste
Lime wedge

Combine all ingredients, except lime wedge, in a cocktail shaker with cracked ice. Shake gently. Strain into chilled highball glass and garnish with lime wedge. Adjust seasonings to taste.

BLUE ANGEL

2 parts brandy (1 oz.)
1 part blue Curaçao (½ oz.)
1 part vanilla liqueur (½ oz.)
1 part half-and half (½ oz.)
Dash lemon juice

Combine all ingredients with cracked ice and shake well in a cocktail shaker. Strain into chilled cocktail glass.

53

BLUE BLAZER FOR TWO

10 parts scotch or blended whiskey (5 oz.)
10 parts boiling water (5 oz.)
Bar sugar (2 tsp.)
2 lemon peels

Warm the coffee mugs by filling them with boiling water and letting them sit for about 5 minutes. Discard water. Pour the scotch into one mug and the boiling water into the other. Ignite the whiskey. While the whiskey is blazing, mix it with the water by carefully pouring them back and forth between the two mugs. Extinguish the flames and serve in two mugs. Add 1 tsp. of sugar and lemon peel to each drink. With some practice, this can be a very dramatic presentation, giving the appearance of liquid fire.

BLUE DEVIL

4 parts gin (2 oz.)
1 part fresh lime juice (½ oz.)
Maraschino liqueur (1 tbsp.)
Blue Curaçao (1 tsp.)

Combine all ingredients with cracked ice in a cocktail shaker and shake well. Strain into chilled cocktail glass.

BLOODY MARY (from J.G. Melon's)

BLUE HAWAIIAN

BLUE GRASS COCKTAIL

4 parts bourbon (2 oz.)
2 parts pineapple juice (1 oz.)
2 parts fresh lemon juice (1 oz.)
Maraschino liqueur (1 tsp.)

Combine all ingredients with crushed ice in a cocktail shaker. Shake well. Strain into chilled cocktail glass.

BLUE HAWAIIAN

4 parts light rum (2 oz.)
4 parts blue Curaçao (2 oz.)
4 parts cream of coconut (2 oz.)
8 parts pineapple juice (4 oz.)
Pineapple spear
Maraschino cherry

Combine all liquid ingredients in a blender with cracked ice and blend at high speed for about ten seconds. Pour into chilled highball glass and garnish with cherry and pineapple spear.

BLUE LADY

5 parts blue Curaçao (2½ oz.)
2 parts white crème de cacao (1 oz.)
2 parts half-and-half (1 oz.)

Combine all ingredients with cracked ice in a cocktail shaker. Shake well and strain into chilled cocktail glass.

BLUE LAGOON

4 parts vodka (2 oz.)
2 parts blue Curaçao (1 oz.)
4 parts pineapple juice (2 oz.)
3 – 5 dashes triple sec
Pineapple spear

Combine all ingredients, except pineapple spear, with cracked ice in a cocktail shaker. Shake well. Strain into chilled cocktail glass and garnish with pineapple.

BLUE MARGARITA

4 parts white tequila (2 oz.)
2 parts blue Curaçao (1 oz.)
Triple sec (1 tbsp.)
3 parts fresh lime juice (1½ oz.)
Coarse salt (2 tsp.)
Lime wedge

Spread the salt in a saucer. Rub the rim of a cocktail glass with the lime wedge and dip the glass into the salt to coat the rim. Save lime for garnish. Combine all liquid ingredients in a cocktail shaker with cracked ice and shake well. Strain into salted cocktail glass and garnish with lime wedge.

BLUE MONDAY

4 parts vodka (2 oz.)
2 parts Cointreau (1 oz.)
1 part blue Curaçao (½ oz.)

Stir all ingredients with cracked ice in a mixing glass. Strain into chilled cocktail glass.

BLUE LAGOON

BLUE MARGARITA

BLUE MOON

4 parts gin (2 oz.)
1 part blue Curaçao (½ oz.)
Lemon twist

Stir liquid ingredients with ice in a mixing glass. Strain into chilled cocktail glass and garnish with lemon twist.

BLUE MOUNTAIN

4 parts dark rum (2 oz.)
2 parts vodka (1 oz.)
2 parts coffee liqueur (1 oz.)
8 parts fresh orange juice (½ cup or 4 oz.)

Combine all ingredients with cracked ice in a cocktail shaker and shake well. Strain into chilled old-fashioned glass.

BLUE SHARK

4 parts vodka (2 oz.)
4 parts white tequila (2 oz.)
Several dashes blue Curaçao

Combine all ingredients with cracked ice in a cocktail shaker. Shake well and strain into chilled old-fashioned glass.

BLUEBERRY SHAKE

Fresh blueberries (½ cup)
Sugar (1 tbsp.)
Milk (1 cup or 8 oz.)

Combine all ingredients in a blender with cracked ice and blend until slushy. Pour into chilled collins glass and garnish with fresh blueberries. Note: Fresh strawberries may also be used.

BOBBY BURNS

4 parts scotch (2 oz.)
2 parts sweet vermouth (1 oz.)
Benedictine (1 tsp.)
Lemon twist

Stir liquid ingredients with cracked ice in a mixing glass. Strain into chilled cocktail glass and garnish with lemon twist.

BOB DANBY

6 parts Dubonnet rouge (3 oz.)
3 parts brandy (1½ oz.)

Stir both ingredients with ice cubes in a mixing glass. Strain into chilled cocktail glass.

BOCCIE BALL

4 parts amaretto (2 oz.)
Fresh orange juice
Orange slice

Pour the amaretto and orange juice into a chilled highball glass with ice cubes. Stir. Garnish with orange slice.

BOILERMAKER

Beer (½ pint)
3 parts whiskey of your choice
(1½ oz.)

Pour the whiskey into a shot glass. Drop shot glass into ½ pint mug of beer.

BOLERO

4 parts light rum (2 oz.)
1 part Calvados or apple brandy
(½ oz.)
1 part sweet vermouth (½ oz.)
Dash Angostura bitters

Combine all ingredients in a mixing glass with cracked ice. Stir well. Strain over ice cubes into a chilled old-fashioned glass.

BOMBAY COCKTAIL

4 parts brandy (2 oz.)
1 part dry vermouth (½ oz.)
1 part sweet vermouth (½ oz.)
Triple sec (½ tsp.)
Dash of Pernod

Stir ingredients with cracked ice in a mixing glass. Strain into chilled cocktail glass.

BOMBAY PUNCH

Brandy (1 liter)
Dry sherry (1 liter)
8 parts triple sec (½ cup or 4 oz.)
8 parts maraschino liqueur (½ cup or 4 oz.)
4 parts kirschwasser (2 oz.)
4 bottles chilled champagne or sparkling wine (750-ml)
Bar sugar (½ cup)
Juice of 12 lemons
Juice of 6 limes
Sparkling water (2 liters)
Fresh fruit in season

Stir the fruit juices and sugar together in a large punch bowl until sugar is dissolved. Add remaining liquid ingredients and stir well. Add one large block of ice. Garnish with sliced seasonal fruit. Serves 25.

BOILERMAKER

BONGO COLA

4 parts gold rum (2 oz.)
2 parts coffee liqueur (1 oz.)
4 parts pineapple juice (2 oz.)
Dash of kirschwasser
Dash of fresh lemon juice
Cola
Maraschino cherry

Combine all ingredients, except cola
and cherry, in a cocktail shaker with
cracked ice. Shake well. Pour into
chilled collins glass over ice cubes.
Top off with cola. Stir gently and
garnish with cherry.

BONNIE PRINCE

4 parts gin (2 oz.)
1 part white wine (½ oz.)
½ part Drambuie (¼ oz.)
Orange peel

Combine all ingredients, except
orange peel, in a cocktail shaker and
shake well. Strain into chilled cocktail
glass and garnish with orange peel.

BOOMERANG

4 parts gin (2 oz.)
1 part dry vermouth (½ oz.)
Dash Angostura bitters
Dash maraschino liqueur
Lemon twist

Stir all liquid ingredients with ice
cubes in a mixing glass. Strain into
cocktail glass and add lemon twist.

BORINQUEN

4 parts white rum (2 oz.)
2 parts fresh lime juice (1 oz.)
2 parts fresh orange juice (1 oz.)
Passion fruit syrup (1 tbsp.)
151-proof rum (1 tsp.)

Combine ingredients with cracked ice in a blender. Blend at low speed for about 10 seconds. Pour into chilled old-fashioned glass.

BOSSA NOVA

4 parts dark rum (2 oz.)
3 parts Galliano (1½ oz.)
2 parts apricot brandy (1 oz.)
8 parts passionfruit juice (½ cup or 4 oz.)

Combine all ingredients in blender with ice cubes. Blend at low speed for about 15 seconds. Pour into chilled highball glass.

BOSOM CARESSER

4 parts brandy (2 oz.)
2 parts Madeira (1 oz.)
2 parts triple sec (1 oz.)
Grenadine (1tsp.)
1 egg yolk

Shake all ingredients vigorously in a cocktail shaker. Strain into chilled red wine glass.

BOSTON COCKTAIL

3 parts gin (1½ oz.)
2 parts apricot brandy (1 oz.)
Fresh lemon juice (1 tsp.)
Grenadine (1tsp.)

Combine all ingredients with cracked ice in a cocktail shaker. Shake well and strain into chilled cocktail glass.

BOSTON COOLER

4 parts light rum (2 oz.)
1 part fresh lemon juice (½ oz.)
Bar sugar (½ tsp.)
Sparkling water
Lemon twist

Combine rum, lemon juice and sugar in a cocktail shaker with cracked ice. Shake well. Strain over ice cubes into a chilled highball glass. Stir. Add sparkling water and lemon twist.

BOSTON SIDECAR

3 parts light rum (1½ oz.)
1 part brandy (½ oz.)
1 part triple sec (½ oz.)
1 part fresh lemon juice (½ oz.)

Combine all ingredients in a cocktail shaker with ice cubes. Shake well. Strain into chilled cocktail glass.

BOSTON SOUR

4 parts whiskey (2 oz.)
2 parts fresh lemon juice (1 oz.)
Bar sugar (1 tsp.)
1 egg white
Lemon slice
Maraschino cherry

Combine all ingredients, except fruit, in a cocktail shaker with cracked ice. Shake vigorously. Strain into chilled sour glass and garnish with cherry and lemon.

BOURBON À LA CRÈME

4 parts bourbon (2 oz.)
1 part dark crème de cacao (½ oz.)
3 vanilla beans

Combine all ingredients in a cocktail shaker with cracked ice. Chill in the refrigerator for at least one hour. When ready, shake well and strain into chilled cocktail glass.

BOURBON AND BRANCH

6 parts single barrel bourbon (3 oz.)
4 parts bottled water (2 oz.)

Pour the bourbon and water over ice cubes in a highball glass. Do not chill the glass. This drink may also be served "straight up" at room temperature.

BOURBON COBBLER

4 parts bourbon (2 oz.)
2 parts Southern Comfort (1 oz.)
Peach brandy (1 tsp.)
Fresh lemon juice (2 tsp.)
Bar sugar (½ tsp.)
Sparkling water
Peach slice

Combine all ingredients, except
sparkling water and peach slice, with
cracked ice in a cocktail shaker. Shake
well. Strain into a chilled highball
glass over ice cubes and top off with
sparkling water. Stir and garnish with
peach slice.

BOURBON COLLINS

4 parts bourbon (2 oz.)
1 part fresh lime juice (½ oz.)
Bar sugar (½ tsp.)
Sparkling water
Lime twist

Combine all ingredients, except
sparkling water and lime twist, in a
cocktail shaker and shake well. Strain
over ice cubes into chilled collins
glass. Fill with sparkling water and
garnish with lime twist.

BOURBON COBBLER

BOURBON COOLER

6 parts bourbon (3 oz.)
1 part grenadine (½ oz.)
Bar sugar (½ tsp.)
3 – 5 dashes peppermint schnapps
3 – 5 dashes orange bitters
Sparkling water
Pineapple spear

Combine all ingredients, except
sparkling water and pineapple spear,
in a cocktail shaker with cracked ice.
Shake well. Pour into chilled collins
glass and fill with sparkling water. Stir
and garnish with pineapple spear.

BOURBON DAISY

4 parts bourbon (2 oz.)
2 parts fresh lemon juice (1 oz.)
Grenadine (2 tsp.)
Southern Comfort (2 tsp.)
Sparkling water
Orange slice

Combine bourbon, lemon juice and
grenadine with cracked ice in a
cocktail shaker. Shake well. Pour into
a chilled highball glass and fill with
sparkling water. Float Southern
Comfort on top and garnish with
orange slice.

BOURBON MILK PUNCH

4 parts bourbon (2 oz.)
6 parts milk (3 oz.)
Honey (1 tsp.)
Dash vanilla extract
Freshly grated nutmeg

Combine all ingredients, except the
nutmeg, in a cocktail shaker with
cracked ice. Shake well. Strain into
chilled old-fashioned glass and
sprinkle with nutmeg.

BOURBON SATIN

3 parts bourbon (1½ oz.)
2 parts white crème de cacao
(1 oz.)
2 parts half-and-half (1 oz.)

Combine all ingredients with cracked
ice in a cocktail shaker and shake
well. Strain into chilled cocktail glass.

BOURBON SIDECAR

4 parts bourbon (2 oz.)
2 parts triple sec (1 oz.)
1 part fresh lemon juice (½ oz.)

Combine all ingredients with cracked
ice in a cocktail shaker and shake
well. Strain into chilled cocktail glass.

BOURBON SLOE GIN FIZZ

4 parts bourbon (2 oz.)
2 parts sloe gin (1 oz.)
Fresh lemon juice (1 tsp.)
Sugar syrup (1 tsp.)
Sparkling water
Lemon slice
Maraschino cherry

Pour all ingredients, except water and
fruit, into a chilled collins glass. Add
some cracked ice and stir. Add three
ice cubes, fill with sparkling water and
garnish with fruit.

BOURBON SOUR

4 parts bourbon (2 oz.)
2 parts fresh lemon juice (1 oz.)
Bar sugar (½ tsp.)
Orange slice

Combine all ingredients, except
orange slice, in a cocktail shaker with
cracked ice. Shake well. Strain into
chilled sour glass and garnish with
orange slice.

BRANDIED APRICOT

4 parts brandy (2 oz.)
1 part apricot brandy (½ oz.)
1 part fresh lemon juice (½ oz.)
Slice fresh apricot

Combine all ingredients, except
apricot, in a cocktail shaker with
cracked ice. Shake well and strain into
chilled cocktail glass. Garnish with
apricot.

BRANDIED MADEIRA

3 parts brandy (1½ oz.)
3 parts Madeira (1½ oz.)
1 part dry vermouth (½ oz.)
Lemon twist

Stir all liquid ingredients in a mixing
glass. Pour into a cocktail glass and
garnish with lemon twist.

BRANDIED PORT

2 parts brandy (1 oz.)
2 parts tawny port (1 oz.)
1 part maraschino liqueur (½ oz.)
2 parts fresh lemon juice (1 oz.)
Orange slice

Combine all ingredients, except
orange slice, with cracked ice in a
cocktail shaker. Shake well. Strain
into chilled cocktail glass and garnish
with orange slice.

BRANDY ALEXANDER

3 parts brandy (1½ oz.)
3 parts dark crème de cacao
(1½ oz.)
3 parts half-and-half (1½ oz.)

Shake all ingredients with cracked ice
in a cocktail shaker. Strain into
chilled cocktail glass.

BRANDY BUCK

4 parts brandy (2 oz.)
1 part white crème de menthe
(½ oz.)
1 part fresh lemon juice (½ oz.)
Sparkling water
Seedless grapes

Combine all ingredients, except water
and grapes, in a cocktail shaker with
cracked ice. Shake well. Pour into
chilled highball glass. Fill with
sparkling water and stir. Garnish with
grapes.

BRANDY CASSIS

4 parts brandy (2 oz.)
1 part crème de cassis (½ oz.)
1 part fresh lemon juice (½ oz.)
Lemon twist

Combine all ingredients, except lemon
twist, in a mixing glass with cracked
ice. Stir well. Strain into chilled
cocktail glass and garnish with lemon
twist.

BRANDY COBBLER

4 parts brandy (2 oz.)
Bar sugar (1 tsp.)
6 parts sparkling water (3 oz.)
Maraschino cherry
Lemon slice

Dissolve the sugar in the sparkling
water in a chilled old-fashioned glass.
Add cracked ice until the glass is
almost full. Add the brandy and stir
well. Garnish with cherry and orange.

BRANDY COCKTAIL

4 parts brandy (2 oz.)
Bar sugar (½ tsp.)
2 dashes Angostura bitters
Lemon twist

Combine liquid ingredients in a
mixing glass and stir until sugar is
dissolved. Pour into cocktail shaker
with cracked ice and shake well.
Strain into chilled cocktail glass and
garnish with lemon twist.

BRANDY CRUSTA

4 parts brandy (2 oz.)
1½ parts Cointreau (¾ oz.)
Maraschino liqueur (2 tsp.)
1 part fresh lemon juice
Bar sugar (1 tbsp.)
Lemon wedge

Rim the edge of a chilled cocktail
glass with sugar by rubbing it with the
lemon wedge and dipping it in the
sugar. Combine all liquid ingredients
in a cocktail shaker with cracked ice.
Shake well and strain into sugar-
rimmed glass.

BRANDY ALEXANDER

BRANDY DAISY

4 parts brandy (2 oz.)
1 part fresh lemon juice (½ oz.)
Grenadine (1 tsp.)
Bar sugar (½ tsp.)
Maraschino cherry

Combine all ingredients, except
cherry, in a cocktail shaker with
cracked ice. Shake well. Pour into
chilled old-fashioned glass and
garnish with cherry.

BRANDY FIX

6 parts brandy (3 oz.)
2 parts fresh lemon juice (1 oz.)
Bar sugar (½ tsp.)
Splash of mineral water

Stir lemon juice, sugar and water in a
chilled highball glass. Fill glass with
cracked ice and brandy. Stir.

BRANDY FIZZ

4 parts brandy (2 oz.)
Bar sugar (½ tsp.)
1 part fresh lemon juice (½ oz.)
Sparkling water

Combine all ingredients, except
sparkling water, in cocktail shaker
with cracked ice and shake well.
Strain into chilled highball glass over
ice cubes and fill with sparkling water.

BRANDY FLIP

4 parts brandy (2 oz.)
Half-and-half (1 tbsp.)
Bar sugar (½ tsp.)
1 egg
Freshly ground nutmeg

Combine all ingredients, except
nutmeg, in a cocktail shaker with
cracked ice. Shake vigorously. Strain
into chilled sour glass and sprinkle
with nutmeg.

BRANDY GUMP

6 parts brandy (3 oz.)
1 part fresh lemon juice (½ oz.)
Grenadine (½ tsp.)

Combine all ingredients with cracked
ice in a cocktail shaker. Shake well
and strain into chilled cocktail glass.

BRANDY MANHATTAN

4 parts brandy (2 oz.)
1 part sweet vermouth (½ oz.)
Dash Angostura bitters
Maraschino cherry

Combine all ingredients, except
cherry, in a mixing glass with cracked
ice. Stir and strain into chilled
cocktail glass. Garnish with cherry.

BRANDY MELBA

4 parts brandy (2 oz.)
1 part peach brandy (½ oz.)
1 part raspberry liqueur (½ oz.)
1 part fresh lemon juice (½ oz.)
3 – 5 dashes orange bitters
Peach slice

Combine all ingredients, except peach
slice, with cracked ice in a cocktail
shaker. Shake well and strain into
chilled cocktail glass. Garnish with
peach.

BRANDY MILK PUNCH

4 parts brandy (2 oz.)
12 parts milk (6 oz.)
Bar sugar (1 tsp.)
Freshly ground nutmeg

Combine all ingredients, except
nutmeg, in a cocktail shaker with
cracked ice. Shake well. Pour into
chilled double old-fashioned glass
and sprinkle nutmeg on top.

BRANDY OLD FASHIONED

6 parts brandy (3 oz.)
3 – 5 dashes Angostura bitters
Sugar cube
Dash of water
Lemon twist

Muddle sugar cube with bitters and
a dash of water in the bottom of a
chilled old-fashioned glass. Add
brandy and ice cubes. Stir and garnish
with lemon peel.

BRANDY SANGAREE

5 parts brandy (2½ oz.)
Bar sugar (½ tsp.)
Dash water
Freshly ground nutmeg

Dissolve sugar with a dash of water in
a chilled double old-fashioned glass.
Add ice cubes and brandy and stir
well. Sprinkle with ground nutmeg.

BRANDY SOUR

5 parts brandy (2½ oz.)
2 parts fresh lemon juice (1 oz.)
Bar sugar (½ tsp.)
Orange slice
Maraschino cherry

Combine all ingredients, except the
fruit, in a cocktail shaker with cracked
ice. Shake well and strain into chilled
sour glass. Garnish with cherry and
orange.

BRANDY SWIZZLE

4 parts brandy (2 oz.)
3 parts fresh lime juice (1½ oz.)
Bar sugar (1 tsp.)
Dash Angostura bitters
Sparkling water

Combine all ingredients, except
sparkling water, in a cocktail shaker
with cracked ice. Shake well. Strain
into collins glass filled with cracked
ice. Add sparkling water. Stir gently
and serve with a swizzle stick.

BRANDY VERMOUTH COCKTAIL

6 parts brandy (3 oz.)
1 part sweet vermouth (½ oz.)
Dash Angostura bitters

Shake all ingredients together with cracked ice in a cocktail shaker. Strain into chilled cocktail glass.

BRAVE BULL

4 parts silver tequila (2 oz.)
2 parts coffee liqueur (1 oz.)
Lemon twist

Pour liquid ingredients into a chilled old-fashioned glass with ice cubes. Stir and garnish with lemon twist.

BRAZIL COCKTAIL

4 parts dry sherry (2 oz.)
3 parts dry vermouth (1½ oz.)
Dash Pernod
Dash Angostura bitters
Lemon twist

Combine all liquid ingredients in a mixing glass with ice cubes and stir well. Strain into chilled cocktail glass and garnish with twist.

BRAZILIAN CHOCOLATE

Unsweetened chocolate (1 solid oz.)
Sugar (¼ cup)
Salt (dash)
16 parts boiling water (8 oz.)
16 parts hot half-and-half (8 oz.)
24 parts strong hot coffee (12 oz.)
Vanilla extract (1 tsp.)
Grated cinnamon (½ tsp.)

Melt chocolate, sugar, and salt in a microwave or a double boiler. Stir in boiling water and continue to heat until mixture is hot and well blended. Add hot half-and-half and coffee. Stir well and add vanilla and cinnamon. Serve in heated coffee mugs Serves 4.

BRIGHTON PUNCH

4 parts B & B (2 oz.)
3 parts bourbon (1½ oz.)
2 parts fresh orange juice (1 oz.)
2 parts fresh lemon juice (1 oz.)
Sparkling water
Orange slice

Combine all ingredients, except water and fruit, with cracked ice in a cocktail shaker. Shake well. Strain into a chilled highball glass over ice cubes. Top off with sparkling water and stir. Garnish with orange.

BRITTANY

4 parts gin (2 oz.)
1 part Amer Picon (½ oz.)
1 part fresh lemon juice (½ oz.)
1 part fresh orange juice (½ oz.)
Bar sugar (½ tsp.)
Orange twist

Combine all ingredients, except orange twist, with cracked ice in a cocktail shaker. Shake well and strain into chilled cocktail glass. Garnish with orange twist.

BRONX CHEER

4 parts apricot brandy (2 oz.)
Raspberry soda
Orange peel
Fresh raspberries

Pour brandy into a chilled collins glass almost filled with ice cubes. Fill with raspberry soda. Stir gently and garnish with orange peel and a few fresh raspberries.

BRONX COCKTAIL

4 parts gin (2 oz.)
1 part dry vermouth (½ oz.)
1 part sweet vermouth (½ oz.)
2 parts fresh orange juice (1 oz.)

Combine all ingredients in a mixing glass with cracked ice. Stir and strain into chilled cocktail glass.

BRONX CHEER

BRONX SILVER COCKTAIL

4 parts gin (2 oz.)
1 part dry vermouth (½ oz.)
1 egg white
2 parts fresh orange juice (1 oz.)

Combine all ingredients with cracked ice in a cocktail shaker. Shake vigorously. Strain into chilled cocktail glass.

BRONX TERRACE COCKTAIL

4 parts gin (2 oz.)
1 part dry vermouth (½ oz.)
2 parts fresh lime juice (1 oz.)
Maraschino cherry

Combine liquid ingredients with cracked ice in a cocktail shaker and shake well. Strain into chilled cocktail glass and garnish with cherry.

BROWN COCKTAIL

3 parts gin (1½ oz.)
2 parts light rum (1 oz.)
1 part dry vermouth (½ oz.)

Stir all ingredients with cracked ice in a mixing glass and strain into chilled cocktail glass.

BUDDHA PUNCH

32 parts Gewurtzaminner
or Riesling wine (2 cups or 16 oz.)
16 parts light rum (1 cup or 8 oz.)
16 parts fresh orange juice (1 cup or 8 oz.)
8 parts fresh lemon juice (½ cup or 4 oz.)
8 parts triple sec (½ cup or 4 oz.)
1 part cherry brandy (½ oz.)
1 part sugar syrup (½ oz.)
Several dashes orange bitters
Champagne or sparkling wine (1 bottle or 750-ml.)
Lime slices

Pre-chill all ingredients. Pour everything, except champagne and lime slices, into chilled punch bowl. Stir. Just before serving, add the champagne and a block of ice. Stir gently and float lime slices on top. Serves 20.

BUDDY'S BLOODY MARY

4 parts vodka (2 oz.)
12 parts V-8 juice (6 oz.)
Fresh lime juice (½ tsp.)
Several dashes Worcestershire sauce
Several dashes Tabasco sauce
White horseradish (1 tsp.)
Freshly ground pepper to taste
Celery salt to taste
Lime wedge

Combine V-8 juice, lime juice, Worcestershire sauce, Tabasco sauce and horseradish in a cocktail shaker. Shake well. Fill a chilled highball glass with ice cubes. Grind pepper and shake celery salt into the glass to make seasoned ice cubes. Pour the juice mixture into the highball glass and stir gently. Squeeze the lime slice over the drink and drop in.

BULLDOG

4 parts cherry brandy (2 oz.)
2 parts light rum (1 oz.)
2 parts fresh lime juice (1 oz.)

Combine all ingredients with cracked ice in a cocktail shaker. Shake well. Strain into chilled cocktail glass.

BULLFROG

4 parts vodka (2 oz.)
Triple sec (1 tsp.)
Limeade
Lime slice

Pour vodka and triple sec over ice cubes into a chilled highball glass. Stir. Top off with limeade. Stir again and garnish with slice of lime.

BULLSHOT

4 parts vodka (2 oz.)
8 parts cold beef bouillon (4 oz.)
Fresh lemon juice (1 tsp.)
Several dashes Worcestershire sauce
Tabasco sauce to taste
Celery salt to taste
Freshly ground pepper to taste

Mix all ingredients in a chilled highball glass with ice cubes.

BUNNY BONANZA

4 parts tequila (2 oz.)
2 parts apple brandy (1 oz.)
1 part fresh lemon juice (½ oz.)
Maple syrup (¾ tsp.)
3 dashes triple sec
Lemon slice

Combine all ingredients, except lemon slice, in a cocktail shaker with cracked ice. Shake well. Strain into chilled old-fashioned glass and garnish with lemon slice.

BURGUNDY PUNCH

Red Burgundy or Cabernet Sauvignon (2 bottles or 750-ml.)
16 parts kirschwasser (1 cup or 8 oz.)
16 parts port (1 cup or 8 oz.)
32 parts fresh orange juice (1 pint or 16 oz.)
8 parts fresh lemon juice (½ cup or 4 oz.)
2 parts sugar syrup (1 oz.)
Orange slices

Pre-chill ingredients. Pour into chilled punch bowl with a block of ice. Stir well and garnish with orange slices. Serves 20.

BUSHRANGER

4 parts light rum (2 oz.)
3 parts Dubonnet rouge (1½ oz.)
Dash Angostura bitters
Lemon twist

Combine all ingredients, except lemon peel, in a cocktail shaker with cracked ice. Shake well. Strain into chilled cocktail glass and garnish with lemon peel.

BUTTON HOOK

2 parts brandy (1 oz.)
2 parts apricot brandy (1 oz.)
2 parts white crème de menthe (1 oz.)
2 parts Pernod (1 oz.)

Combine all ingredients with cracked ice in a cocktail shaker and shake well. Strain into chilled cocktail glass.

BUTTAFUOCO

4 parts white tequila (2 oz.)
1 part Galliano (½ oz.)
1 part cherry liqueur (½ oz.)
1 part fresh lemon juice (½ oz.)
Club soda
Maraschino cherry

Combine all ingredients with cracked ice in a cocktail shaker, except club soda and cherry. Shake well. Strain into highball glass over ice cubes and fill with club soda. Stir gently. Top off with cherry.

BULL'S MILK

5 parts brandy (2½ oz.)
2 parts dark rum (1 oz.)
10 parts milk (5 oz.)
Bar sugar (½ tsp.)
Freshly grated nutmeg

Combine all ingredients, except nutmeg, with cracked ice in a mixing glass. Stir well. Pour into chilled highball glass and sprinkle with nutmeg.

BYRRH CASSIS

4 parts byrrh (2 oz.)
2 parts crème de cassis (1 oz.)
Sparkling water

Mix byrrh and crème de cassis in a chilled balloon wine glass. Add ice cubes and top off with chilled sparkling water.

C

CABARET

4 parts gin (2 oz.)
3 parts Dubonnet rouge
(1½ oz.)
3 – 5 dashes Angostura bitters
3 – 5 dashes Pernod
Maraschino cherry

Combine all ingredients, except
cherry, in a cocktail shaker and shake
well. Strain into chilled cocktail glass
and garnish with cherry.

CABLEGRAM

4 parts blended whiskey
(2 oz.)
1 part fresh lemon juice (½ oz.)
Bar sugar (½ tsp.)
Ginger ale

Stir all ingredients, except ginger ale,
in a mixing glass with cracked ice.
Strain into chilled highball glass over
ice cubes. Top off with ginger ale and
stir again.

CADIZ

3 parts dry sherry (1½ oz.)
2 parts blackberry brandy (1 oz.)
1 part triple sec (½ oz.)
1 part half-and-half (½ oz.)

Combine all ingredients with cracked
ice in a cocktail shaker with cracked
ice. Shake well. Strain into chilled
old-fashioned glass.

CAFÉ AU LAIT

Hot coffee
Hot milk
Sugar (optional)

Combine equal parts of each liquid in
a heated coffee mug. Sweeten to taste.

CAFÉ BRULOT

16 parts cognac (1 cup
or 8 oz.)
4 parts white Curaçao (2 oz.)
64 parts hot black coffee (1 quart or
32 oz.)
2 cinnamon sticks
12 whole cloves
Peels of 2 lemons and 2 oranges cut
into thin strips
4 sugar cubes

In a large punch bowl, mash together
the cinnamon, cloves, fruit peel and
sugar. Sit in the brandy and Curaçao.
Ignite and gradually add hot coffee,
stirring gently until the flames are
extinguished. Serve in warmed mugs.
Serves 6 – 8.

CAFÉ DE PARIS COCKTAIL

4 parts gin (2 oz.)
Pernod (1 tsp.)
Half-and half (1 tsp.)
1 egg white

Combine all ingredients with cracked
ice in a cocktail shaker. Shake
vigorously. Strain into chilled cocktail
glass.

CAFÉ DIABLO

4 parts cognac (2 oz.)
2 parts Cointreau (1 oz.)
2 parts white Curaçao (1 oz.)
32 parts hot black coffee (1 pint or
16 oz.)
2 cinnamon sticks
8 whole cloves
6 coffee beans

Place all ingredients, except coffee, in
chafing dish. Warm the contents over
low, direct heat. Ignite. Add the coffee
and stir until flames are extinguished.
Serve in warmed mugs. Serves 4.

CAFÉ ROMANO

2 parts white Sambuca (1 oz.)
2 parts coffee liqueur (1 oz.)
2 parts half-and-half (1 oz.)

Combine all ingredients in a cocktail
shaker with cracked ice and shake
well. Strain into chilled cocktail glass.

CAFÉ ROYALE

4 parts brandy or cognac
(2 oz.)
1 sugar cube
Hot black coffee (1 cup)
Half-and-half to taste

Pour hot coffee into mug. Rest a
tablespoon on top of the cup and put
the sugar cube in it. Soak the sugar
with the brandy. After the spoon heats
up, ignite the sugar. Hold until flame
burns out and pour the sugar/brandy
mixture into the coffee. Float half-
and-half on top.

CAIPIRINHA

4 parts Cachaça (Brazilian sugar
cane alcohol) (2 oz.)
1 part fresh lime juice (1 oz.)
Granulated sugar (1 tbsp.)
Lime rinds

Combine all ingredients in a cocktail
shaker with cracked ice. Shake well.
Strain into chilled old-fashioned glass
over ice cubes.

CAJUN MARTINI

6 parts pepper vodka (3 oz.)
Dash of dry vermouth
Large slice of pickled jalapeño pepper

Combine vodka and vermouth in a
mixing glass with cracked ice and stir
well. Strain into cocktail glass. Drop
in the jalapeño.

NOTE: For a Cajun martini with extra
kick, steep pickled jalapeños in the
vodka for at least an hour in the
freezer before preparing the drink.

CAFÉ ROYALE

CAIPIRINHA (from The Coffee Shop)

CALIFORNIA LEMONADE

4 parts blended whiskey (2 oz.)
2 parts fresh lemon juice (1 oz.)
2 parts fresh lime juice (1 oz.)
Bar sugar (1 tsp.)
Sparkling water
Orange slice

Combine whiskey, juices and sugar in a cocktail shaker with cracked ice. Shake well. Strain into a chilled highball glass almost filled with ice cubes. Top off with sparkling water. Stir gently and garnish with orange slice.

CALIFORNIA SMOOTHIE

1 banana, sliced thin
Fresh strawberries (½ cup)
Pitted dates, chopped (½ cup)
3 parts honey (1½ oz.)
16 parts cold fresh orange juice (8 oz.)
Cracked ice

Combine fruits and honey in a blender and blend until smooth. Add orange juice and cracked ice and blend until smooth. Pour into chilled collins glass.

CALM VOYAGE

3 parts light rum (1½ oz.)
2 parts Strega (½ oz.)
Passionfruit syrup (1 tbsp.)
Fresh lemon juice (1 tbsp.)
½ egg white

Combine all ingredients in a blender with cracked ice. Blend at low speed until smooth and pour into chilled champagne flute.

CALYPSO

4 parts gold rum (2 oz.)
2 parts pineapple juice (1 oz.)
1 part fresh lemon juice (½ oz.)
Falernum (1 tsp.)
Dash Angostura bitters
Freshly grated nutmeg

Combine all ingredients, except
nutmeg, with cracked ice in a cocktail
shaker. Shake well and strain into
chilled cocktail glass. Sprinkle with
nutmeg.

CAMPARI-SODA

4 parts Campari (2 oz.)
Sparkling water
Lime wedge

Fill a highball glass with ice cubes
and pour the Campari into the glass.
Fill with Pellegrino water and stir
gently. Squeeze the lime over the drink
and drop it in.

CANADIAN AND CAMPARI

3 parts Canadian whisky
(1½ oz.)
2 parts Campari (1 oz.)
1 part dry vermouth (½ oz.)
Lemon twist

Stir all ingredients, except lemon
twist, in a mixing glass with cracked
ice. Strain into chilled cocktail glass
and garnish with lemon twist.

CANADIAN APPLE

4 parts Canadian whisky
(2 oz.)
1 part apple brandy (½ oz.)
Sugar syrup (1 tsp.)
Fresh lemon juice (1½ tsp.)
Ground cinnamon
Lemon slice

Combine all ingredients except lemon
slice in a cocktail shaker with cracked
ice and shake well. Pour into chilled
old-fashioned glass and garnish with
lemon slice.

CANADIAN BLACKBERRY COCKTAIL

4 parts Canadian whisky (2 oz.)
1 part blackberry brandy (½ oz.)
1 part fresh orange juice (½ oz.)
Fresh lemon juice (1 tsp.)
Bar sugar (½ tsp.)

Combine all ingredients with cracked
ice in a cocktail shaker and shake well.
Strain into a chilled old-fashioned
glass.

CANADIAN CHERRY

4 parts Canadian whisky
(2 oz.)
2 part cherry brandy (1 oz.)
Fresh lemon juice (2 tsp.)
Fresh orange juice (2 tsp.)
Bar sugar

Rim a chilled cocktail glass with
sugar by pouring one part of the
cherry brandy into a saucer and
dipping the glass into it. Pour some
sugar into another saucer and dip the
moistened rim into the sugar. Shake
all ingredients in a cocktail shaker
with cracked ice and strain into the
glass.

CANADIAN COCKTAIL

4 parts Canadian whisky (2 oz.)
Triple sec (2 tsp.)
Dash Angostura bitters
Bar sugar (½ tsp.)

Combine all ingredients in cocktail
shaker and shake with cracked ice.
Strain into chilled old-fashioned glass.

CANADIAN DAISY

CANADIAN DAISY

4 parts Canadian whisky
(2 oz.)
Brandy (1 tsp.)
1 part fresh lemon juice (½ oz.)
Raspberry syrup (1 tsp.)
Sparkling water
Fresh raspberries

Combine whiskey, lemon juice and
raspberry syrup in a cocktail shaker
with ice cubes and shake well. Pour
into a chilled highball glass and
top off with sparkling water. Float
brandy on top and garnish with fresh
raspberries.

CANADIAN OLD FASHIONED

4 parts Canadian whisky (2 oz.)
Triple sec (1 tsp.)
Dash fresh lemon juice
Dash Angostura bitters
Lemon twist
Orange twist

Combine all ingredients, except twists,
in a cocktail shaker with cracked ice.
Shake well and pour into chilled old-
fashioned glass. Garnish with twists.

CANADIAN PINEAPPLE

4 parts Canadian whisky (2 oz.)
Pineapple juice (1 tbsp.)
Maraschino liqueur (2 tsp.)
Fresh lemon juice (2 tsp.)
Pineapple spear

Combine all ingredients, except the pineapple spear, in a cocktail shaker with cracked ice. Shake well. Strain into chilled cocktail glass and garnish with pineapple spear.

CANTALOUPE CUP

4 parts light rum (2 oz.)
1 part fresh lime juice (½ oz.)
1 part fresh orange juice (½ oz.)
Diced ripe cantaloupe (⅓ cup)
Bar sugar (½ tsp.)
Cantaloupe slice

Combine all ingredients, except cantaloupe slice, in a blender with cracked ice. Blend until smooth. Pour into chilled old-fashioned glass and garnish with cantaloupe slice.

CAPE COD COOLER

4 parts sloe gin (2 oz.)
2 parts gin (1 oz.)
1 part fresh lime juice (½ oz.)
1 part orgeat (almond) syrup (½ oz.)
10 parts cranberry juice (5 oz.)
Lime slice

Combine all ingredients, except lime slice, in a cocktail shaker with cracked ice. Shake well. Pour into chilled collins glass and garnish with lime.

CAPE COD SUNRISE

6 parts cranberry juice (3 oz.)
2 parts fresh lime juice (1 oz.)
Lime slice
Fresh mint sprig

Combine ingredients with crushed ice in a cocktail shaker. Shake well and pour into chilled wine glass. Garnish with lime slice and mint.

CAPE CODDER

4 parts vodka (2 oz.)
12 parts cranberry juice (6 oz.)
Lime wedge

Stir vodka and juice in a chilled highball glass with ice cubes. Squeeze the lime wedge over the drink and drop it in.

CAPRI

2 parts white crème de cacao (1 oz.)
2 parts crème de bananes (1 oz.)
2 parts half-and-half (1 oz.)

Shake all ingredients with cracked ice in a cocktail shaker. Strain into chilled old-fashioned glass over ice cubes.

CARA SPOSA

3 parts coffee liqueur (1½ oz.)
2 parts Cointreau (1 oz.)
2 parts half-and-half (1 oz.)

Combine all ingredients with cracked ice in a blender. Blend until smooth. Pour into chilled cocktail glass.

CAPE CODDER

CARDINAL

4 parts light rum (2 oz.)
1 part amaretto (½ oz.)
1 part triple sec (½ oz.)
2 parts fresh lime juice (1 oz.)
Grenadine (½ tsp.)
Lime slice

Combine all ingredients, except lime slice, in a cocktail shaker with cracked ice. Pour into chilled old-fashioned glass and garnish with lime slice.

CARIBBEAN CHAMPAGNE

Chilled champagne or sparkling wine
Light rum (½ tsp.)
Crème de bananes (½ tsp.)
Banana slice

Pour rum and crème de bananes in a chilled champagne flute. Fill with champagne and stir gently. Garnish with banana slice.

CHAMBORLADA (from The Shark Bar)

CAROLINA

6 parts gold tequila (3 oz.)
2 parts half-and-half (1 oz.)
Grenadine (1 tsp.)
Vanilla extract (1 tsp.)
1 egg white
Ground cinnamon
Maraschino cherry

Combine all ingredients, except
cinnamon and cherry, in a cocktail
shaker with cracked ice. Shake
vigorously. Strain into chilled cocktail
glass. Sprinkle with cinnamon and
top with cherry.

CARROL COCKTAIL

4 parts brandy (2 oz.)
1 part sweet vermouth (½ oz.)
Maraschino cherry

Stir liquid ingredients with cracked ice
in a mixing glass. Strain into chilled
cocktail glass and garnish with cherry.

CARROT COCKTAIL

6 parts pineapple juice (3 oz.)
Crushed pineapple (¼ cup)
Carrots, chopped (2 small or 1 large)

Combine all ingredients with cracked
ice in a blender. Blend until slushy
and pour into chilled highball glass.

CARUSO

4 parts gin (2 oz.)
1 part dry vermouth (½ oz.)
1 part green crème de menthe (½ oz.)

Combine ingredients in mixing glass
with cracked ice and stir. Strain into
chilled cocktail glass.

CASA BLANCA

4 parts light rum (2 oz.)
1 part triple sec (½ oz.)
1 part cherry liqueur (½ oz.)
1 part fresh lime juice (½ oz.)

Combine all ingredients with cracked
ice in a cocktail shaker and shake
well. Strain into chilled cocktail glass.

CASINO

5 parts gin (2½ oz.)
1 part fresh lemon juice (½ oz.)
Maraschino liqueur (1 tsp.)
2 dashes orange bitters

Combine all ingredients with cracked ice in a cocktail shaker and shake well. Strain into chilled cocktail glass.

CHAMBORLADA

4 parts light rum (2 oz.)
2 parts dark rum (1 oz.)
6 parts pineapple juice (3 oz.)
4 parts coconut cream (2 oz.)
4 parts Chambord

Combine all ingredients, except Chambord, with cracked ice in a blender. Blend until smooth. Pour the Chambord into the bottom of the balloon wine glass. Then pour the piña colada mixture on top of that, keeping it layered. Top off the piña colada mixture with a little more Chambord.

CHAMPAGNE COCKTAIL

1 sugar cube
Several dashes Angostura bitters
Chilled champagne
Lemon twist

Place sugar cube in bottom of chilled champagne flute. Douse with bitters. Fill with chilled champagne and stir. Garnish with lemon twist.

CHAMPAGNE COOLER

3 parts brandy (1½ oz.)
2 parts triple sec (1 oz.)
Champagne or sparkling wine
Fresh mint

Pour brandy and triple sec into a chilled red wine glass, fill with champagne, and stir. Garnish with sprig of fresh mint.

CHAMPAGNE COCKTAIL
(from The Promenade Bar at the Rainbow Room)

CHAMPAGNE CUP

1 part cognac (½ oz.)
1 part white Curaçao (½ oz.)
Champagne or sparkling wine
Orange slice
Fresh mint sprig

Pour cognac and Curaçao into chilled wine glass, add one ice cube and fill with champagne. Garnish with orange slice and mint sprig.

CHAMPAGNE PUNCH

16 parts cognac (1 cup or 8 oz.)
16 parts cherry liqueur (1 cup or 8 oz.)
16 parts triple sec (1 cup or 8 oz.)
8 parts sugar syrup (½ cup or 4 oz.)
8 parts fresh lemon juice (½ cup or 4 oz.)
Champagne or sparkling wine (2 bottles or 750-ml.)

Pre-chill ingredients. Pour all ingredients except champagne into a large punch bowl with a block of ice and stir well. Before serving, add champagne and stir gently. Serves 15 – 20.

CHAMPAGNE SORBET PUNCH

Champagne or sparkling wine
(2 bottles – 750-ml. each)
White dessert wine (1 bottle –
750-ml.)
Lemon sorbet (1 quart)

Combine champagne and wine in a
punch bowl with a block of ice. Stir
gently. Add a block of ice and scoops of
the sorbet. Serves 20 – 25.

CHAMPS ELYSÉES

4 parts cognac (2 oz.)
1 part yellow Chartreuse (½ oz.)
1 part fresh lemon juice (½ oz.)
Bar sugar (½ tsp.)
Dash Angostura bitters

Combine all ingredients with cracked
ice in a cocktail shaker and shake
well. Pour into chilled cocktail glass.

CHANGUIRONGO

4 parts silver tequila (2 oz.)
Ginger ale
Lime wedge

Pour tequila and soda into a chilled
collins glass filled with ice cubes. Stir
and garnish with lime wedge.

CHANTICLEER

4 parts gin (2 oz.)
2 parts fresh lemon juice (1 oz.)
Raspberry syrup (1 tbsp.)
1 egg white

Combine all ingredients with cracked
ice in a cocktail shaker and shake
vigorously. Strain into a chilled old-
fashioned glass.

CHAPALA

4 parts gold tequila (2 oz.)
1 part triple sec (½ oz.)
4 parts fresh orange juice (2 oz.)
2 parts fresh lime juice (1 oz.)
1 part grenadine (½ oz.)

Combine all ingredients in a cocktail
shaker and shake well. Pour into a
chilled highball glass half-filled with
cracked ice and stir.

CHAPEL HILL

4 parts bourbon (2 oz.)
1 part white Curaçao (½ oz.)
1 part fresh lemon juice (½ oz.)
Orange slice

Combine all ingredients, except
orange slice, with cracked ice in a
cocktail shaker. Shake well and strain
into chilled cocktail glass. Garnish
with orange slice.

CHARLES COCKTAIL

4 parts brandy (2 oz.)
1 part sweet vermouth (½ oz.)
2 – 3 dashes Angostura bitters

Combine all ingredients in a mixing
glass with cracked ice and stir. Strain
into chilled cocktail glass.

CHARLIE CHAPLIN

4 parts sloe gin (2 oz.)
4 parts apricot brandy (2 oz.)
3 parts fresh lemon juice (1½ oz.)

Combine all ingredients with cracked
ice in a cocktail shaker and shake
well. Strain over ice cubes into a
chilled old-fashioned glass.

CHARMER

3 parts scotch (1½ oz.)
1 part blue Curaçao (½ oz.)
Dash dry vermouth
Dash orange bitters

Mix all ingredients with cracked ice in
a cocktail shaker. Strain in to chilled
cocktail glass.

CHATHAM COCKTAIL

4 parts gin (2 oz.)
1 part ginger brandy (½ oz.)
1 part fresh lemon juice (½ oz.)
Bar sugar (½ tsp.)
Small piece of candied ginger

Combine all ingredients, except
ginger, in a cocktail shaker with
cracked ice. Shake well. Strain into
chilled cocktail glass and garnish with
ginger.

CHEERY CHERRY

8 parts unsweetened cherry
cider (4 oz.)
2 parts fresh lime juice (1 oz.)
Sparkling water
Lemon slice

Pour cider and sparkling water into a
chilled highball glass over ice. Stir
and garnish with lemon slice.

CHELSEA SIDECAR

4 parts gin (2 oz.)
1 part triple sec (½ oz.)
1 part fresh lemon juice (½ oz.)

Combine all ingredients with cracked
ice in a cocktail shaker and shake
well. Strain into chilled cocktail glass.

CHATHAM

CHERRY BLOSSOM

4 parts brandy (2 oz.)
2 parts kirschwasser (1 oz.)
1 part triple sec (½ oz.)
1 part fresh lemon juice (½ oz.)
Grenadine (1 tbsp.)
Bar sugar (½ tsp.)

Combine all ingredients with cracked ice in a cocktail shaker and shake well. Strain into chilled cocktail glass.

CHERRY COBBLER

4 parts gin (2 oz.)
1 part cherry Heering (½ oz.)
1 part crème de cassis (½ oz.)
1 part fresh lemon juice (½ oz.)
Sugar syrup (1 tbsp.)
Maraschino cherry
Lemon slice

Combine all ingredients, except lemon slice and cherry, in a cocktail shaker with cracked ice. Shake well and strain into chilled old-fashioned glass. Garnish with cherry and lemon slice.

CHERRY COOLER

4 parts kirschwasser (2 oz.)
Cola
Lemon slice

Pour kirschwasser and cola into a
chilled highball glass over ice. Stir
and garnish with lemon slice.

CHERRY DAIQUIRI

4 parts light rum (2 oz.)
1 part cherry liqueur (½ oz.)
1 part fresh lime juice (½ oz.)
Kirschwasser (¼ tsp.)
Lime twist

Combine all ingredients, except lime
twist, in a cocktail shaker with cracked
ice. Shake well and strain into chilled
cocktail glass. Garnish with lime twist.

CHERRY FIZZ

4 parts kirschwasser (2 oz.)
1 part fresh lemon juice (½ oz.)
Bar sugar (½ tsp.)
Sparkling water
Maraschino cherry

Combine all ingredients, except water
and cherry, in a cocktail shaker with
cracked ice. Shake well. Strain over ice
cubes into a chilled collins glass. Fill
with sparkling water and stir gently.
Garnish with cherry.

CHERRY RASPBERRY
SHAKE

8 parts unsweetened cherry cider
(4 oz.)
8 parts raspberry sorbet (4 oz.)
Fresh lemon juice (1 tsp.)

Combine all ingredients with cracked
ice in a blender. Blend untilslushy and
pour into chilled collins glass.

CHERRY RUM

4 parts light rum (2 oz.)
2 parts cherry brandy (1 oz.)
1 part half-and-half (½ oz.)

Combine all ingredients with cracked
ice in a cocktail shaker and shake
well. Strain into chilled cocktail glass.

CHI-CHI

CHI-CHI

4 parts light rum (2 oz.)
1 part blackberry brandy (½ oz.)
Pineapple juice

Stir rum and pineapple juice together
in a chilled highball glass almost
filled with ice cubes. Float brandy on
top.

CHICAGO

4 parts brandy (2 oz.)
Dash triple sec
Dash Angostura bitters
Champagne or sparkling wine
Lemon wedge
Bar sugar

Rim a chilled balloon wine glass with
sugar by moistening the rim of the
glass with the lemon wedge and
rolling it in sugar. Mix brandy, triple
sec and bitters with cracked ice in a
mixing glass and strain into wine
glass. Fill with champagne.

CHOCOLATE COCKTAIL

CHICAGO FIZZ

3 parts gold rum (1½ oz.)
2 parts port (1 oz.)
1 part fresh lemon juice (½ oz.)
Bar sugar (½ tsp.)
1 egg white
Sparkling water

Combine all ingredients, except
sparkling water, with cracked ice in a
cocktail shaker. Shake vigorously.
Strain into chilled collins glass over
ice cubes and fill with sparkling water.
Stir gently.

CHICKEN SHOT

4 parts chilled chicken
bouillon (2 oz.)
4 parts chilled beef bouillon (2 oz.)
1 part fresh lemon juice (½ oz.)
Tabasco sauce to taste
Worcestershire sauce to taste
Freshly ground pepper to taste
Celery salt to taste

Combine all ingredients in a mixing
glass with cracked ice. Stir well. Pour
into chilled old-fashioned glass.

CHINESE COCKTAIL

4 parts dark rum (2 oz.)
Grenadine (1 tbsp.)
3 – 5 dashes white Curaçao
3 – 5 dashes maraschino liqueur
Dash Angostura bitters

Combine all ingredients with cracked
ice in a cocktail shaker and shake
well. Strain into chilled cocktail glass.

PLEASE NOTE: Blue icons represent
alcoholic drinks. Green icons represent
non-alcoholic drinks.

CHIQUITA

4 parts vodka (2 oz.)
1 part banana liqueur
(½ oz.)
1 part fresh lime juice (½ oz.)
¼ cup sliced bananas
Orgeat (almond) syrup (1 tsp.)

Combine all ingredients in a mixing
glass with cracked ice and stir well.
Pour into chilled deep-saucer
champagne glass.

CHOCOLATE COCKTAIL

6 parts port (3 oz.)
1 part yellow chartreuse (1 oz.)
1 egg yolk
Grated semi-sweet chocolate (1 tbsp.)

Combine port, chartreuse and egg
yolk with cracked ice in a blender.
Blend until smooth. Pour into chilled
cocktail glass and sprinkle with
chocolate.

CHOCOLATE RUM

4 parts light rum (2 oz.)
2 parts dark crème de cacao (1 oz.)
2 parts white crème de menthe (1 oz.)
1 part 151-proof rum (½ oz.)
2 parts half-and-half (1 oz.)

Shake all ingredients with cracked ice
in a cocktail shaker. Strain over ice
cubes into a chilled old-fashioned
glass.

CHOCOLATIER CAKE

2 parts crème de cacao (1 oz.)
2 parts brandy (1 oz.)
2 parts heavy cream (1 oz.)

Prechill all ingredients. Using a bar
spoon, carefully pour each ingredient
into a chilled pony glass in the order
listed.

CHOCOLATÍER CAKE

CHRYSANTHEMUM COCKTAIL

4 parts dry vermouth (2 oz.)
3 parts Benedictine (1½ oz.)
Pernod (¼ tsp.)
Orange twist

Combine the vermouth and Benedictine in a mixing glass with cracked ice and stir. Strain into chilled cocktail glass. Add the Pernod and stir. Drop the orange twist into the drink.

CIDER CUP

8 parts brandy (4 oz.)
4 parts Cointreau (2 oz.)
32 parts apple cider (16 oz.)
16 parts sparkling water (8 oz.)
Bar sugar (4 tsp.)
Apple slices
Fresh mint sprigs

Stir all ingredients, except apples and mint, with ice cubes in a large pitcher. Garnish with apple slices and mint. Serve in red wine glasses. Serves 3 – 4.

CLAM DIGGER

16 parts Clamato juice (8 oz.)
2 parts fresh lime juice (1 oz.)
Tabasco sauce (3 – 5 dashes)
Worcestershire sauce (3 – 5 dashes)
Freshly ground pepper to taste
Celery salt to taste
White horseradish (¼ tsp.)
Celery stalk
Lime wedge

Combine all ingredients with cracked ice in a cocktail shaker and shake well. Strain into chilled collins glass over ice cubes and garnish with lime wedge and celery stalk.

CLARET COBBLER

8 parts chilled claret or
Cabernet Sauvignon (4 oz.)
Fresh lemon juice (1 tsp.)
Bar sugar (1 tsp.)
4 parts chilled sparkling water (2 oz.)
Orange slice

In a chilled wine glass, dissolve sugar in lemon juice and water. Add claret and cracked ice. Stir gently and garnish with orange slice.

CLARET CUP

32 parts claret or
Cabernet Sauvignon
(16 oz.)
4 parts brandy (2 oz.)
2 parts Cointreau (1 oz.)
Bar sugar (3 tsp.)
16 parts sparkling water (8 oz.)
Orange slices
Fresh mint sprigs

Stir all ingredients, except orange slices and mint sprigs, in a large pitcher with ice cubes. Garnish with fruit and mint. Serve in red wine glasses. Serves 3 – 4.

CLARET PUNCH

Claret or Cabernet
Sauvignon (3 bottles – 750 ml. each)
32 parts brandy (16 oz.)
16 parts Cointreau (8 oz.)
Fresh lemon juice (24 oz.)
Bar sugar (½ –1 cup to taste)
Sliced fruits in season

Stir all ingredients except fruit in a large punch bowl. Add one block of ice. Decorate with sliced seasonal fruits. Serves 15 – 20.

CLARIDGE COCKTAIL

4 parts gin (2 oz.)
1 part dry vermouth (½ oz.)
1 part apricot brandy (½ oz.)
1 part triple sec (½ oz.)

Combine all ingredients in a cocktail shaker with cracked ice. Shake well and strain into chilled cocktail glass.

CLASSIC COCKTAIL

4 parts brandy (2 oz.)
1 part white Curaçao (½ oz.)
1 part maraschino liqueur (½ oz.)
1 part fresh lemon juice (½ oz.)
Lemon twist
Lemon wedge
Bar sugar

Rim a chilled cocktail glass with sugar by moistening the edge with the lemon wedge and dipping in sugar. Combine remaining ingredients, except lemon twist, in a cocktail shaker with cracked ice. Shake well. Strain into sugar-rimmed cocktail glass and garnish with lemon twist.

CLOISTER

4 parts gin (2 oz.)
1 part yellow Chartreuse (½ oz.)
1 part fresh grapefruit juice (½ oz.)
Fresh lemon juice (1 tsp.)
Bar sugar (½ tsp.)

Combine all ingredients with cracked ice in a cocktail shaker. Shake well and strain into chilled cocktail glass.

CLOVER CLUB COCKTAIL

4 parts gin (2 oz.)
2 part fresh lemon juice (1 oz.)
Grenadine (2 tsp.)
1 egg white

Combine all ingredients with cracked ice in a cocktail shaker and shake vigorously. Strain into chilled cocktail glass.

COCK N'BULL SHOT

4 parts vodka (2 oz.)
4 parts chicken bouillon (2 oz.)
4 parts beef bouillon (2 oz.)
1 part fresh lemon juice (½ oz.)
Tabasco sauce to taste
Worcestershire sauce to taste
Freshly ground pepper to taste
Celery salt to taste

Combine all ingredients in a mixing glass with cracked ice. Stir well. Pour into chilled old-fashioned glass.

COCO CHANEL

3 parts gin (1½ oz.)
3 parts coffee liqueur (1½ oz.)
3 parts half-and-half (1½ oz.)

Combine all ingredients with cracked ice in a cocktail shaker. Shake well and strain into chilled cocktail glass.

COCO COLA

4 parts coconut milk (2 oz.)
2 parts fresh lime juice (1 oz.)
Cola
Lime wedge

Combine coconut milk and lime juice in a cocktail shaker and shake well. Pour over ice into a chilled highball glass. Fill with colaand garnish with lime wedge.

COCO LOCO

1 fresh coconut with coconut water
Crushed ice (1 cup)
4 parts silver tequila (2 oz.)
2 parts gin (1 oz.)
2 parts light rum (1 oz.)
4 parts pineapple juice (2 oz.)
Sugar syrup (1 tsp.)
½ lime

Open a fresh coconut by sawing off the top. Do not discard the water inside. Add the crushed ice to the coconut and pour in all liquid ingredients. Squeeze the lime half over the drink and drop it in. Stir well.

COCONUT COOLER

4 parts coconut milk (2 oz.)
4 parts fresh lime juice (2 oz.)
Sparkling water
Fresh mint sprig

Combine coconut milk and lime juice in a cocktail shaker and shake well. Pour over ice cubes into a chilled collins glass. Fill with sparkling water and stir gently. Garnish with mint sprig.

COFFEE COCKTAIL

6 parts ruby port (3 oz.)
2 parts brandy (1 oz.)
2 – 3 dashes white Curaçao
1 egg yolk
Bar sugar (½ tsp.)
Freshly grated nutmeg

Combine all ingredients, except nutmeg, in a blender with cracked ice. Blend until smooth. Pour into chilled sour glass and sprinkle with nutmeg.

COCO LOCO

COFFEE EGG NOG

4 parts blended whiskey (2 oz.)
2 parts coffee liqueur (1 oz.)
12 parts milk (6 oz.)
2 parts half-and-half (1 oz.)
Sugar syrup (1 tsp.)
Instant coffee (½ tsp.)
1 egg
Freshly ground nutmeg

Combine all ingredients, except
nutmeg, with cracked ice in a blender.
Blend until smooth and pour into
chilled collins glass. Sprinkle with
nutmeg.

COFFEE FLIP

4 parts cognac (2 oz.)
2 parts ruby port (1 oz.)
10 parts cold coffee (5 oz.)
Bar sugar (½ tsp.)
1 egg
Freshly ground nutmeg

Combine all ingredients, except
nutmeg, in a blender with cracked ice.
Blend until smooth. Pour into chilled
red wine glass and sprinkle with
nutmeg.

COFFEE GRASSHOPPER

3 parts coffee liqueur (1½ oz.)
2 parts white crème de menthe (1 oz.)
2 parts half-and-half (1 oz)

Combine all ingredients with cracked ice in a cocktail shaker and shake well. Strain into chilled old-fashioned glass over ice cubes.

COGNAC COUPLING

4 parts cognac (2 oz.)
2 parts tawny port (1 oz.)
1 part Pernod (½ oz.)
2 – 3 dashes Peychaud's bitters
Fresh lemon juice (1 tsp.)

Shake all ingredients with cracked ice in a cocktail shaker. Strain over ice into a chilled old-fashioned glass.

COLD AND CLAMMY BLOODY MARY

4 parts iced vodka (2 oz.)
12 parts Clamato juice (6 oz.)
Fresh lime juice (½ tsp.)
Worcestershire sauce (½ tsp.)
Several dashes Tabasco sauce
Freshly ground pepper to taste
Salt to taste
Slice of green onion

Combine all ingredients, except onion, in cocktail shaker with cracked ice. Shake well. Strain over ice cubes into chilled highball glass. Garnish with green onion. Adjust seasonings if necessary.

COLD DECK

4 parts brandy (2 oz.)
1 part sweet vermouth (½ oz.)
1 part white crème de menthe (½ oz.)

Combine all ingredients with cracked ice in a cocktail shaker and shake well. Strain into chilled cocktail glass.

COLONIAL COCKTAIL

4 parts gin (2 oz.)
Maraschino liqueur (1 tsp.)
1 part grapefruit juice (½ oz.)
1 cocktail olive

Shake all ingredients, except olive, in a cocktail shaker with cracked ice. Strain into chilled cocktail glass and garnish with olive.

COLONY CLUB

4 parts gin (2 oz.)
Pernod (1 tsp.)
3 – 5 dashes orange bitters

Combine all ingredients in a cocktail shaker with cracked ice and shake well. Strain into chilled cocktail glass..

COLUMBIA

4 parts brandy (2 oz.)
1 part sweet vermouth (½ oz.)
Fresh lemon juice (1 tbsp.)
Grenadine (1tsp.)
Dash Angostura bitters

Combine all ingredients with cracked ice in a cocktail shaker. Shake well and strain into chilled cocktail glass.

COMBO

4 parts dry vermouth (2 oz.)
Brandy (1 tsp.)
Cointreau (½ tsp.)
Bar sugar (½ tsp.)
Dash Angostura bitters

Shake all ingredients with cracked ice in a cocktail shaker. Strain into chilled old-fashioned glass over ice cubes.

COMMODORE COCKTAIL

4 parts bourbon (2 oz.)
2 parts white crème de cacao (1 oz.)
1 part fresh lemon juice (½ oz.)

Combine ingredients with cracked ice in a cocktail shaker and shake well. Strain into chilled cocktail glass.

COMMONWEALTH COCKTAIL

4 parts Canadian whiskey (2 oz.)
1 part Grand Marnier (½ oz.)
Fresh lemon juice (1 tsp.)
Orange twist

Combine all ingredients, except orange twist, in a mixing glass with cracked ice. Stir well. Pour into chilled cocktail glass and garnish with orange twist.

CONEY ISLAND BABY

4 parts peppermint schnapps (2 oz.)
2 parts dark crème de cacao (1 oz.)
Seltzer

Combine schnapps and crème de cacao in a cocktail shaker with cracked ice. Shake well. Strain over ice cubes into a chilled highball glass. Fill with seltzer and stir gently.

CONFETTI

8 parts unsweetened cherry cider (4 oz.)
2 parts orgeat (almond) syrup (1 oz.)
Chopped fresh apples (2 oz.)
Chopped fresh pears (2 oz.)
Chopped fresh peaches (2 oz.)

Combine all ingredients in a blender with cracked ice. Blend until smooth and pour into chilled highball glass. Note: if you must used canned fruit, use the kind that is packed in its own juice with no added sugar.

CONTINENTAL COCKTAIL

4 parts light rum (2 oz.)
1 part green crème de menthe (½ oz.)
1 part fresh lime juice (½ oz.)
Bar sugar (½ tsp.)

Combine all ingredients with cracked ice in a cocktail shaker and shake well. Strain into chilled cocktail glass.

COOL COLLINS

4 parts fresh lemon juice (2 oz.)
Bar sugar (1 tsp.)
Fresh mint leaves (7)
Sparkling water
Lemon slice
Mint sprigs

Pour lemon juice and sugar into a chilled collins glass. Drop in the mint leaves and crush them with a bar spoon. Add ice cubes and fill with sparkling water. Stir gently and garnish with lemon slice and mint sprigs.

COOL COLONEL

4 parts bourbon (2 oz.)
2 parts Southern Comfort (1 oz.)
8 parts strong iced tea (4 oz.)
1 part fresh lemon juice (½ oz.)
Bar sugar (½ tsp.)
Sparkling water
Lemon twist

Combine all ingredients, except lemon twist and water, in a mixing glass with cracked ice. Stir well. Pour into a chilled Collins glass, fill with sparkling water and stir gently. Garnish with lemon twist.

COOPERSTOWN COCKTAIL

4 parts gin (2 oz.)
1 part dry vermouth (½ oz.)
1 part sweet vermouth (½ oz.)
Fresh mint sprig

Combine all ingredients, except mint, with cracked ice in a cocktail shaker and shake well. Strain into chilled cocktail glass and garnish with mint.

CORKSCREW

4 parts light rum (2 oz.)
1 part dry vermouth (½ oz.)
1 part peach liqueur (½ oz.)
Lime slice

Combine all ingredients, except lime, in a cocktail shaker with cracked ice. Shake well. Strain into chilled cocktail glass and garnish with lime slice.

CORNELL COCKTAIL

4 parts gin (2 oz.)
1 part maraschino liqueur
(½ oz.)
½ egg white

Combine ingredients with cracked ice
in a cocktail shaker. Shake vigorously.
Strain into chilled cocktail glass.

CORONADO

4 parts gin (2 oz.)
1 part white Curaçao (½ oz.)
4 parts pineapple juice (2 oz.)
3 – 5 dashes kirschwasser
Maraschino cherry

Combine all ingredients, except
cherry, with cracked ice in a cocktail
shaker. Shake well and strain into
chilled old-fashioned glass. Garnish
with cherry.

CORPSE REVIVER

4 parts apple brandy (2 oz.)
2 parts brandy (1 oz.)
1 part sweet vermouth (½ oz.)

Combine all ingredients in a cocktail
shaker with cracked ice. Shake well.
Strain into chilled cocktail glass.

COSMOPOLITAN

4 parts vodka (2 oz.)
2 parts triple sec (1 oz.)
2 parts cranberry juice (1 oz.)
1 part fresh lime juice (½ oz.)

Combine ingredients, with cracked ice
in a cocktail shaker. Shake well. Pour
into chilled cocktail glass.

COSMOPOLITAN (from Odeon)

COSSACK

4 parts vodka (2 oz.)
2 parts cognac (1 oz.)
2 parts fresh lime juice (1 oz.)
Bar sugar (½ tsp.)

Combine all ingredients in a cocktail shaker with cracked ice. Shake well. Strain into chilled cocktail glass.

COSTA DEL SOL

4 parts gin (2 oz.)
2 parts apricot brandy (1 oz.)
2 parts Cointreau (1 oz.)

Combine all ingredients with cracked ice in a cocktail shaker. Shake well and pour into chilled old-fashioned glass.

COUNT STROGANOFF

4 parts vodka (2 oz.)
2 parts white crème de cacao (1 oz.)
1 part fresh lemon juice (½ oz.)

Combine all ingredients with cracked ice in a cocktail shaker and shake well. Strain into chilled cocktail glass.

COUNTRY CLUB COOLER

8 parts Lillet blanc (4 oz.)
Grenadine (1tsp.)
Sparkling water
Orange twist

Pour Lillet and grenadine into a chilled collins glass and stir. Add ice cubes and fill with sparkling water. Stir gently and garnish with orange twist.

COWBOY COCKTAIL

6 parts rye (3 oz.)
Half-and-half (2 tbsp.)

Combine ingredients with cracked ice in a cocktail shaker and shake well. Strain into chilled cocktail glass.

COWGIRL'S PRAYER

4 parts gold tequila (2 oz.)
Home made fresh lemonade
2 parts fresh lime juice (1 oz.)
Lemon slice
Lime slice

Pour the tequila and lime juice over ice cubes in a chilled collins glass. Fill with lemonade and stir. Garnish with lemon and lime slices.

CRANBERRY CREAM COCKTAIL

5 parts cranberry juice (2½ oz.)
4 parts apple juice (2 oz.)
1 part coconut cream (½ oz.)
2 parts fresh lime juice (1 oz.)
Grenadine (2 dashes)

Combine all ingredients in a blender with cracked ice and blend until smooth. Pour into chilled wine glass.

CREAMSICLE

4 parts vanilla liqueur (2 oz.)
8 parts fresh orange juice (4 oz.)
4 parts half-and-half (2 oz.)
Orange slice

Combine all ingredients, except orange slice, in a cocktail shaker with cracked ice. Shake well and strain over ice cubes into a chilled highball glass. Garnish with orange slice.

CREAMY ORANGE

2 parts cream sherry (1 oz.)
2 parts fresh orange juice (1 oz.)
1 part brandy (½ oz.)
1 part half-and-half (½ oz.)

Combine all ingredients with cracked ice in a cocktail shaker. Shake well and strain into chilled cocktail glass.

CREAMSICLE

CREAMY SCREWDRIVER

4 parts vodka (2 oz.)
1 egg yolk
Bar sugar (½ tsp.)
12 parts fresh orange juice (6 oz.)

Combine all ingredients with cracked ice in a blender and blend until smooth. Pour into chilled collins glass over ice cubes.

CRÈME DE MENTHE FRAPPE

4 parts green crème de menthe (2 oz.)
Shaved ice

Fill an old-fashioned glass with shaved ice. Add crème de menthe and serve with short straw.

CUBA LIBRE

CREOLE

4 parts light rum (2 oz.)
Fresh lemon juice (1 tsp.)
Tabasco sauce to taste
Freshly ground pepper to taste
Salt to taste
Beef bouillon

Combine rum, lemon juice and
Tabasco sauce with cracked ice in a
cocktail shaker and shake well. Strain
into chilled old-fashioned glass over
ice cubes. Fill with bouillon and stir.
Season with salt and pepper.

CREOLE LADY

4 parts bourbon (2 oz.)
3 parts Madeira (1½ oz.)
Grenadine (1tsp.)
Red maraschino cherry
Green maraschino cherry

Stir liquid ingredients with ice in a
mixing glass. Strain into chilled
cocktail glass and garnish with
cherries.

CRIMSON

4 parts gin (2 oz.)
1 part ruby port (½ oz.)
Fresh lime juice (2 tsp.)
Grenadine (1tsp.)

Shake all ingredients, except port, with cracked ice in a cocktail shaker. Strain into chilled cocktail glass and float port on top.

CUBA LIBRE

4 parts light rum (2 oz.)
Cola
Lime wedge

Pour the rum and cola into a chilled highball glass filled with ice cubes. Stir and garnish with lime.

CURAÇAO COOLER

CUBAN COCKTAIL

4 parts brandy (2 oz.)
2 parts apricot brandy (1 oz.)
Light rum (1 tsp.)
2 parts fresh lime juice (1 oz.)

Combine ingredients in a cocktail shaker with cracked ice and shake well. Strain into chilled cocktail glass.

CUBAN SPECIAL

4 parts light rum (2 oz.)
Triple sec (1 tsp.)
2 parts fresh lime juice (1 oz.)
Pineapple juice (1 tbsp.)
Pineapple spear

Combine all ingredients with cracked ice in a cocktail shaker and shake well. Strain into chilled cocktail glass and garnish with pineapple spear.

CUBANO

4 parts light rum (2 oz.)
2 parts fresh lime juice (1 oz.)
Bar sugar (½ tsp.)

Combine all ingredients with cracked ice in a cocktail shaker. Shake well and strain into chilled cocktail glass.

CULROSS

4 parts light rum (2 oz.)
1 part apricot brandy (½ oz.)
1 part Lillet blanc (½ oz.)
Fresh lemon juice (1 tsp.)

Combine ingredients with cracked ice in a cocktail shaker. Shake well and strain into chilled cocktail glass.

CURAÇAO COOLER

4 parts dark rum (2 oz.)
3 parts white Curaçao (1½ oz.)
2 parts fresh lime juice (1 oz.)
Sparkling water
Orange slice

Combine all ingredients, except sparkling water and orange slice, in a cocktail shaker with cracked ice. Shake well. Pour into chilled highball glass and fill with sparkling water. Stir gently and garnish with orange slice.

D

DAIQUIRI

4 parts light rum (2 oz.)
1½ parts fresh lime juice (¾ oz.)
Sugar syrup (½ tsp.)

Combine all ingredients with cracked
ice in a cocktail shaker. Shake well.
Strain into chilled cocktail glass.

DAMN THE WEATHER

4 parts gin (2 oz.)
Sweet vermouth (1 tbsp.)
Triple sec (2 tsp.)
1 part fresh orange juice (½ oz.)

Combine all ingredients with cracked
ice in a cocktail shaker and shake
well. Strain into chilled cocktail glass.

DANIEL'S COCKTAIL

4 parts fresh orange juice
(2 oz.)
3 parts fresh lime juice (1½ oz.)
Grenadine (2 tsp.)

Combine all ingredients with cracked
ice in a cocktail shaker and shake
well. Strain into chilled cocktail glass.

DANISH GIN FIZZ

4 parts gin (2 oz.)
1 part cherry Heering (½ oz.)
Kirschwasser (1 tsp.)
1 part fresh lime juice (½ oz.)
Bar sugar (½ tsp.)
Sparkling water
Lime slice
Maraschino cherry

Combine all ingredients, except
sparkling water and fruit, in a cocktail
shaker with cracked ice. Shake well
and strain over ice cubes into a chilled
highball glass. Fill with sparkling
water and stir gently. Garnish with
lime slice and cherry.

DARB

3 parts gin (1½ oz.)
2 parts dry vermouth (1 oz.)
2 parts apricot brandy (1 oz.)
1 part fresh lemon juice (½ oz.)

Combine all ingredients with cracked
ice in a cocktail shaker and shake
well. Strain into chilled cocktail glass.

DAYDREAM

3 parts passion fruit syrup
(1½ oz.)
Fresh orange juice
Freshly ground nutmeg

Pour passion fruit syrup into a chilled
collins glass filled with ice cubes. Fill
with orange juice and stir. Sprinkle
nutmeg on top.

DEAUVILLE

3 parts brandy (1½ oz.)
2 parts apple brandy (1 oz.)
1 part Cointreau (½ oz.)
1 part fresh lemon juice (½ oz.)

Combine ingredients with cracked ice
in a cocktail shaker and shake well.
Strain into chilled cocktail glass.

DEEP SEA

4 parts gin (2 oz.)
2 parts dry vermouth (1 oz.)
Pernod (½ tsp.)
Dash orange bitters

Stir ingredients with cracked ice in a
mixing glass. Strain into chilled
cocktail glass.

DELMONICO COCKTAIL

3 parts gin (1½ oz.)
2 parts brandy (1 oz.)
1 part dry vermouth (½ oz.)
1 part sweet vermouth (½ oz.)
2 dashes Angostura bitters
Lemon twist

Combine liquid ingredients in a mixing glass with ice cubes and stir well. Strain into cocktail glass and garnish with lemon twist.

DELTA

4 parts blended whiskey (2 oz.)
1 part Southern Comfort (½ oz.)
1 part fresh lime juice (½ oz.)
Bar sugar (½ tsp.)
Orange slice
Fresh peach slice

Combine all ingredients, except fruit, with cracked ice in a cocktail shaker. Shake well. Pour into chilled old-fashioned glass and garnish with fruit.

DEMPSEY

4 parts gin (2 oz.)
2 parts apple brandy (1 oz.)
Pernod (1 tsp.)
Grenadine (1tsp.)

Combine ingredients with cracked ice in a mixing glass and stir. Strain into chilled cocktail glass.

DEPTH BOMB

4 parts brandy (2 oz.)
2 parts apple brandy (1 oz.)
Fresh lemon juice (½ tsp.)
Grenadine (½ tsp.)

Combine all ingredients in a cocktail shaker with cracked ice and shake well. Strain over ice cubes into chilled old-fashioned glass.

DEPTH CHARGE

4 parts schnapps, flavor of your choice (2 oz.)
Beer (1 pint or 16 oz.)

Pour the schnapps, then the beer, into a frosted mug.

DERBY DAIQUIRI

4 parts light rum (2 oz.)
2 parts fresh orange juice (1 oz.)
1 part fresh lime juice (½ oz.)
Bar sugar (1 tsp.)

Combine all ingredients with cracked ice in a blender. Blend at low speed until smooth. Pour into chilled champagne flute.

DERBY FIZZ

4 parts scotch (2 oz.)
Triple sec (1 tsp.)
1 part fresh lemon juice (½ oz.)
Bar sugar (½ tsp.)
1 whole egg
Sparkling water

Combine all ingredients, except water, with cracked ice in a cocktail shaker and shake vigorously. Pour over ice cubes into a chilled collins glass. Fill with sparkling water and stir gently.

DERBY SPECIAL

4 parts light rum (2 oz.)
1 part Cointreau (½ oz.)
2 parts fresh orange juice (1 oz.)
1 part fresh lime juice (½ oz.)

Combine all ingredients in a blender with cracked ice. Blend until smooth and thick. Pour into chilled cocktail glass.

DEVIL'S COCKTAIL

4 parts ruby port (2 oz.)
2 parts dry vermouth (1 oz.)
Lemon juice (½ tsp.)

Stir ingredients with cracked ice in a mixing glass. Strain into chilled cocktail glass.

DEVIL'S TAIL

4 parts light rum (2 oz.)
2 parts vodka (1 oz.)
Apricot brandy (2 tsp.)
1 part fresh lime juice (½ oz.)
Grenadine (2 tsp.)
Lime twist

Combine all ingredients, except lime twist, with cracked ice in a blender. Blend at low speed until smooth. Pour into chilled champagne flute and garnish with lime twist.

DIABLO

4 parts white port (2 oz.)
2 parts dry vermouth (1 oz.)
Fresh lemon juice (¼)
Lemon twist

Combine all ingredients, except lemon twist, in a cocktail shaker with cracked ice. Shake well and strain onto chilled cocktail glass. Garnish with lemon twist.

DIAMOND FIZZ

4 parts gin (2 oz.)
1 part fresh lemon juice (½ oz.)
Bar sugar (1 tsp.)
Champagne or sparkling wine

Shake all ingredients, except champagne, with cracked ice in a cocktail shaker. Strain over ice cubes in a chilled highball glass and fill with champagne. Stir gently.

DIAMOND HEAD

4 parts gin (2 oz.)
1 part apricot brandy (½ oz.)
2 parts fresh lemon juice (1 oz.)
Bar sugar (½ tsp.)
½ egg white

Combine all ingredients in cocktail shaker with cracked ice. Shake vigorously and strain into chilled cocktail glass.

DIANA

4 parts white crème de menthe (2 oz.)
1 part cognac (½ oz.)
Crushed ice

Pour the crème de menthe into a snifter filled with crushed ice. Float cognac on top.

DINAH

4 parts blended whiskey (2 oz.)
1 part fresh lemon juice (½ oz.)
Bar sugar (½ tsp.)
Fresh mint sprig

Shake all ingredients, except mint, in a cocktail shaker with cracked ice. Strain into chilled cocktail glass and garnish with mint sprig.

DIPLOMAT

4 parts dry vermouth (2 oz.)
1 part sweet vermouth (½ oz.)
Maraschino liqueur (½ tsp.)
3 dashes Angostura bitters
Lemon slice
Maraschino cherry

Combine liquid ingredients in a mixing glass with cracked ice and stir well. Strain into chilled cocktail glass and garnish with fruit.

DIXIE

4 parts gin (2 oz.)
2 parts Pernod (1 oz.)
1 part dry vermouth (½ oz.)
4 parts fresh orange juice (2 oz.)
Grenadine (¼ tsp.)

Shake all ingredients with cracked ice in a cocktail shaker. Strain into a chilled old-fashioned glass.

DIXIE WHISKEY COCKTAIL

4 parts bourbon (2 oz.)
Cointreau (½ tsp.)
White crème de menthe (½ tsp.)
Bar sugar (½ tsp.)
Dash Angostura bitters

Shake all ingredients with cracked ice in a cocktail shaker. Strain into chilled cocktail glass.

DOUBLE STANDARD SOUR

3 parts blended whiskey (1½ oz.)
3 parts gin (1½ oz.)
2 parts fresh lemon juice (1 oz.)
Bar sugar (½ tsp.)
Grenadine (1tsp.)
Maraschino cherry
Orange slice

Combine all ingredients, except fruit, in a cocktail shaker with cracked ice. Shake well. Strain into chilled sour glass and garnish with fruit.

DREAM COCKTAIL

4 parts brandy (2 oz.)
2 parts triple sec (1 oz.)
Pernod (½ tsp.)

Combine ingredients with cracked ice in a cocktail shaker and shake well. Strain into chilled cocktail glass.

DRY MANHATTAN

6 parts rye (3 oz.)
2 parts dry vermouth (1 oz.)
Dash Angostura bitters
Maraschino cherry

Combine all ingredients, except cherry, in a mixing glass with ice cubes. Stir well and strain into chilled cocktail glass. Garnish with cherry.

DUBARRY COCKTAIL

4 parts gin (2 oz.)
1 part dry vermouth (½ oz.)
Pernod (½ tsp.)
Dash orange bitters
Orange slice

Stir all ingredients, except orange slice, in a mixing glass with cracked ice. Strain into chilled cocktail glass and garnish with orange.

DUBONNET COCKTAIL

4 parts gin (2 oz.)
3 parts Dubonnet rouge (1½ oz.)
Dash of Angostura bitters
Lemon twist

Stir liquid ingredients with cracked ice in a mixing glass. Strain into chilled cocktail glass and garnish with lemon twist.

DUBONNET FIZZ

4 parts Dubonnet rouge (2 oz.)
2 parts cherry Heering (1 oz.)
2 parts fresh orange juice (1 oz.)
1 part fresh lemon juice (½ oz.)
Sparkling water
Lemon slice

Combine all ingredients, except sparkling water and lemon slice, in a cocktail shaker with cracked ice. Shake well. Strain into chilled highball glass over ice cubes. Fill with sparkling water and stir gently. Garnish with lemon slice.

DUCHESS

4 parts Pernod (2 oz.)
1 part dry vermouth (½ oz.)
1 part sweet vermouth (½ oz.)

Shake all ingredients with cracked ice in a cocktail shaker. Strain into chilled cocktail glass.

E

EARTHQUAKE

4 parts blended whiskey
(2 oz.)
2 parts gin (1 oz.)
2 parts Pernod (1 oz.)

Combine all ingredients with cracked
ice in a cocktail shaker. Shake well
and strain into chilled cocktail glass.

EAST INDIA

4 parts brandy (2 oz.)
1½ parts triple sec (¾ oz.)
1½ parts pineapple juice (¾ oz.)
2 dashes Angostura bitters

Combine ingredients in a mixing
glass with cracked ice. Stir well and
strain into chilled cocktail glass.

ECLIPSE

4 parts sloe gin (2 oz.)
2 parts gin (1 oz.)
Grenadine
Maraschino cherry
Orange twist

Put the cherry in a chilled cocktail
glass and cover with grenadine. Shake
the gins together with cracked ice in a
cocktail shaker. Carefully strain into
the cocktail glass so the gins do not
mix with with the grenadine. Garnish
with orange twist.

EGG CREAM

2 parts chocolate syrup (1 oz.)
7 parts cold milk (3½ oz.)
Seltzer

Put syrup in the bottom of glass. Add
milk and stir. Add seltzer and stir
vigorously so a foamy head appears.

EGG NOG

Brandy (1 bottle –
750-ml.)
Milk (1½ quarts)
Whipped heavy cream (1 pint)
Bar sugar (1 cup or 8 oz.)
Dozen eggs
Freshly grated nutmeg

Separate the eggs and beat the yolks
with the sugar in a large punch bowl.
Reserve the whites. Stir in the milk
and whipped cream. Add the brandy
and refrigerate for at least one hour.
Before serving, whip the egg whites
stiff and fold into the egg nog.
Sprinkle with freshly grated nutmeg.
Serves 25.

EGG NOG

(NON-ALCOHOLIC)

16 parts milk (8 oz.)
1 egg
Sugar (1 tbsp.)
Almond extract (¼ tsp.)
Vanilla extract (¼ tsp.)
Whipped cream
Freshly grated nutmeg

Beat the egg well and pour into
cocktail shaker with cold milk, sugar
and extracts. Shake well and pour into
chilled mug. Top with whipped cream
and sprinkle nutmeg on top.

EGG SOUR

4 parts brandy (2 oz.)
1 part fresh lemon juice (½ oz.)
Cointreau (½ tsp.)
Bar sugar (½ tsp.)
1 whole egg

Shake all ingredients vigorously with
cracked ice. Pour into chilled sour
glass.

EGG NOG

ELK'S OWN

4 parts rye (2 oz.)
2 parts ruby port (1 oz.)
1 part fresh lemon juice (½ oz.)
1 egg white
Bar sugar (1 tsp.)
Pineapple spear

Combine all ingredients, except
pineapple spear, with cracked ice in a
cocktail shaker and shake vigorously.
Strain into chilled cocktail glass.

EL PRESIDENTE

4 parts light rum (2 oz.)
2 parts fresh lime juice (1 oz.)
Grenadine (1tsp.)
Pineapple juice (1 tsp.)

Shake ingredients with cracked ice in
cocktail shaker. Strain into chilled
cocktail glass.

EMERALD ISLE COCKTAIL

5 parts gin (2½ oz.)
Green crème de menthe (2 tsp.)
3 dashes Angostura bitters
Green maraschino cherry

Stir liquid ingredients in a mixing glass with cracked ice. Strain into chilled cocktail glass and garnish with cherry.

EMERSON

4 parts gin (2 oz.)
2 parts sweet vermouth (1 oz.)
1 part fresh lime juice (½ oz.)
Maraschino liqueur (1 tsp.)

Combine all ingredients with cracked ice in a cocktail shaker. Shake well. Strain into chilled cocktail glass.

EYE OPENER

EVERYBODY'S IRISH

4 parts Irish whiskey (2 oz.)
1 part green Chartreuse (½ oz.)
1 part green crème de menthe (½ oz.)

Stir all ingredients with cracked ice in a mixing glass. Strain into chilled cocktail glass.

EXIT 13-E

8 parts loganberry juice (4 oz.)
8 parts pineapple juice (4 oz.)
1 part fresh lime juice (½ oz.)

Combine ingredients in a mixing glass with cracked ice and stir well. Strain into chilled collins glass over ice cubes.

EYE OF THE HURRICANE

4 parts passion fruit syrup (2 oz.)
2 parts fresh lime juice (1 oz.)
Bitter lemon soda
Lime slice

Combine syrup and juice with cracked ice in a mixing glass. Strain into chilled highball glass over ice cubes and fill with bitter lemon soda. Stir gently and garnish with lime slice.

EYE-OPENER

4 parts light rum (2 oz.)
Pernod (1 tsp.)
Cointreau (1 tsp.)
White crème de cacao (1 tsp.)
Bar sugar (½ tsp.)
1 egg yolk

Shake all ingredients vigorously with cracked ice in a cocktail shaker. Strain into chilled sour glass.

F

FAIR AND WARMER

4 parts light rum (2 oz.)
1 part sweet vermouth (½ oz.)
3 dashes white Curaçao
Lemon twist

Shake all ingredients, except lemon,
with cracked ice in a cocktail shaker.
Strain into chilled cocktail glass and
garnish with lemon twist.

FAIRY BELLE COCKTAIL

4 parts gin (2 oz.)
2 parts apricot brandy (1 oz.)
Grenadine (1tsp.)
1 egg white

Combine all ingredients with cracked
ice in a cocktail shaker and shake
vigorously. Strain into chilled cocktail
glass.

FALLEN ANGEL

4 parts gin (2 oz.)
White crème de menthe (1 tsp.)
2 parts fresh lime juice (1 oz.)
Dash Angostura bitters
Maraschino cherry

Combine all ingredients, except
cherry, with cracked ice in a cocktail
shaker. Shake well and strain into
chilled cocktail glass. Garnish with
cherry.

FANCY BRANDY

4 parts brandy (2 oz.)
Cointreau (½ tsp.)
Bar sugar (½ tsp.)
3 dashes Angostura bitters
Lemon twist

Combine all ingredients, except
lemon, in a cocktail shaker with
cracked ice. Shake well and strain
into chilled cocktail glass. Garnish
with lemon twist.

FANCY WHISKEY

4 parts whiskey (2 oz.)
Cointreau (½ tsp.)
Bar sugar (½ tsp.)
3 dashes Angostura bitters
Lemon twist

Combine all ingredients, except lemon
twist, with cracked ice in a cocktail
shaker. Shake well and strain into
chilled cocktail glass, drop lemon
twist on top.

FANTASIO

4 parts brandy (2 oz.)
2 parts dry vermouth (1 oz.)
Maraschino liqueur (2 tsp.)
White crème de menthe (2 tsp.)

Combine all ingredients with cracked
ice in a mixing glass and stir well.
Strain into chilled cocktail glass.

FARE THE WELL

4 parts gin (2 oz.)
1 part dry vermouth (½ oz.)
Dash sweet vermouth
Dash Cointreau

Combine all ingredients with cracked
ice and shake well. Strain into chilled
old-fashioned glass.

FARMER'S COCKTAIL

4 parts gin (2 oz.)
1 part dry vermouth (1 oz.)
1 part sweet vermouth (1 oz.)
3 dashes Angostura bitters

Combine all ingredients with cracked
ice in a cocktail shaker and shake
well. Strain into chilled cocktail glass.

FAUX KIR

2 parts raspberry syrup (1 oz.)
White grape juice
Lemon twist

Pour syrup over ice cubes in a chilled
wine glass. Fill with white grape juice
and stir well. Garnish with lemon
twist.

FAUX KIR ROYALE

3 parts raspberry syrup
(1½ oz.)
Sparkling cider

Stir the syrup with cracked ice in a
mixing glass. Pour into chilled wine
glass and fill with cold sparkling cider.
Stir gently.

FAVORITE

3 parts gin (1½ oz.)
2 parts apricot brandy (1 oz.)
2 parts dry vermouth (1 oz.0
Lemon juice (½ tsp.)

Combine all ingredients with cracked
ice in a cocktail shaker and shake
well. Strain into chilled cocktail glass.

FERDINAND THE BULL

8 parts tomato juice (4 oz.)
8 parts chilled beef bouillon (4 oz.)
2 parts lime juice (1 oz.)
Tabasco sauce to taste
Worcestershire sauce to taste
Freshly ground pepper to taste
Lime wedge

Combine all ingredients, except
pepper and lime wedge, with cracked
ice in a cocktail shaker and shake
well. Strain over ice cubes into chilled
collins glass. Grind pepper over drink
and garnish with lime wedge.

FERN GULLY

4 parts dark rum (2 oz.)
3 parts light rum (1½ oz.)
1 part amaretto (½ oz.)
1 part coconut cream (½ oz.)
2 parts fresh orange juice (1 oz.)
2 parts fresh lime juice (1 oz.)

Combine all ingredients with cracked
ice in a blender. Blend at low speed
until smooth. Pour into chilled red
wine glass.

FERRARI

4 parts dry vermouth (2 oz.)
2 parts amaretto (1 oz.)
Dash orange bitters
Lemon twist

Combine all ingredients, except
lemon, in a cocktail shaker with
cracked ice. Shake well and strain over
ice cubes into a chilled old-fashioned
glass. Garnish with lemon twist.

FIFTH AVENUE

3 parts dark crème de cacao
(1½ oz.)
3 parts apricot brandy (1½ oz.)
1½ parts half-and-half (¾ oz.)

Layer ingredients in the order given
into a pousse-café glass.

FIFTY-FIFTY

4 parts gin (2 oz.)
4 parts dry vermouth (2 oz.)
Spanish olive

Stir liquid ingredients in mixing glass
with cracked ice. Strain into chilled
cocktail glass and garnish with olive.

FINE AND DANDY

4 parts gin (2 oz.)
2 parts triple sec (1 oz.)
2 parts fresh lemon juice (1 oz.)
Dash orange bitters

Combine all ingredients with cracked
ice in a cocktail shaker and shake
well. Strain into chilled cocktail glass.

FIREMAN'S SOUR

4 parts light rum (2 oz.)
3 parts fresh lime juice (1½ oz.)
Bar sugar (½ tsp.)
Grenadine (1 tbsp.)
Lemon slice
Maraschino cherry

Combine all ingredients, except fruit,
with cracked ice in a cocktail shaker.
Shake well and strain into chilled sour
glass. Garnish with cherry and lemon.

FISH HOUSE PUNCH

Dark rum (2 liters)
Cognac (1 liter)
8 parts peach brandy (4 oz.)
Fresh lemon juice (1 liter)
Bottled spring water (non-sparkling) (2 liters)
Bar sugar (1½ cups or to taste)
Fresh peach slices

In a chilled punch bowl, dissolve sugar in water and lemon juice. Stir in remaining ingredients. Add large block of ice and garnish with peach slices. Serves 40.

FINO MARTINI

6 parts gin or vodka (3 oz.)
Fino sherry (1 tsp.)
Lemon twist

Stir gin (or vodka) and sherry in a mixing glass with ice cubes. Strain into chilled cocktail glass and garnish with lemon twist.

FJORD

4 parts brandy (2 oz.)
2 parts aquavit (1 oz.)
4 parts fresh orange juice (2 oz.)
2 parts fresh lime juice (1 oz.)
Grenadine (2 tsp.)

Combine all ingredients with cracked ice in a cocktail shaker and shake well. Strain into chilled cocktail glass.

FLAMINGO

4 parts gin (2 oz.)
1 part apricot brandy (½ oz.)
1 part fresh lime juice (½ oz.)
Grenadine (1tsp.)

Combine all ingredients with ice in a cocktail shaker and shake well. Strain into chilled cocktail glass.

FLORADORA

4 parts gin (2 oz.)
4 parts fresh lime juice (2 oz.)
Grenadine (1 tbsp.)
Bar sugar (½ tsp.)
Sparkling water

Combine all ingredients, except sparkling water, with cracked ice in a cocktail shaker. Shake well and strain over ice cubes into a chilled highball glass. Fill with sparkling water and stir gently.

FLORIDA

4 parts gin (2 oz.)
1 part kirschwasser (½ oz.)
1 part Cointreau (½ oz.)
Fresh lemon juice (1 tbsp.)
Fresh orange juice

Combine all ingredients, except orange juice, in a cocktail shaker with cracked ice. Shake well and strain over ice cubes into a chilled highball glass. Fill with orange juice and stir again.

FLYING DUTCHMAN

4 parts gin (2 oz.)
Pernod (1 tsp.)

Stir ingredient with ice cubes in a chilled old-fashioned glass.

FLYING GRASSHOPPER

4 parts vodka (2 oz.)
1 part green crème de menthe (½ oz.)
1 part white crème de menthe (½ oz.)

Combine all ingredients with cracked ice in a blender and blend at low speed until slushy. Pour into a chilled old-fashioned glass.

FLYING SCOTSMAN

4 parts scotch (2 oz.)
2 parts sweet vermouth (1 oz.)
Bar sugar (¼ tsp.)
3 – 5 dashes Angostura bitters

Combine all ingredients with cracked ice in a blender and blend at low speed until slushy. Pour into chilled old-fashioned glass.

FOG CUTTER

4 parts light rum (2 oz.)
2 parts brandy (1 oz.)
2 parts gin (1 oz.)
Sweet sherry (1 tsp.)
3 parts fresh lemon juice (1½ oz.)
2 parts fresh orange juice (1 oz.)
Orgeat (almond) syrup (1 tsp.)

Combine all ingredients, except sherry, with cracked ice in a cocktail shaker and shake well. Strain over ice cubes into chilled collins glass. Float sherry on top.

FORESTER

4 parts bourbon (2 oz.)
1 part cherry liqueur (½ oz.)
Fresh lemon juice (1 tsp.)
Maraschino cherry

Combine all ingredients, except cherry, with cracked ice in a cocktail shaker. Shake well. Pour into a chilled old-fashioned glass and garnish with cherry.

FORT LAUDERDALE

4 parts light rum (2 oz.)
1 part sweet vermouth (½ oz.)
2 parts fresh lime juice (1 oz.)
2 parts fresh orange juice (1 oz.)
Orange slice

Combine all ingredients, except orange slice, with cracked ice in a cocktail shaker. Shake well and strain into chilled old-fashioned glass over ice cubes. Garnish with orange.

FOX RIVER COCKTAIL

4 parts rye (2 oz.)
1 part dark crème de cacao (½ oz.)
3 – 5 dashes Angostura bitters
Lemon twist

Combine all ingredients, except lemon, in a mixing glass with cracked ice and stir. Strain into chilled cocktail glass and garnish with lemon twist.

FOGHORN

4 parts gin (2 oz.)
Chilled ginger beer
Lemon slice

Fill a chilled pilsner glass almost to the top with ginger beer. Pour in gin and stir gently. Garnish with lemon slice.

FRAISE FIZZ

4 parts gin (2 oz.)
2 parts strawberry liqueur (1 oz.)
1 part fresh lemon juice (½ oz.)
Bar sugar (½ tsp.)
Sparkling water
Lemon twist
1 fresh strawberry

Combine gin, liqueur, lemon juice, and sugar with cracked ice in a cocktail shaker. Shake well and strain into chilled highball glass over ice cubes. Fill with sparkling water and stir gently. Garnish with lemon twist and strawberry.

FRANKENJACK

4 parts gin (2 oz.)
2 parts dry vermouth (1 oz.)
2 parts apricot brandy (1 oz.)
2 parts triple sec (1 oz.)
Maraschino cherry

Combine all ingredients, except cherry, with cracked ice in a cocktail shaker. Shake well and pour into chilled old-fashioned glass. Garnish with cherry.

FREE SILVER

4 parts gin (2 oz.)
2 parts dark rum (1 oz.)
2 parts fresh lemon juice (1 oz.)
Bar sugar (½ tsp.)
Milk (1 tbsp.)
Sparkling water

Combine all ingredients, except sparkling water, with cracked ice in a cocktail shaker and shake well. Strain over ice cubes into chilled collins glass. Fill with sparkling water and stir gently.

FRENCH CONNECTION

4 parts cognac (2 oz.)
2 parts amaretto (1 oz.)

Pour ingredients into a chilled old-fashioned glass over ice cubes. Stir well.

FRENCH KISS

4 parts bourbon (2 oz.)
2 parts apricot liqueur (1 oz.)
Fresh lemon juice (1 tsp.)
Grenadine (2 tsp.)

Combine all ingredients with cracked ice in a cocktail shaker and shake well. Strain into chilled cocktail glass.

FRENCH '75'

4 parts cognac (2 oz.)
Sugar syrup (1 tbsp.)
2 parts fresh lemon juice (1 oz.)
Champagne
Lemon twist

Combine all ingredients, except champagne and lemon twist, with cracked ice in a cocktail shaker. Shake well and pour into chilled highball glass. Fill with cold champagne and garnish with lemon twist.

FRIAR TUCK

4 parts Frangelico (2 oz.)
4 parts fresh lemon (2 oz.)
Grenadine (1tsp.)
Orange slice

Combine all ingredients in a blender with cracked ice. Blend until smooth and pour into chilled old-fashioned glass. Garnish with orange slice.

FROTH BLOWER

4 parts gin (2 oz.)
Grenadine (1tsp.)
1 egg white

Combine all ingredients with cracked ice in a blender. Blend until smooth and pour into a chilled old-fashioned glass.

FROUPE

4 parts brandy (2 oz.)
3 parts sweet vermouth (1½ oz.)
Benedictine (1 tsp.)

Combine all ingredients in a mixing glass with ice cubes. Stir well and strain into chilled old-fashioned glass.

FROSTBITE

4 parts white tequila (2 oz.)
1 part white crème de cacao (½ oz.)
2 parts blue Curaçao (1 oz.)
4 parts half-and-half (2 oz.)

Combine all ingredients in a cocktail shaker with cracked ice and shake well. Pour into chilled sour glass.

FROZEN APPLE

4 parts apple brandy (2 oz.)
1 part fresh lime juice (½ oz.)
Bar sugar (1 tsp.)
½ egg white
1 apple slice

Combine all ingredients, except apple slice, with a cup of crushed ice in a blender. Blend at low speed until slushy and pour into chilled old fashioned glass.

FROZEN BERKELEY

4 parts light rum (2 oz.)
1 part brandy (½ oz.)
Passion fruit syrup (1 tbsp.)
Fresh lime juice (1 tbsp.)

Combine all ingredients with ½ cup of crushed ice in a blender. Blend until slushy and pour into chilled champagne flute.

FROZEN DAIQUIRI

FROZEN BRANDY AND RUM

4 parts brandy (2 oz.)
3 parts light rum (1½ oz.)
Fresh lemon juice (1 tbsp.)
1 egg yolk
Bar sugar (1 tsp.)

Combine all ingredients with 1 cup of crushed ice in a blender. Blend at low speed until slushy and pour into chilled old-fashioned glass.

FROZEN DAIQUIRI

4 parts light rum (2 oz.)
2 parts fresh lime juice (1 oz.)
Bar sugar (1 tsp.)
Lime slice

Combine all ingredients, except lime slice, with ½ cup of cracked ice in a blender. Blend at low speed until slushy and pour into chilled champagne flute. Garnish with lime slice.

107

FROZEN MARGARITA

4 parts white tequila (2 oz.)
1 parts triple sec (½ oz.)
2 parts fresh lime juice (1 oz.)
Lime slice

Combine all ingredients, except lime slice, with ½ cup of cracked ice in a blender. Blend at low speed until slushy and pour into chilled cocktail glass. Garnish with lime slice.

FROZEN MATADOR

4 parts gold tequila (2 oz.)
4 parts pineapple juice (2 oz.)
1 part fresh lime juice (½ oz.)
Lime slice

Combine all ingredients, except lime slice, with ½ cup of cracked ice in a blender. Blend until smooth. Garnish with lime slice.

FROZEN MINT DAIQUIRI

4 parts light rum (2 oz.)
1 part fresh lime juice (½ oz.)
6 fresh mint leaves
Bar sugar (1 tsp.)

Combine all ingredients with ½ cup
of cracked ice in a blender and blend
until slushy. Pour into chilled old-
fashioned glass.

FROZEN MINT JULEP

4 parts bourbon (2 oz.)
2 parts fresh lemon juice (1 oz.)
2 parts sugar syrup (1 oz.)
6 fresh mint leaves
Fresh mint sprig

Muddle all ingredients, except mint
sprig, in a glass. Pour into a blender
with ½ cup of cracked ice and blend
at low speed until slushy. Pour into
chilled highball glass and garnish
with mint sprig.

FROZEN PEACH DAIQUIRI

4 parts light rum (2 oz.)
2 parts fresh lime juice (1 oz.)
Sugar syrup (1 tsp.)
4 parts fresh peaches, chopped fine
(2 oz.)
Fresh peach slice

Combine all ingredients, except peach
slice, in a blender with ½ cup cracked
ice. Blend until slushy and pour into
cocktail glass. Garnish with peach
slice.

FROZEN PINEAPPLE DAIQUIRI

4 parts light rum (2 oz.)
2 parts fresh lime juice (1 oz.)
Pineapple syrup (½ tsp.)
4 parts fresh pineapple, chopped fine
(2 oz.)
Pineapple spear

Combine all ingredients, except
pineapple spear, with ½ cup cracked
ice in a blender. Blend until slushy
and pour into a cocktail glass.
Garnish with pineapple spear.

FUZZY NAVEL

FRUIT JUICE SPRITZER

6 parts fruit juice of your choice
(3 oz.)
Sparkling water
Lemon twist

Pour juice into chilled wine glass over
ice cubes. Fill with sparkling water
and garnish with lemon twist.

FUZZY NAVEL

4 parts vodka (2 oz.)
2 parts peach schnapps (1 oz.)
16 parts fresh orange juice (8 oz.)
Orange slice

Combine all ingredients, except
orange slice, with cracked ice in a
cocktail shaker. Shake well and pour
into chilled collins glass and garnish
with orange slice.

G

GAUGUIN

4 parts light rum (2 oz.)
1 part fresh lemon juice (½ oz.)
1 part fresh lime juice (½ oz.)
1 part passion fruit syrup (½ oz.)
Maraschino cherry

Combine all ingredients, except
cherry, in a blender with cracked ice.
Blend at low speed until smooth. Pour
into chilled old-fashioned glass and
garnish with cherry.

GAZETTE

4 parts brandy (2 oz.)
1 part sweet vermouth (½ oz.)
Fresh lemon juice (1 tsp.)
Bar sugar (½ tsp.)

Combine all ingredients with cracked
ice in a cocktail shaker. Shake well
and strain into chilled cocktail glass.

GAZPACHO COCKTAIL

12 parts tomato juice (6 oz.)
2 parts fresh lemon juice (1 oz.)
2 cucumber slices chopped
1 scallion white part only, sliced
Garlic clove, crushed
Oregano (⅛ tsp.)
Tabasco sauce (3 – 5 dashes)
Freshly ground pepper to taste
Salt to taste
Cucumber slice, whole
Avocado slice

Combine all ingredients, except whole
cucumber and avocado slices, in a
blender with cracked ice and blend
until smooth. Pour into chilled collins
glass and garnish with cucumber and
avocado slices.

GENERAL HARRISON'S EGG NOG

1 Egg
Bar sugar (1 tsp.)
Dry red wine (note: you may
substitute hard cider for wine)
Freshly ground nutmeg

Combine egg and sugar in a cocktail
shaker with cracked ice. Shake
vigorously. Strain into chilled highball
glass and fill with red wine. Stir and
sprinkle nutmeg on top.

GENOA

4 parts gin (2 oz.)
3 parts grappa (1½ oz.)
1 part white Sambuca (½ oz.)
Dry vermouth (2 tsp.)
Green cocktail olive

Stir liquid ingredients with cracked ice
in a mixing glass. Strain into chilled
cocktail glass and garnish with the
olive.

GENOA VODKA

4 parts vodka (2 oz.)
2 parts Campari (1 oz.)
6 parts fresh orange juice (3 oz.)

Combine all ingredients with cracked
ice in a cocktail shaker and shake
well. Pour into chilled old-fashioned
glass.

GENTLE BEN

4 parts white tequila (2 oz.)
2 parts vodka (1 oz.)
2 parts gin (1 oz.)
Fresh orange juice (½ cup or 4 oz.)
Sloe gin (1 tsp.)
Orange slice

Combine all liquid ingredients, except
sloe gin and orange slice, in a cocktail
shaker with cracked ice. Pour into a
chilled highball glass and float sloe
gin on top. Garnish with orange slice.

GEORGIA PEACH

GENTLE BULL

4 parts white tequila (2 oz.)
2 parts coffee liqueur (1 oz.)
3 parts half-and-half (1½ oz.)

Combine all ingredients with cracked
ice in a cocktail shaker and shake
well. Strain into chilled cocktail glass.

GEORGIA PEACH

4 parts vodka (2 oz.)
2 parts peach brandy (1 oz.)
Fresh lemon juice (1 tsp.)
Peach preserves (1 tsp.)
1 wedge peeled fresh peach, chopped
fine (about 2 oz.)

Combine all ingredients with cracked
ice in a blender. Blend until smooth
and pour into chilled highball glass.

GEORGIA PEACH FIZZ

4 parts brandy (2 oz.)
2 parts peach brandy (1 oz.)
2 parts fresh lemon juice (1 oz.)
Crème de bananes (1 tbsp.)
Sugar syrup (1 tsp.)
Sparkling water
Fresh peach slice

Combine all ingredients in a mixing
glass, except sparkling water and
peach slice, with cracked ice. Stir well
and pour into chilled collins glass. Fill
with club soda and stir gently. Garnish
with peach slice.

GIBSON (from The Polo Lounge)

GIBSON

6 parts gin or vodka (3 oz.)
3 – 5 dashes dry vermouth
(to taste)
Cocktail onions

Pour gin and vodka in a mixing glass
with ice cubes and stir well. Pour into
chilled cocktail glass and garnish with
2 or 3 cocktail onions.

GILROY

4 parts gin (2 oz.)
2 parts cherry brandy (1 oz.)
1 part dry vermouth (½ oz.)
1 part fresh lemon juice (½ oz.)
3 – 5 dashes orange bitters

Combine all ingredients with cracked
ice in a cocktail shaker and shake
well. Pour into chilled old-fashioned
glass.

GIMLET

GIN AND GINGER

4 parts gin (2 oz.)
Ginger ale
Lemon twist

Pour gin into chilled highball glass filled with ice cubes. Twist lemon over glass and drop in. Fill with ginger ale and stir gently.

GIN AND IT

6 parts gin (3 oz.)
2 parts sweet vermouth (1 oz.)

Stir ingredients without ice in a mixing glass. Pour into cocktail glass.

GIN AND SIN

4 parts gin (2 oz.)
4 parts fresh lemon juice (2 oz.)
4 parts fresh orange juice (2 oz.)
2 dashes grenadine

Combine all ingredients with cracked ice in a cocktail shaker. Strain into chilled cocktail glass.

GIN AND TONIC

4 parts gin (2 oz.)
Tonic water
Lime wedge

Pour gin and tonic water into a chilled collins glass. Add ice cubes and stir. Squeeze lime wedge over drink and drop in.

GIN BUCK

4 parts gin (2 oz.)
2 parts fresh lemon juice (1 oz.)
Ginger ale

Pour all ingredients into chilled old fashioned glass over ice cubes. Stir well.

GIN CASSIS

4 parts gin (2 oz.)
1 part crème de cassis (½ oz.)
1 part fresh lemon juice (½ oz.)

Combine all ingredients with cracked ice in a cocktail shaker and shake well. Pour into chilled old-fashioned glass.

GIMLET

6 parts gin (3 oz.)
2 parts Rose's lime juice (1 oz.)

Combine ingredients with cracked ice in a cocktail shaker and shake well. Strain into chilled cocktail glass.

GIN ALOHA

4 parts gin (2 oz.)
3 parts triple sec (1½ oz.)
1 part unsweetened pineapple juice (½ oz.)
Dash orange bitters

Combine all ingredients with cracked ice in a cocktail shaker. Shake well and strain into chilled cocktail glass.

GIN AND BITTERS (PINK GIN)

1 tsp. Angostura bitters
Gin

Pour bitters into cocktail glass and swirl around until it is entirely coated with bitters. Fill with gin. This drink should be served at room temperature

113

GIN COBBLER

4 parts gin (2 oz.)
Sugar syrup (1 tsp.)
Sparkling water
Orange slice

Stir gin and sugar syrup with cracked
ice in a chilled highball glass. Fill
with sparkling water and garnish with
orange slice.

GIN COOLER

4 parts gin (2 oz.)
Bar sugar (½ tsp.)
Sparkling water
Lemon peel

Mix gin with sugar in the bottom of a
chilled collins glass. Add ice cubes and
fill with sparkling water. Stir gently
and garnish with lemon peel.

GIN DAISY

6 parts gin (3 oz.)
2 parts fresh lemon juice (1 oz.)
Grenadine (1 tbsp.)
Sugar syrup (1 tsp.)
Sparkling water
Orange slice

Combine all ingredients, except
orange slice and sparkling water, in a
cocktail shaker with cracked ice.
Shake well. Pour into chilled highball
glass. Top off with sparkling water, stir
gently, and garnish with orange slice.

GIN FIX

6 parts gin (3 oz.)
2 parts fresh lemon juice (1 oz.)
Water (1 tsp.)
Bar sugar (1 tsp.)
Lemon slice

Dissolve sugar in lemon juice and
water in the bottom of a chilled
highball glass. Add gin and stir. Fill
glass with ice cubes and garnish with
lemon slice.

GIN FIZZ

4 parts gin (2 oz.)
2 parts fresh lemon juice (1 oz.)
Bar sugar (1 tsp.)
Sparkling water

Combine all ingredients, except sparkling water, in a cocktail shaker with
cracked ice. Shake well and strain over
ice cubes into chilled highball. Fill
with sparkling water and stir gently.

GIN MILK PUNCH

4 parts gin (2 oz.)
12 parts milk (6 oz.)
Bar sugar (½ tsp.)
Freshly ground nutmeg

Combine all ingredients, except
nutmeg, in a cocktail shaker with
cracked ice. Shake well and pour into
chilled highball glass. Sprinkle with
nutmeg.

GIN RICKEY

4 parts gin (2 oz.)
2 parts fresh lime juice (1 oz.)
Sparkling water

Pour gin and lime juice over ice cubes
into chilled highball glass. Fill with
sparkling water and stir gently.

GIN SANGAREE

4 parts gin (2 oz.)
Ruby port (1 tbsp.)
Water (1 tsp.)
Bar sugar (½ tsp.)
Sparkling water

Dissolve sugar in water in the bottom
of a chilled highball glass. Add gin
and stir. Add ice cubes and fill glass
with sparkling water. Stir gently and
float port on top.

GIN SIDECAR

4 parts gin (2 oz.)
2 parts triple sec (1 oz.)
2 parts fresh lemon juice (1 oz.)

Combine all ingredients with cracked
ice in a cocktail shaker and shake
well. Pour into chilled old-fashioned
glass.

GIN SLING

4 parts gin (2 oz.)
1 part fresh lemon juice (1 oz.)
Water (1 tsp.)
Bar sugar (1 tsp.)
Orange twist

In the bottom of a mixing glass, dissolve sugar in water and lemon juice. Add gin and stir. Pour over ice cubes into a chilled old-fashioned glass and garnish with orange twist.

GIN SMASH

6 parts gin (3 oz.)
2 parts sparkling water (1 oz.)
Bar sugar (1 tsp.)
4 fresh mint sprigs
Lemon twist

In the bottom of a chilled old-fashioned glass, muddle the mint sprigs with the sugar and sparkling water. Fill the glass with ice cubes and add gin. Stir well and garnish with lemon twist.

GIN SOUR

4 parts gin (2 oz.)
2 parts fresh lemon juice (1 oz.)
Bar sugar (½ tsp.)
Orange slice
Maraschino cherry

Combine all ingredients, except fruit,
with cracked ice in a cocktail shaker.
Shake well and strain into a chilled
sour glass. Garnish with orange slice
and cherry.

GIN SWIZZLE

4 parts gin (2 oz.)
3 parts fresh lime juice (1½ oz.)
2 dashes Angostura bitters
Bar sugar (1 tsp.)
Sparkling water

Combine all ingredients, except
sparkling water, in a cocktail shaker
with cracked ice. Strain over ice cubes
into chilled collins glass. Fill with
sparkling water and stir gently. Serve
with a swizzle stick.

GINGER BEER

4 parts ginger brandy (2 oz.)
Dark beer

Fill a frosted beer mug with dark beer
and add ginger brandy. Do not stir.

GINGERSNAP

6 parts vodka (3 oz.)
2 parts ginger wine (1 oz.)
Sparkling water
Slice of candied ginger

Combine vodka and wine in a chilled
highball glass. Add ice cubes and fill
with sparkling water. Stir gently and
drop in candied ginger.

GINZA MARY

4 parts vodka (2 oz.)
3 parts sake (1½ oz.)
4 parts tomato juice (2 oz.)
1 part fresh lemon juice (½ oz.)
3 – 5 dashes Tabasco sauce
2 dashes soy sauce
Freshly ground pepper to taste

Combine all ingredients with cracked
ice in a mixing glass. Stir well and
pour into chilled old-fashioned glass.

GLAD EYES

4 parts Pernod (2 oz.)
2 parts peppermint schnapps (1 oz.)

Combine ingredients with cracked ice
in a mixing glass and stir well. Strain
into chilled cocktail glass.

GLASGOW

4 parts scotch (2 oz.)
Dry vermouth (1 tsp.)
Fresh lemon juice (1 tbsp.)
Almond extract (1 tsp.)

Combine all ingredients with cracked
ice in a cocktail shaker. Shake well
and strain over ice into a chilled old-
fashioned glass.

GLOGG

Dry red wine
(2 bottles – 750-ml. each)
Brandy (1 bottle 750-ml.)
Aquavit (1 pint or 16 oz.)
25 whole cloves
20 crushed cardamom seeds
4 cinnamon sticks
Dried orange peel (2 oz.)
Blanched almonds (2 cups)
Raisins (2 cups)
Sugar cubes (1 pound or 16 oz.)

Put all ingredients, except sugar and
aquavit, in a large kettle and bring to
a boil. Turn down heat immediately
and simmer for 15 – 20 minutes,
stirring occasionally. Place a rack or
mesh strainer over the kettle and
spread the sugar cubes over it.
Saturate the sugar with the aquavit.
Ignite and let the sugar melt into the
glogg. Stir again. Serve hot in heated
mugs. Serves 10.

GLOOM LIFTER

4 parts blended whiskey (2 oz.)
2 parts brandy (1 oz.)
Raspberry liqueur (1 tbsp.)
1 part fresh lemon juice (½ oz.)
Bar sugar (½ tsp.)
½ egg white

Combine all ingredients in cocktail shaker with cracked ice. Shake vigorously. Strain into chilled highball glass over ice cubes.

GLUHWEIN

12 parts dry red wine
(6 oz.)
Lemon peel
Orange peel
1 cinnamon stick, broken in pieces
5 whole cloves
Pinch freshly ground nutmeg
Honey (1 tsp.)

Combine all ingredients in a saucepan and stir until honey is dissolved. Do not boil. Serve in a heated mug.

GODCHILD

3 parts amaretto (1½ oz.)
2 parts vodka (1 oz.)
2 parts half-and-half (1 oz.)

Combine all ingredients with cracked ice in a blender and blend until smooth. Serve in chilled champagne flute.

GODFATHER

4 parts scotch (2 oz.)
2 parts amaretto (1 oz.)

Pour ingredients into a chilled old-fashioned glass filled with ice cubes. Stir well.

GODMOTHER

4 parts vodka (2 oz.)
2 parts amaretto (1 oz.)

Pour ingredients into a chilled old-fashioned glass filled with ice cubes. Stir well.

GOLDEN CADILLAC

4 parts Galliano (2 oz.)
2 parts white crème de cacao
(1 oz.)
2 parts half-and-half (1 oz.)

Combine all ingredients with cracked ice in a blender. Blend until smooth and pour into chilled cocktail glass.

GOLDEN DAWN

4 parts gin (2 oz.)
2 parts apricot liqueur (1 oz.)
2 parts fresh lime juice (1 oz.)
4 parts fresh orange juice (2 oz.)
Dash grenadine

Combine all ingredients with cracked ice in a cocktail shaker and shake well. Strain into chilled cocktail glass.

GOLDEN DAZE

4 parts gin (2 oz.)
2 parts peach brandy (1 oz.)
2 parts fresh orange juice (1 oz.)

Combine all ingredients with cracked ice in a cocktail shaker. Shake well and strain into chilled cocktail glass.

GOLDEN DRAGON

4 parts brandy (2 oz.)
4 parts yellow Chartreuse
(2 oz.)
Lemon twist

Stir liquid ingredients with cracked ice in a mixing glass and strain into chilled cocktail glass. Garnish with lemon twist.

GOLDEN DREAM

4 parts Galliano (2 oz.)
2 parts Cointreau (1 oz.)
2 parts fresh orange juice (1 oz.)
Half-and-half (1 tsp.)

Combine all ingredients with cracked ice in a cocktail shaker. Shake well and strain into chilled cocktail glass.

GOLDEN FIZZ

5 parts gin (2½ oz.)
2 parts fresh lime juice (1 oz.)
Bar sugar (½ tsp.)
1 egg yolk
Sparkling water
Lemon slice

Combine all ingredients, except sparkling water and lemon, in a cocktail
shaker with cracked ice. Shake
vigorously and pour into chilled
collins glass. Fill with sparkling water
and stir gently. Garnish with lemon
slice.

GOLDEN FROG

2 parts vodka (1 oz.)
2 parts Galliano (1 oz.)
2 parts Strega (1 oz.)
2 parts fresh lemon juice (1 oz.)

Combine all ingredients with cracked
ice in a blender and blend until
slushy. Pour into chilled cocktail
glass.

GOLDEN GATE

4 parts light rum (2 oz.)
2 parts gin (1 oz.)
2 parts white crème de cacao (1 oz.)
4 parts fresh lemon juice (2 oz.)
151-proof rum (1 tsp.)
Orgeat (almond) syrup (1 tsp.)
Orange slice

Combine all ingredients, except
orange slice, in a cocktail shaker with
cracked ice. Shake well and pour into
chilled old-fashioned glass. Garnish
with orange slice.

GOLDEN GLOW

4 parts bourbon (2 oz.)
2 parts dark rum (1 oz.)
4 parts fresh orange juice (2 oz.)
Fresh lemon juice (1 tbsp.)
Sugar syrup (½ tsp.)
Dash grenadine

Combine all ingredients, except
grenadine, with cracked ice in a
cocktail shaker. Shake well and strain
into a chilled cocktail glass. Float
grenadine on top.

GOLDEN HORNET

4 parts gin (2 oz.)
1 part scotch (½ oz.)
1 part amontillado sherry (½ oz.)
Lemon twist

Stir gin and sherry in a mixing glass
with ice cubes. Pour into chilled old-
fashioned glass. Float scotch on top
and garnish with lemon twist.

GOLDEN ROOSTER

4 parts gin (2 oz.)
1 part dry vermouth (½ oz.)
1 part Cointreau (½ oz.)
1 part apricot brandy (½ oz.)
Maraschino cherry

Combine all ingredients, except
cherry, with cracked ice in a cocktail
shaker. Shake well and pour into a
chilled old-fashioned glass. Garnish
with cherry.

GOLDEN SLIPPER

4 parts apricot brandy (2 oz.)
2 parts yellow Chartreuse (1 oz.)
1 egg yolk

Combine ingredients with cracked ice
in a blender. Blend until smooth and
pour into chilled old-fashioned glass.

GOLF COCKTAIL

6 parts gin (3 oz.)
2 parts dry vermouth (1 oz.)
3 dashes Angostura bitters

Stir ingredients with cracked ice in a
mixing glass and strain into chilled
cocktail glass.

GOOD AND PLENTY

2 parts vodka (1 oz.)
2 parts coffee liqueur (1 oz.)
Dash Pernod
½ scoop vanilla ice cream

Combine all ingredients in a blender.
Blend for a few seconds at low speed.
Pour into chilled red wine glass.

GRADEAL SPECIAL

4 parts gin (2 oz.)
2 parts light rum (1 oz.)
2 parts apricot brandy (1 oz.)

Combine all ingredients with cracked
ice in a cocktail shaker and shake
well. Strain into chilled cocktail glass.

GRENADA

3 parts brandy (1½ oz.)
2 parts dry sherry (1 oz.)
1 part white Curaçao (½ oz.)
Tonic water
Orange slice

Combine all ingredients, except tonic
and orange, with cracked ice in a
cocktail shaker and shake well. Pour
into chilled highball glass and fill
with tonic water. Stir gently and
garnish with orange slice.

GRAND APPLE

4 parts Calvados (2 oz.)
2 parts cognac (1 oz.)
2 parts Grand Marnier (1 oz.)

Combine ingredients in a mixing
glass with cracked ice. Stir well. Strain
over ice cubes into a chilled old-
fashioned glass.

GRAND OCCASION

4 parts light rum (2 oz.)
1 part Grand Marnier (½ oz.)
1 part white crème de cacao (½ oz.)
1 part lemon juice (½ oz.)

Combine all ingredients with cracked
ice and shake well. Strain into chilled
cocktail glass.

GRAND PASSION

4 parts gin (2 oz.)
2 parts dry vermouth (1 oz.)
2 parts passion fruit syrup (1 oz.)
1 part fresh lemon juice (½ oz.)
Orange peel

Combine all liquid ingredients with
cracked ice in a cocktail shaker and
shake well. Strain into chilled cocktail
glass and garnish with orange twist.

GRAND ROYAL FIZZ

4 parts gin (2 oz.)
Maraschino liqueur (1 tsp.)
3 parts fresh orange juice (1½ oz.)
2 parts fresh lemon juice (1 oz.)
Bar sugar (½ tsp.)
Half-and-half (2 tsp.)
Sparkling water

Combine all ingredients, except
sparkling water, with cracked ice in a
cocktail shaker and shake well. Strain
into a chilled highball glass over ice
cubes. Fill with sparkling water and
stir gently.

GRANVILLE

4 parts gin (2 oz.)
Grand Marnier (1 tsp.)
Calvados (1 tsp.)
Fresh lemon juice (1 tsp.)

Combine all ingredients with cracked
ice in a cocktail shaker and shake
well. Strain into chilled cocktail glass.

GRAPEFRUIT
COCKTAIL

4 parts gin (2 oz.)
4 parts grapefruit juice (2 oz.)
Maraschino liqueur (2 tsp.)
Maraschino cherry

Combine liquid ingredients with
cracked ice in a cocktail shaker and
shake well. Strain into chilled cocktail
glass and garnish with cherry.

GRAPESHOT

4 parts gold tequila (2 oz.)
1 part white Curaçao (1 oz.)
3 parts white grape juice (1½ oz.)

Combine all ingredients with cracked
ice in a cocktail shaker. Shake well
and strain into chilled cocktail glass.

GRAPEVINE

4 parts gin (2 oz.)
4 parts red grape juice (2 oz.)
2 parts fresh lemon juice (1 oz.)
Sugar syrup (½ tsp.)
Dash grenadine

Pour all ingredients over ice cubes into a chilled old-fashioned glass and stir well.

GRASSHOPPER

4 parts green crème de menthe (2 oz.)
4 parts white crème de cacao (2 oz.)
4 parts half-and-half (2 oz.)

Combine all ingredients with cracked ice in a cocktail shaker and shake well. Strain into chilled cocktail glass.

GRASSHOPPER

GREAT DANE

4 parts gin (2 oz.)
2 parts cherry Herring (1 oz.)
1 part dry vermouth (½ oz.)
Kirschwasser (1 tsp.)
Lemon twist

Combine all ingredients, except lemon
twist, with cracked ice in a cocktail
shaker and shake well. Strain into
chilled cocktail glass and garnish with
lemon twist.

GREAT SECRET

4 parts gin (2 oz.)
2 parts Lillet blanc
3 – 5 dashes Angostura bitters
Orange twist

Combine all ingredients, except
orange twist, with cracked ice in a
cocktail shaker and shake well. Strain
into chilled cocktail glass and garnish
with orange twist.

GREENBACK

4 parts gin (2 oz.)
2 parts green crème de menthe (1 oz.)
2 parts fresh lemon juice (1 oz.)

Combine ingredients with cracked ice
in a cocktail shaker and shake well.
Strain into chilled old-fashioned glass
over ice cubes.

GREEN DEVIL

4 parts gin (2 oz.)
4 parts green crème de menthe (2 oz.)
1 part fresh lime juice (½ oz.)

Combine all ingredients with cracked
ice in a cocktail shaker and shake
well. Strain over ice cubes into chilled
old-fashioned glass.

GREEN DRAGON

GREEN DRAGON

4 parts gin (2 oz.)
2 parts green crème de
menthe (1 oz.)
1 part Jagermeister (½ oz.)
1 part fresh lime juice (½ oz.)
3 – 5 dashes orange bitters

Combine all ingredients with cracked
ice in a cocktail shaker and shake
well. Strain into chilled cocktail glass.

GREEN ROOM

4 parts dry vermouth (2 oz.)
2 parts brandy (1 oz.)
Several dashes triple sec
Orange twist

Stir all ingredients, except orange
twist, in a mixing glass with cracked
ice. Strain into chilled cocktail glass
and garnish with orange twist.

PLEASE NOTE: Blue icons represent
alcoholic drinks. Green icons represent
non-alcoholic drinks.

GREEN SUMMER COOLER

4 parts fresh lime juice (2 oz.)
6 parts pineapple juice (3 oz.)
2 parts green peppermint syrup (1 oz.)
Ginger ale
Cucumber slice
Lime slice

Combine juices and syrup in a cocktail shaker with cracked ice. Strain into chilled collins glass over ice cubes. Top off with ginger ale and stir gently. Garnish with cucumber and lime slice.

GRINGO SWIZZLE

4 parts silver tequila (2 oz.)
1 part crème de cassis (½ oz.)
2 parts fresh lime juice (1 oz.)
2 parts fresh orange juice (1 oz.)
2 parts pineapple juice (1 oz.)
Ginger ale

Combine all ingredients, except ginger ale, in a cocktail shaker with cracked ice. Shake well and pour into chilled collins glass. Fill with cold ginger ale and stir gently.

GUACAMOLE COCKTAIL

1 California avocado, diced
10 parts chilled tomato juice (5 oz.)
4 parts chilled fresh lime juice (2 oz.)
1 small green chile, chopped
1 garlic clove, minced
Salt to taste
Freshly ground black pepper to taste
Lime wedge

Combine all ingredients, except lime wedge, in a blender. Blend until smooth but not too watery. Chill mixture for 1 hour and pour into chilled collins glass. Garnish with lime wedge.

GYPSY COCKTAIL

4 parts gin (2 oz.)
2 parts sweet vermouth (1 oz.)
Maraschino cherry

Stir gin and vermouth with cracked ice in a mixing glass. Strain into a chilled cocktail glass and garnish with cherry.

H

HABITANT COCKTAIL

4 parts Canadian whiskey (2 oz.)
2 parts fresh lemon juice (1 oz.)
1 tsp. maple syrup
Orange slice
Maraschino cherry

Combine all ingredients, except fruit, in a cocktail shaker with cracked ice. Shake well and strain into chilled cocktail glass. Garnish with fruit.

HAIR RAISER COCKTAIL

4 parts vodka (2 oz.)
1 part rock & rye (½ oz.)
2 parts fresh lemon juice (1 oz.)

Combine all ingredients with cracked ice in a cocktail shaker and shake well. Strain into chilled cocktail glass.

HALLEY'S COMFORT

4 parts Southern Comfort (2 oz.)
4 parts peach schnapps (2 oz.)
Sparkling water
Lemon slice

Pour Southern Comfort and schnapps into a chilled collins glass filled with ice cubes. Fill with sparkling water. Stir gently and garnish with lemon slice.

HAMMERHEAD

4 parts amaretto (2 oz.)
4 parts white Curaçao (2 oz.)
4 parts gold rum (2 oz.)
Dash Southern Comfort

Combine all ingredients with cracked ice in a cocktail shaker and shake well. Strain into chilled cocktail glass.

HAPPY APPLE

4 parts gold rum (2 oz.)
6 parts apple cider (3 oz.)
1 part fresh lemon juice (½ oz.)
Lime twist

Combine all ingredients, except lime twist, with cracked ice in a cocktail shaker. Shake well and pour into chilled old-fashioned glass. Garnish with lime twist.

HARLEM COCKTAIL

4 parts gin (2 oz.)
3 parts pineapple juice (1½ oz.)
Maraschino liqueur (1 tsp.)
Diced fresh pineapple (1 tbsp.)

Combine all ingredients with cracked ice in a cocktail shaker. Shake well. Strain into chilled old-fashioned glass.

HARVARD COCKTAIL

4 parts brandy (2 oz.)
1 part sweet vermouth (½ oz.)
Fresh lemon juice (2 tsp.)
Grenadine (1 tsp.)
1 dash Angostura bitters

Combine all ingredients with cracked ice in a cocktail shaker and shake well. Strain into chilled cocktail glass.

HARVARD COOLER

4 parts apple brandy (2 oz.)
Bar sugar (1 tsp.)
Sparkling water
Lemon twist

Dissolve sugar in brandy in a chilled collins glass. Add ice cubes and fill with sparking water. Garnish with lemon twist and stir gently.

HARVEY WALLBANGER

4 parts vodka (2 oz.)
2 parts Galliano (1 oz.)
10 parts orange juice (5 oz.)

Pour vodka and orange juice over ice cubes in chilled collins glass. Stir. Float Galliano on top.

123

HASTY COCKTAIL

4 parts gin (2 oz.)
1 part dry vermouth (½ oz.)
3 – 5 dashes Pernod
Grenadine (1 tsp.)

Combine all ingredients with cracked ice in a mixing glass. Stir well and strain into chilled cocktail glass.

HAVANA BANANA FIZZ

4 parts light rum (2 oz.)
5 parts pineapple juice (2½ oz.)
3 parts fresh lime juice (1½ oz.)
3 – 5 dashes Peychaud's bitters
⅓ banana, sliced
Bitter lemon soda

Combine all ingredients, except soda, with cracked ice in a blender. Blend at low speed until smooth. Pour into a chilled old fashioned glass, fill with bitter lemon soda and stir.

HAVANA CLUB

6 parts light rum (3 oz.)
1 part dry vermouth (½ oz.)

Combine ingredients with cracked ice in a mixing glass. Stir well and strain into chilled cocktail glass.

HAVANA COCKTAIL

4 parts light rum (2 oz.)
4 parts pineapple juice (2 oz.)
1 part fresh lemon juice (½ oz.)

Combine all ingredients with cracked ice in a cocktail shaker. Shake well and strain into chilled cocktail glass.

HAWAIIAN COCKTAIL

4 parts gin (2 oz.)
1 part triple sec (½ oz.)
1 part pineapple juice (½ oz.)

Combine ingredients in cocktail shaker with cracked ice. Shake well and strain into chilled cocktail glass.

HAWAIIAN EYE

4 parts bourbon (2 oz.)
2 parts vodka (1 oz.)
2 parts coffee liqueur (1 oz.)
1 part Pernod (½ oz.)
2 parts half-and-half (1 oz.)
4 parts maraschino cherry juice
(2 oz.)
1 egg white
Pineapple spear
Maraschino cherry

Combine all ingredients, except fruit, in a blender with cracked ice. Blend until smooth and pour into chilled old-fashioned glass. Garnish with fruit.

HAWAIIAN LEMONADE

6 parts pineapple juice (3 oz.)
Fresh lemonade
Pineapple spear

Pour pineapple juice into a chilled collins glass over ice cubes. Fill with lemonade and stir. Garnish with pineapple spear.

HAWAIIAN ORANGE BLOSSOM

4 parts gin (2 oz.)
2 parts triple sec (1 oz.)
4 parts fresh orange juice (2 oz.)
2 parts pineapple juice (1 oz.)

Combine all ingredients with cracked ice in a cocktail shaker and shake well. Strain into chilled sour glass.

HEART'S COCKTAIL

4 parts Irish whiskey (2 oz.)
2 parts sweet vermouth (1 oz.)
2 parts Pernod (1 oz.)
3 – 5 dashes Angostura bitters

Combine all ingredients in a cocktail shaker with cracked ice. Shake well and pour into chilled old-fashioned glass.

HEAVENLY DAYS

4 parts hazelnut syrup (2 oz.)
4 parts fresh lemon juice (2 oz.)
Grenadine (1 tsp.)
Sparkling water
Orange slice

Combine all ingredients, except orange slice and water, in a cocktail shaker with cracked ice. Shake well and pour over ice into a chilled highball glass. Fill with sparkling water and stir gently. Garnish with orange slice.

HENRY MORGAN'S GROG

4 parts blended whiskey (2 oz.)
2 parts Pernod (1 oz.)
1 part dark rum (½ oz.)
2 parts half-and-half (1 oz.)
Freshly ground nutmeg

Combine all ingredients, except nutmeg, in a cocktail shaker with cracked ice. Shake well and pour into chilled old-fashioned glass. Sprinkle with nutmeg.

HIGHLAND COOLER

4 parts scotch (2 oz.)
4 parts sparkling water (2 oz.)
Bar sugar (1 tsp.)
Ginger ale
Lemon twist

In a chilled collins glass, dissolve the sugar in the water. Add scotch and ice cubes. Fill with ginger ale and stir gently. Garnish with lemon twist.

HIGHLAND FLING

4 parts scotch (2 oz.)
2 parts sweet vermouth (1 oz.)
3 – 5 dashes orange bitters
Spanish olive

Stir liquid ingredients with cracked ice in a mixing glass. Strain into chilled cocktail glass and drop in the olive.

HOFFMAN HOUSE COCKTAIL

4 parts gin (2 oz.)
1 part dry vermouth (½ oz.)
3 dashes orange bitters
Cocktail olive

Stir all ingredients, except olive, in a mixing glass. Strain into chilled cocktail glass and garnish with olive.

HOLE-IN-ONE

4 parts scotch (2 oz.)
1 part dry vermouth (½ oz.)
Fresh lemon juice (½ tsp.)
Dash orange bitters

Combine all ingredients with cracked ice in a cocktail shaker and shake well. Strain into chilled cocktail glass.

HOMESTEAD COCKTAIL

4 parts gin (2 oz.)
2 parts sweet vermouth (1 oz.)
Orange slice

Stir gin and vermouth with ice cubes in a mixing glass. Strain into chilled cocktail glass and garnish with orange slice.

HONEY BEE

4 parts light rum (2 oz.)
1 part honey (½ oz.)
1 part fresh lemon juice (½ oz.)

Combine all ingredients in a cocktail shaker with cracked ice and shake well. Strain into chilled cocktail glass.

HONEYMOON

4 parts apple brandy (2 oz.)
2 parts Benedictine (1 oz.)
2 parts fresh lemon juice (1 oz.)
Triple sec (1 tsp.)

Combine all ingredients with cracked ice and shake well. Strain into chilled cocktail glass.

HONOLULU COCKTAIL

4 parts gin (2 oz.)
2 parts pineapple juice (1 oz.)
Fresh lemon juice (1 tsp.)
Fresh lime juice (1 tsp.)
Fresh orange juice (1 tsp.)
Dash orange bitters
Bar sugar (½ tsp.)

Combine all ingredients in a cocktail shaker with cracked ice and shake well. Strain into chilled cocktail glass.

HOOPLA

2 parts brandy (1 oz.)
2 parts Cointreau (1 oz.)
2 parts Lillet blanc (1 oz.)
2 parts fresh lemon juice (1 oz.)

Combine all ingredients with cracked ice in a cocktail shaker. Shake well and strain into chilled cocktail glass.

HOOT MON

4 parts scotch (2 oz.)
1 part Lillet blanc (½ oz.)
1 part sweet vermouth (½ oz.)

Combine all ingredients with cracked ice in a cocktail shaker. Shake well and strain into chilled cocktail glass.

HOP TOAD

4 parts light rum (2 oz.)
3 parts apricot brandy (1½ oz.)
2 parts fresh lime juice (½ oz.)

Combine all ingredients in a mixing glass with ice cubes and stir well. Strain into chilled cocktail glass.

HORSE'S NECK

4 parts blended whiskey (2 oz.)
Ginger ale
3 dashes Angostura bitters
Rind of one lemon, peeled in a spiral

Put the lemon spiral in a chilled collins glass and hand one end over the rim. Fill with ice cubes and add whiskey. Fill with ginger ale and stir well.

HOT BRANDY FLIP

4 parts brandy (2 oz.)
Whole egg
Bar sugar (1 tsp.)
Hot milk
Cinnamon stick

In a small bowl, beat egg, sugar and brandy. Pour into warmed mug and fill with hot milk. Stir with a cinnamon stick and leave it in for garnish.

HOT BRICK TODDY

4 parts blended whiskey (2 oz.)
2 parts hot water (1 oz.)
Bar sugar (1 tsp.)
Butter (1 tsp.)
Ground cinnamon to taste
Boiling water

Dissolve all ingredients, except whiskey, in hot water in a warmed coffee mug or punch cup. Add whiskey and boiling water. Stir well.

HOT BUTTERED RUM

HOT BUTTERED RUM

4 parts dark rum (2 oz.)
Brown sugar (1 tsp.)
Pat of butter
Boiling water
Freshly ground nutmeg

Put sugar into warmed mug and fill two-thirds with boiling water. Add rum and stir. Float butter on top and sprinkle with nutmeg.

HOTEL PLAZA COCKTAIL

2 parts dry vermouth (1 oz.)
2 parts sweet vermouth (1 oz.)
2 parts gin (1 oz.)
Maraschino cherry

Stir liquid ingredients with ice cubes in a mixing glass. Strain into chilled cocktail glass and garnish with cherry.

HOT MILK PUNCH

6 parts whiskey (3 oz.)
16 parts milk (8 oz.)
Bar sugar (1 tsp.)
Cinnamon stick
Freshly ground nutmeg

Heat all ingredients, except nutmeg and cinnamon stick, in a sauce pan over low heat. Stir regularly until mixture is very hot. Pour into warmed mug and stir with cinnamon stick. Sprinkle with nutmeg.

127

HOT PANTS

4 parts silver tequila (2 oz.)
1 part peppermint schnapps (½ oz.)
1 part grapefruit juice (½ oz.)
Bar sugar (½ tsp.).

Rim a chilled old-fashioned glass with
salt. Combine all ingredients with ice
cubes in a cocktails shaker and shake
well. Pour into salted old-fashioned
glass.

HOT TODDY

6 parts chosen liquor
(3 oz.)
2 parts honey or sugar
syrup (1 oz.)
2 parts fresh lemon juice (1 oz.)
5 whole cloves
Ground cinnamon to taste
Lemon slice
Boiling water or hot tea
Freshly grated nutmeg
Cinnamon stick

Add all ingredients, except nutmeg,
boiling water and cinnamon stick, to
a warmed coffee mug. Fill with
boiling water and stir. Garnish with
cinnamon stick and nutmeg.

128

HOT TOT TODDY

Hot tea
2 parts honey (1 oz.)
2 parts fresh lemon juice (1 oz.)
5 whole cloves
Ground cinnamon to taste
Lemon slice
Freshly grated nutmeg
Cinnamon stick

Mull all ingredients, except nutmeg,
tea and cinnamon stick, in the bottom
of a warmed coffee mug. Fill with hot
tea and stir. Garnish with cinnamon
stick and nutmeg.

HUDSON BAY

4 parts gin (2 oz.)
2 parts cherry brandy (1 oz.)
151-proof rum (1 tbsp.)
1 part fresh orange juice (½ oz.)
Fresh lime juice (1 tbsp.)

Combine all ingredients with cracked
ice in a cocktail shaker. Shake well
and strain into chilled cocktail glass.

HUDSON BAY

HULA-HULA

4 parts gin (2 oz.)
2 parts fresh orange juice (1 oz.)
Triple sec (1 tbsp.)

Combine all ingredients with cracked
ice in a cocktail shaker. Strain into
chilled cocktail glass.

HUNTER'S COCKTAIL

4 parts rye (2 oz.)
1 part cherry brandy (½ oz.)
Maraschino cherry

Pour rye and brandy into a chilled
old-fashioned glass filled with ice
cubes. Stir well and garnish with
cherry.

HUNTRESS COCKTAIL

4 parts bourbon (2 oz.)
2 parts cherry liqueur (1 oz.)
2 parts half-and-half (1 oz.)
Dash Cointreau

Combine all ingredients in a cocktail
shaker with cracked ice and shake
well. Strain into chilled cocktail glass.

HUNTSMAN COCKTAIL

4 parts vodka (2 oz.)
2 parts dark rum (1 oz.)
2 parts fresh lime juice (1 oz.)
Bar sugar (½ tsp.)

Combine all ingredients with cracked
ice in a cocktail shaker. Shake well
and strain into chilled cocktail glass.

HURRICANE

3 parts dark rum (1½ oz.)
3 parts light rum (1½ oz.)
2 parts passion fruit syrup (1 oz.)
Fresh lime juice (1 tbsp.)

Shake all ingredients with cracked ice
in a cocktail shaker. Strain into
chilled cocktail glass.

I

ICE PICK

4 parts vodka (2 oz.)
Iced tea
Lime wedge

Pour vodka and iced tea into a chilled collins glass filled with ice cubes. Squeeze the lime wedge over drink and drop in. Stir.

ICED TEA

Loose tea of your choice
(2 heaping tsp.)
12 parts water (6 oz.)
Sugar to taste
Fresh mint sprig
Lemon wedge

Put tea in a heated ceramic tea pot and add boiling water. Steep for 5 minutes. Stir and strain into a chilled collins glass filled with ice cubes. Add more ice if necessary. Add sugar to taste and garnish with mint and lemon.

ICH BIEN

4 parts apple brandy (2 oz.)
1 part white Curaçao (½ oz.)
4 parts half-and-half (2 oz.)
1 egg yolk
Freshly grated nutmeg

Combine all ingredients, except nutmeg, with cracked ice in a blender. Blend until smooth and pour into chilled sour glass. Sprinkle with nutmeg.

IDEAL COCKTAIL

4 parts gin (2 oz.)
2 parts dry vermouth (1 oz.)
Maraschino liqueur (½ tsp.)
Fresh lemon juice (1 tsp.)
Maraschino cherry

Combine all ingredients, except cherry, with cracked ice in a cocktail shaker. Shake well and pour into chilled cocktail glass. Garnish with cherry.

IMPERIAL COCKTAIL

4 parts gin (2 oz.)
2 parts dry vermouth (1 oz.)
Maraschino liqueur (½ tsp.)
2 dashes Angostura bitters

Combine all ingredients in a mixing glass with ice cubes and stir well. Strain into chilled cocktail glass.

IMPERIAL FIZZ

4 parts blended whiskey (2 oz.)
2 parts light rum (1 oz.)
2 parts fresh lemon juice (1 oz.)
Bar sugar (½ tsp.)
Sparkling water

Combine all ingredients, except water, with cracked ice in a cocktail shaker. Strain into chilled highball glass and add ice cubes. Fill with sparkling water and stir gently.

INCA COCKTAIL

4 parts gin (2 oz.)
2 parts dry vermouth (1 oz.)
2 parts sweet vermouth (1 oz.)
2 parts dry sherry (1 oz.)
Dash orange bitters
Dash orgeat (almond) syrup

Combine all ingredients in a mixing glass with cracked ice and stir well. Strain into chilled cocktail glass.

INCOME TAX COCKTAIL

4 parts gin (2 oz.)
Dry vermouth (1 tbsp.)
Sweet vermouth (1 tbsp.)
3 parts fresh orange juice (1½ oz.)
3 dashes Angostura bitters

Combine all ingredients with cracked ice in a cocktail shaker. Shake well and strain into chilled cocktail glass.

INDEPENDENCE
SWIZZLE

4 oz. dark rum (2 oz.)
3 parts fresh lime juice (1½ oz.)
Honey (1 tsp.)
3 – 5 dashes Angostura bitters
Lime slice

Dissolve honey in a little warm water.
Stir it with remaining ingredients,
except lime slice, in a chilled old-
fashioned glass filled with crushed ice.
Garnish with lime slice and serve with
swizzle stick.

INDIAN RIVER

4 parts blended whiskey (2 oz.)
1 part raspberry liqueur (½ oz.)
1 part sweet vermouth (½ oz.)
2 parts grapefruit juice (1 oz.)

Combine all ingredients with cracked
ice in a cocktail shaker. Shake well
and strain into chilled cocktail glass.

INDIAN SUMMER

4 parts apple brandy (2 oz.)
Hot apple cider
Ground cinnamon
Cinnamon stick

Rim a sour glass with cinnamon by
wetting the rim and dipping in
cinnamon. Add brandy and hot cider.
Stir and garnish with cinnamon stick.

INK STREET

4 parts rye (2 oz.)
4 parts fresh lemon street (2 oz.)
4 parts fresh orange juice (2 oz.)

Combine all ingredients with cracked
ice in a cocktail shaker. Shake well
and strain into chilled cocktail glass.

INTERNATIONAL
COCKTAIL

4 parts cognac (2 oz.)
1 part Pernod (½ oz.)
1 part triple sec (½ oz.)
Vodka (2 tsp.)

Combine all ingredients with cracked
ice in a cocktail shaker. Shake well
and strain into chilled cocktail glass.

IRISH CANADIAN
SANGAREE

4 parts Canadian whiskey (2 oz.)
2 parts Irish mist (1 oz.)
2 parts fresh lemon juice (1 oz.)
2 parts fresh orange juice (1 oz.)
Freshly grated nutmeg

Pour all ingredients, except nutmeg,
into a chilled old-fashioned glass and
stir with ice cubes. Sprinkle with
nutmeg.

IRISH COFFEE

4 parts Irish whiskey (2 oz.)
Hot black coffee
Whipped cream
Granulated sugar

Rim the cup with sugar and pour in
Irish whiskey. Fill the cup to within
½ inch of the rim with coffee. Stir.
Top off with whipped cream.

IRISH COW

4 parts Irish whiskey (2 oz.)
16 parts hot milk (1 cup or
8 oz.)
Bar sugar (1 tsp.)

Pour the milk into a warmed coffee
mug. Add the whiskey and sugar and
stir well.

IRISH COFFEE (from Old Town Bar)

IRISH FIX

4 parts Irish whiskey (2 oz.)
2 parts Irish mist (1 oz.)
1 part fresh lemon juice (½ oz.)
1 part pineapple juice (½ oz.)
Lemon slice
Orange slice
Pineapple spear

Combine all ingredients, except fruit, in a blender with cracked ice. Blend until smooth. Pour into chilled old-fashioned glass and garnish with fruit

IRISH KILT

4 parts Irish whiskey (2 oz.)
2 parts scotch (1 oz.)
2 parts fresh lemon juice (1 oz.)
2 parts sugar syrup (1 oz.)
3 – 5 dashes orange bitters

Combine all ingredients with cracked ice in a cocktail shaker. Shake well and strain into chilled cocktail glass.

133

IRISH SHILLELAGH

4 parts Irish whiskey (2 oz.)
1 part light rum (½ oz.)
1 part sloe gin (½ oz.)
2 parts fresh lemon juice (1 oz.)
Bar sugar (½ tsp.)
Fresh peaches, diced (¼ cup)
Fresh raspberries

Combine all ingredients, except
raspberries, in a blender with cracked
ice. Blend until smooth and pour into
chilled old-fashioned glass. Garnish
with a few raspberries.

ISLAND COOLER

2 parts fresh lemon juice (1 oz.)
4 parts fresh orange juice (2 oz.)
2 parts papaya juice (1 oz.)
2 parts pineapple juice (1 oz.)
Grenadine (½ tsp.)
Sparkling water
Maraschino cherry
Pineapple spear

Combine juices and grenadine in a
cocktail shaker with cracked ice.
Shake well and pour over ice cubes
into a chilled collins glass. Fill with
sparkling water and stir gently.
Garnish with fruit.

ISLE OF THE BLESSED
COCONUT

4 parts light rum (2 oz.)
1 part fresh lemon juice (½ oz.)
1 part fresh lime juice (½ oz.)
1 part fresh orange juice (½ oz.)
Cream of coconut (1 tsp.)
Orgeat (almond) syrup (1 tsp.)

Combine all ingredients with cracked
ice in a blender and blend until
smooth. Pour into a chilled cocktail
glass.

ISLE OF PINES

4 parts light rum (2 oz.)
1 part fresh lime juice (½ oz.)
Peppermint schnapps (1 tsp.)
6 fresh mint leaves

Combine all ingredients with cracked
ice in a blender. Blend until slushy
and pour into chilled cocktail glass.

ITALIAN SODA

2 parts Italian syrup of your
choice (1 oz.)*
Sparkling water
Lemon or lime slice

Add syrup to a chilled collins glass
filled with ice cubes. Add sparkling
water and stir gently. Garnish with
slice of lemon or lime. If you prefer a
sweeter soda, use more syrup.

*Note: Italian syrups come in a
variety of flavors and are available at
specialty food stores and Italian
grocery stores. Flavors vary from
orgeat (almond) and hazelnut to
almost all fruits, as well as peppermint
and other unusual and refreshing
choices.

ITALIAN STALLION

4 parts bourbon (2 oz.)
2 parts Campari (1 oz.)
1 part sweet vermouth
Dash Angostura bitters
Lemon twist

Combine all ingredients, except
lemon, in a mixing glass with ice
cubes and stir well. Strain into chilled
cocktail glass and garnish with lemon
twist.

IXTAPA

4 parts coffee liqueur (2 oz.)
2 parts silver tequila (1 oz.)

Stir ingredients with cracked ice in a
mixing glass and pour into chilled
cocktail glass.

J

JACK-IN-THE-BOX

4 parts apple jack or apple
brandy (2 oz.)
2 parts fresh lemon juice (1 oz.)
2 parts pineapple juice (1 oz.)
3 – 5 dashes Angostura bitters

Combine all ingredients with cracked
ice in a cocktail shaker. Shake well
and strain into chilled cocktail glass.

JACK ROSE

4 parts applejack or apple
brandy (2 oz.)
1 part fresh lime juice (½ oz.)
Grenadine (1 tsp.)

Combine all ingredients with cracked
ice in a cocktail shaker. Shake well
and strain into chilled cocktail glass.

JADE

Blue Curaçao (¼ tsp.)
Melon liqueur (¼ tsp.)
Fresh lime juice (¼ tsp.)
Dash Angostura bitters
Champagne or sparkling wine
Lime slice

Combine all ingredients, except
champagne and lime slice, in a
cocktail shaker with cracked ice.
Shake well and strain into champagne
flute. Fill with champagne and
garnish with lime slice.

JAMAICAN COFFEE

4 parts coffee liqueur
(2 oz.)
3 parts light rum (1½ oz.)
Hot black coffee
Whipped cream
Freshly ground allspice

Pour rum and liqueur into a mug of
hot coffee. Stir. Top with whipped
cream and sprinkle with ground
allspice.

JAMAICA EGG CREAM

4 parts dark rum (2 oz.)
2 parts gin (1 oz.)
2 parts half-and-half (1 oz.)
Fresh lemon juice (1 tbsp.)
Bar sugar (1 tsp.)
Sparkling water

Combine all ingredients, except water,
in a cocktail shaker with cracked ice
and shake well. Pour into chilled
highball glass and fill with sparkling
water. Stir gently.

JAMAICA GLOW

4 parts gin (2 oz.)
1 part dry red wine (½ oz.)
Dark rum (1 tbsp.)
1 part fresh orange juice (½ oz.)

Combine all ingredients with cracked
ice in a cocktail shaker. Shake well
and strain into chilled cocktail glass.

JAMAICA HOP

4 parts coffee liqueur (2 oz.)
2 parts white crème de cacao
(1 oz.)
4 parts half-and-half (2 oz.)

Combine ingredients with cracked ice
in a cocktail shaker. Shake well and
strain into chilled cocktail glass.

JAMAICA MULE

4 parts light rum (2 oz.)
2 parts dark rum (1 oz.)
2 parts 151-proof rum (1 oz.)
2 parts Falernum (1 oz.)
2 parts fresh lime juice (1 oz.)
Ginger beer
Pineapple spear
Slice candied ginger

Combine all ingredients, except ginger
beer, pineapple and ginger, with
cracked ice in a cocktail shaker. Shake
well and strain into chilled collins
glass. Fill with ginger beer and stir
gently. Garnish with pineapple spear
and ginger.

JAMAICA SHAKE

4 parts bourbon (2 oz.)
3 parts dark rum (1½ oz.)
3 parts half-and-half (1½ oz.)

Combine all ingredients with cracked ice in a cocktail shaker and shake well. Strain into chilled cocktail glass.

JAPANESE

4 parts brandy (2 oz.)
Fresh lime juice (1 tbsp.)
Orgeat (almond) syrup (2 tsp.)
Dash Angostura bitters
Lime twist

Combine all ingredients, except lime twist, in a cocktail shaker with cracked ice. Shake well and strain into chilled cocktail glass. Garnish with lime twist.

JAPANESE FIZZ

4 parts blended whiskey (2 oz.)
Port (1 tbsp.)
2 parts fresh lemon juice (1 oz.)
Bar sugar (1 tsp.)
1 egg white
Sparkling water
Pineapple spear

Combine all ingredients, except sparkling water and pineapple, in a cocktail shaker with cracked ice. Shake vigorously. Strain into chilled highball glass over ice cubes and fill with sparkling water. Stir gently and garnish with pineapple.

JERSEY LIGHTNING

4 parts apple brandy (2 oz.)
2 parts sweet vermouth (1 oz.)
4 parts fresh lime juice (2 oz.)

Combine ingredients with cracked ice in a cocktail shaker and shake well. Strain into chilled cocktail glass.

JEWEL COCKTAIL

4 parts gin (2 oz.)
3 parts green Chartreuse (1½ oz.)
2 parts sweet vermouth (1 oz.)
3 dashes orange bitters
Maraschino cherry

Combine liquid ingredients with cracked ice in a mixing glass and stir well. Strain into chilled cocktail glass and garnish with cherry.

JOCKEY CLUB COCKTAIL

4 parts gin (2 oz.)
White crème de cacao (½ tsp.)
1 part fresh lemon juice (½ oz.)
Dash Angostura bitters

Combine all ingredients with cracked ice in a cocktail shaker. Shake well and strain into chilled cocktail glass.

JOCOSE JULEP

6 parts bourbon (3 oz.)
2 parts green crème de menthe (1 oz.)
3 parts fresh lime juice (1½ oz.)
Bar sugar (1 tsp.)
5 fresh mint leaves
Sparkling water
Sprig of fresh mint

Combine all ingredients, except sparkling water and mint sprig, in a blender with cracked ice. Blend until smooth and pour into chilled collins glass over ice cubes. Fill with sparkling water and garnish with mint sprig. Stir gently.

JOHN COLLINS

4 parts blended whiskey (2 oz.)
2 parts fresh lemon juice (1 oz.)
Bar sugar (1 tsp.)
Sparkling water
Lemon slice
Orange slice
Maraschino cherry

Combine all ingredients, except sparkling water and fruit, in a cocktail shaker with cracked ice. Shake well and strain over ice cubes into a chilled collins glass. Fill with sparkling water and stir gently. Garnish with fruits.

JOHNNY COCKTAIL

4 parts sloe gin (2 oz.)
2 parts triple sec (1 oz.)
Pernod (1 tsp.)

Combine ingredients with cracked ice in a cocktail shaker. Shake well and strain into chilled cocktail glass.

136

JOLLY ROGER

4 parts light rum (2 oz.)
2 parts Drambuie (1 oz.)
2 parts fresh lime juice (1 oz.)
Scotch (¼ tsp.)
Sparkling water

Combine all ingredients, except sparkling water, with cracked ice in a cocktail shaker. Shake well and pour into chilled highball glass. Fill with sparkling water and stir gently.

JOSIAH'S BAY FLOAT

2 parts gold rum (1 oz.)
1 part Galliano (½ oz.)
2 parts pineapple juice (1 oz.)
Lime juice (2 tsp.)
Sugar syrup (2 tsp.)
Champagne or sparkling wine
Lime slice
Maraschino cherry
Pineapple shell, carved out (optional)

Mix all ingredients, except chamapgne, lime, and cherry, with cracked ice in a cocktail shaker or blender. Pour into chilled collins glass or pineapple shell. Fill with champagne. Stir gently and garnish with lime slice and cherry.

137

JOULOUVILLE

4 parts gin (2 oz.)
2 parts apple brandy (1 oz.)
Sweet vermouth (1 tbsp.)
1 part fresh lemon juice (½ oz.)
3 dashes grenadine

Combine all ingredients with cracked
ice in a cocktail shaker. Shake well
and strain into chilled cocktail glass.

PLEASE NOTE: Blue icons represent
alcoholic drinks. Green icons represent
non-alcoholic drinks.

JOURNALIST

4 parts gin (2 oz.)
Dry vermouth (1 tsp.)
Sweet vermouth (1 tsp.)
Triple sec (1 tsp.)
Fresh lime juice (1 tsp.)
Dash Angostura bitters

Combine all ingredients with cracked
ice in a cocktail shaker. Shake well
and strain into chilled cocktail glass.

JUICY JULEP

2 parts fresh lime juice (1 oz.)
2 parts fresh orange juice (1 oz.)
2 parts pineapple juice (1 oz.)
1 part raspberry syrup (½ oz.)
5 fresh crushed mint leaves
Ginger ale
Mint sprig

Combine all ingredients, except ginger
ale and mint sprig, in a cocktail
shaker with cracked ice. Shake well
and pour into chilled collins glass. Fill
with cold ginger ale and stir gently.
Garnish with mint sprig.

JUDGE, JR.

4 parts gin (2 oz.)
4 parts light rum (2 oz.)
2 parts fresh lemon juice (1 oz.)
Grenadine (2 tsp.)

Combine all ingredient with cracked
ice in a cocktail shaker. Shake well
and strain into chilled cocktail glass.

JUDGETTE COCKTAIL

4 parts gin (2 oz.)
3 parts peach brandy (1½ oz.)
2 parts dry vermouth (1 oz.)
Fresh lime juice (½ tsp.)

Combine ingredients with cracked ice
in a cocktail shaker. Shake well and
strain into chilled cocktail glass.

JUNGLE JAMES

4 parts vodka (2 oz.)
4 parts crème de bananes (2 oz.)
4 parts milk (2 oz.)

Combine all ingredients with cracked
ice in a blender and blend until
smooth. Pour into chilled old-
fashioned glass.

JUPITER COCKTAIL

4 parts gin (2 oz.)
2 parts dry vermouth (1 oz.)
Crème de violette (2 tsp.)
Fresh orange juice (2 tsp.)

Combine all ingredients with cracked
ice in a cocktail shaker. Shake well
and strain into chilled cocktail glass.

K

KAHLUA TOREADOR

4 parts brandy (2 oz.)
2 parts Kahlua or coffee liqueur
(1 oz.)
½ egg white

Combine all ingredients with cracked ice in a blender. Blend until smooth and pour into chilled cocktail glass.

KAMEHAMEHA PUNCH

6 parts pineapple juice (3 oz.)
2 parts orgeat (almond) syrup (1 oz.)
4 parts fresh lime juice (2 oz.)
2 parts fresh lemon juice (1 oz.)
1 part blackberry syrup (½ oz.)
Pineapple spear

Combine all ingredients, except blackberry syrup and pineapple spear, in a cocktail shaker with cracked ice. Shake well and pour into chilled highball glass. Float syrup on top and garnish with pineapple spear.

KAMEHAMEHA RUM PUNCH

4 parts light rum (2 oz.)
2 parts dark rum (1 oz.)
Blackberry brandy (2 tsp.)
4 parts pineapple juice (2 oz.)
2 parts orgeat (almond) syrup (1 oz.)
2 parts fresh lime juice (1 oz.)
Fresh lemon juice (1 tsp.)
Pineapple spear

Combine all ingredients, except dark rum and pineapple spear, in a cocktail shaker with cracked ice. Shake well and pour into chilled highball glass. Float dark rum on top and garnish with pineapple spear.

KAMIKAZE

6 parts vodka (3 oz.)
Triple sec (½ tsp.)
Fresh lime juice (½ tsp.)
Lime wedge

Combine all ingredients, except lime wedge, in a cocktail glass with cracked ice and shake well. Strain into chilled cocktail glass and garnish with lime wedge.

KANGAROO

4 parts vodka (2 oz.)
2 parts dry vermouth (1 oz.)
Lemon twist

Stir the vodka and vermouth in a mixing glass with ice cubes. Strain over ice cubes into a chilled old-fashioned glass. Twist lemon over drink and drop in.

KAPTAIN KIRK

5 parts pineapple juice (2½ oz.)
3 parts fresh lime juice (1½ oz.)
½ banana, sliced
Bitter lemon soda

Combine all ingredients, except soda, with cracked ice in a blender. Blend until smooth. Pour into chilled highball glass, fill with bitter lemon soda and stir.

KEMPINSKY FIZZ

4 parts vodka (2 oz.)
2 parts crème de cassis (1 oz.)
Fresh lemon juice (2 tsp.)
Bitter lemon soda (ginger ale or seltzer may be substituted)

Pour all ingredients, except soda, into a chilled highball glass filled with ice cubes. Fill with soda and stir.

KENTUCKY COCKTAIL

6 parts bourbon (3 oz.)
2 parts pineapple juice (1 oz.)

Combine ingredients with cracked ice in a cocktail shaker. Shake well and strain into chilled cocktail glass.

KENTUCKY COLONEL COCKTAIL

6 parts bourbon (3 oz.)
2 parts Benedictine (1 oz.)
Lemon twist

Stir liquid ingredients with ice cubes in a mixing glass. Strain into chilled cocktail glass and garnish with lemon twist.

KENTUCKY ORANGE BLOSSOM

4 parts bourbon (2 oz.)
1 part Cointreau (½ oz.)
2 parts fresh orange juice (1 oz.)
Lemon twist

Combine all ingredients, except lemon twist, with cracked ice in a cocktail shaker. Shake well and pour into chilled old-fashioned glass. Garnish with lemon twist.

KERRY COOLER

4 parts Irish whiskey (2 oz.)
3 parts fino sherry (1½ oz.)
2 parts orgeat (almond) syrup (1 oz.)
2 parts fresh lemon juice (1 oz.)
Sparkling water
Lemon slice

Combine all ingredients, except lemon slice and water, in a cocktail shaker with cracked ice. Shake well and strain into chilled highball glass filled with ice cubes. Fill with sparkling water and stir gently.

KEY CLUB COCKTAIL

4 parts gin (2 oz.)
1 part dark rum (½ oz.)
1 part Falernum (½ oz.)
1 part fresh lime juice (½ oz.)
Pineapple spear

Combine all ingredients, except pineapple, in a cocktail shaker with cracked ice. Shake well and strain into chilled cocktail glass. Garnish with pineapple spear.

K.G.B. COCKTAIL

1½ parts kirschwasser (¾ oz.)
4 parts gin (2 oz.)
Apricot brandy (½ tsp.)
Lemon twist

Combine all ingredients, except lemon, with cracked ice in a cocktail glass. Shake well and strain into chilled cocktail glass. Garnish with lemon twist.

KING COLE COCKTAIL

4 parts blended whiskey (2 oz.)
Orange slice
Pineapple slice
Sugar (½ tsp.)

Muddle fruit and sugar in an old-fashioned glass. Add whiskey and ice cubes. Stir well.

KING'S PEG

2 parts cognac (1 oz.)
Champagne

Pour cognac into a champagne flute. Fill with chilled champagne and stir gently.

KINGSTON COCKTAIL

4 parts dark rum (2 oz.)
1½ parts coffee liqueur (¾ oz.)
Fresh lime juice (2 tsp.)

Combine ingredients with cracked ice in a cocktail shaker. Shake well and strain into chilled cocktail glass.

KIR

4 parts crème de cassis
(2 oz.)
White wine
Lemon twist

Pour cassis over ice cubes in a chilled wine glass. Fill with white wine and stir well. Garnish with lemon twist.

KIR ROYALE

4 parts crème de cassis (2 oz.)
Champagne

Stir the cassis with cracked ice in a
mixing glass. Pour into chilled wine
glass and fill with cold champagne.
Stir gently.

KIRSCH RICKEY

4 parts kirschwasser (2 oz.)
Fresh lime juice (1 tbsp.)
Sparkling water
2 pitted black cherries

Pour kirschwasser and lime juice into
a chilled highball glass filled with ice
cubes. Fill with sparking water and stir
gently. Garnish with cherries.

KIRSCH RICKEY

KISS ME QUICK

4 parts Pernod (2 oz.)
White Curaçao (½ tsp.)
3 – 5 dashes Angostura bitters
Sparkling water

Combine all ingredients, except water, with cracked ice in a cocktail shaker. Shake well and pour into chilled highballglass. Fill with sparkling water and stir gently.

KISS THE BOYS GOOD-BYE

4 parts brandy (2 oz.)
2 parts sloe gin (1 oz.)
3 parts fresh lemon juice (1½ oz.)
1 egg white

Combine all ingredients in a cocktail shaker with cracked ice and shake vigorously. Strain into chilled cocktail glass.

KLONDIKE COOLER

4 parts blended whiskey (2 oz.)
4 parts sparkling water (2 oz.)
Bar sugar (½ tsp.)
Ginger ale
Lemon peel spiral

Mix powdered sugar and ginger ale in
a chilled collins glass. Fill glass with
ice cubes and add whiskey. Fill with
sparkling water and stir well. Garnish
with lemon spiral.

KNICKERBOCKER
COCKTAIL

4 parts gin (2 oz.)
2 parts dry vermouth (1 oz.)
Sweet vermouth (½ tsp.)
Lemon twist

Stir liquid ingredients with ice cubes
in a mixing glass. Strain into chilled
cocktail glass and garnish with lemon
twist.

KNICKERBOCKER
SPECIAL COCKTAIL

4 parts light rum (2 oz.)
Triple sec (½ tsp.)
Raspberry syrup (1 tsp.)
Pineapple syrup (1 tsp.)
Fresh lime juice (1 tsp.)
Fresh orange juice (1 tsp.)
Pineapple spear

Combine liquid ingredients with
cracked ice in a cocktail shaker and
shake well. Strain into chilled cocktail
glass and garnish with pineapple.

KNICKS VICTORY
COOLER

4 parts apricot nectar (2 oz.)
Raspberry soda
Orange peel
Fresh raspberries

Pour apricot nectar into a chilled
collins glass almost filled with ice
cubes. Fill with raspberry soda. Stir
gently and garnish with orange peel
and a few fresh raspberries.

KNOCKOUT COCKTAIL

4 parts dry vermouth (2 oz.)
3 parts gin (1½ oz.)
2 parts Pernod (1 oz.)
White crème de menthe (2 tsp.)
Maraschino cherry

Combine liquid ingredients with ice
cubes in a mixing glass and stir well.
Strain into chilled cocktail glass and
garnish with cherry.

KREMLIN COCKTAIL

4 parts vodka (2 oz.)
3 parts crème de cacao (1½ oz.)
3 parts half-and-half (1½ oz.)

Combine ingredients in a blender with
cracked ice. Blend until smooth and
pour into chilled cocktail glass.

KRETCHMA
COCKTAIL

4 parts vodka (2 oz.)
3 parts white crème de cacao (1½ oz.)
2 parts fresh lemon juice (1 oz.)
2 dashes grenadine

Combine all ingredients with cracked
ice in a cocktail shaker. Shake well
and strain into chilled cocktail glass.

KUP'S INDISPENSIBLE
COCKTAIL

4 parts gin (2 oz.)
1½ parts dry vermouth (¾ oz.)
1½ parts sweet vermouth (¾ oz.)
Orange twist

Combine liquid ingredients with ice
cubes in a mixing glass and stir well.
Strain into chilled cocktail glass and
garnish with orange twist.

KYOTO COCKTAIL

4 parts gin (2 oz.)
2 parts melon liqueur (1 oz.)
1 part dry vermouth
Fresh lemon juice (¼ tsp.)

Combine ingredients with cracked ice
in a cocktail shaker. Shake well and
strain into chilled cocktail glass.

L

LA BOMBA

4 parts light rum (2 oz.)
2 parts apricot brandy (1 oz.)
2 parts Pernod (1 oz.)
2 parts triple sec (1 oz.)
2 parts fresh lemon juice (1 oz.)
Pineapple spear

Combine all ingredients, except pineapple, in a cocktail shaker with cracked ice. Shake well and strain into chilled old-fashioned glass. Garnish with pineapple spear.

LA JOLLA

4 parts brandy (2 oz.)
2 parts crème de bananes (1 oz.)
Fresh lemon juice (1 tbsp.)
Fresh orange juice (1 tsp.)

Combine ingredients with cracked ice in a cocktail shaker. Shake well and strain into chilled cocktail glass.

LADIES' COCKTAIL

4 parts blended whiskey (2 oz.)
Pernod (1 tsp.)
3 – 5 dashes Angostura bitters
Pineapple spear

Combine all ingredients, except pineapple, in a cocktail shaker with cracked ice. Shake well and strain into chilled cocktail glass.

LADY BE GOOD

4 parts brandy (2 oz.)
1 part white crème de menthe (½ oz.)
1 part sweet vermouth (½ oz.)

Combine ingredients with cracked ice in a cocktail shaker. Shake well and strain into chilled cocktail glass.

LADY FINGER

4 parts gin (2 oz.)
3 parts wishniak (1½ oz.)
2 parts kirschwasser (1 oz.)

Combine ingredients with cracked ice in a cocktail shaker. Shake well and strain into chilled cocktail glass.

LAFAYETTE

4 parts bourbon (2 oz.)
1 part dry vermouth (½ oz.)
1 part Dubonnet rouge (½ oz.)
Bar sugar (½ tsp.)
½ egg white

Combine all ingredients with cracked ice in a cocktail shaker. Shake vigorously and pour into chilled old-fashioned glass.

LALLAH ROOKH

4 parts light rum (2 oz.)
2 parts cognac (1 oz.)
1 part vanilla extract
Bar sugar (½ tsp.)
Whipped cream

Combine all ingredients, except whipped cream, with cracked ice in a blender. Blend at low speed until smooth. Pour into chilled wine glass and top with whipped cream.

LAWHILL COCKTAIL

4 parts blended whiskey (2 oz.)
2 part dry vermouth (1 oz.)
Pernod (½ tsp.)
Maraschino liqueur (½ tsp.)
Dash Angostura bitters

Combine ingredients with ice cubes in a mixing glass and stir well. Strain into chilled cocktail glass.

LEAP FROG HIGHBALL

4 parts gin (2 oz.)
3 parts fresh lemon juice (1½ oz.)
Ginger ale

Pour gin and lemon juice into a
chilled highball glass over ice cubes.
Fill with ginger ale and stir gently.

LEAP YEAR COCKTAIL

4 parts gin (2 oz.)
1 parts sweet vermouth (½ oz.)
1 part Grand Marnier (½ oz.)
Fresh lemon juice (½ tsp.)

Combine ingredients with cracked ice
in a cocktail shaker. Shake well and
strain into chilled cocktail glass.

LEMON DROP

4 parts frozen vodka (2 oz.)
Sugar
Lemon wedge

Pour vodka into shot glass. Dampen
the space between your thumb and
forefinger and coat with sugar. Suck
the sugar off your hand, drink the
shot in one swallow, then bite and
suck on the lemon. Repeat as
necessary.

LEMONADE

32 parts sugar
syrup (16 oz.or 2 cups)
32 parts fresh lemon juice (16 oz.
or 2 cups)
40 parts cold water (80 oz.
or 10 cups)
10 Fresh mint sprigs
Lemon slices

Pour lemon juice into pitcher and add
cold water. Add one cup of the sugar
syrup and mint sprigs and stir. Taste
and add more sugar syrup if necessary.
Stir well and add several ice cubes.
Float several lemon slices on top.
Serves 10.

Note: To make pink lemonade, add
½ cup of raspberry or strawberry syrup
and decrease the amount of sugar
syrup accordingly. To make LIMEADE,
substitute fresh lime juice for lemon
juice.

LEMON-LIME COOLER

6 parts fresh lime juice (3 oz.)
1 part sugar syrup (½ oz.)
Bitter lemon soda
Lime slice

Combine lime juice and sugar syrup
in a cocktail shaker with cracked ice.
Shake well and strain into a chilled
collins glass over ice cubes. Fill with
bitter lemon soda. Stir gently and
garnish with lime slice.

LEPRECHAUN

4 parts Irish whiskey (2 oz.)
2 parts light rum (1 oz.)
1 part sloe gin (½ oz.)
2 parts fresh lemon juice (1 oz.)
Bar sugar (½ tsp.)
¼ fresh peach, peeled and diced
Fresh raspberries

Combine all ingredients, except the
raspberries, in a blender with cracked
ice. Blend until slushy and pour into
chilled old-fashioned glass. Garnish
with fresh raspberries.

LEXINGTON AVE.
EXPRESS

4 parts 151-proof rum (2 oz.)
2 parts fresh lime juice (1 oz.)
Grenadine (1 tsp.)

Combine ingredients with cracked ice
in a cocktail shaker. Shake well and
strain into a chilled old-fashioned
glass over ice cubes.

LIBERTY COCKTAIL

4 parts apple brandy (2 oz.)
2 parts light rum (1 oz.)
Bar sugar (¼ tsp.)

Combine ingredients with cracked ice
in a mixing glass. Stir well and strain
into chilled cocktail glass.

LIBERTY COCKTAIL

LIEBFRAUMILCH

4 parts white crème de cacao
(2 oz.)
4 parts half-and-half (2 oz.)
4 parts fresh lime juice (2 oz.)

Combine all ingredients with cracked
ice in a cocktail shaker. Shake well
and strain into chilled cocktail glass.

LIL NAUE

4 parts brandy (2 oz.)
2 parts ruby port (1 oz.)
2 parts apricot brandy (1 oz.)
Bar sugar (1 tsp.)
1 egg yolk
Ground cinnamon

Combine all ingredients, except
cinnamon, with cracked ice in a
blender. Blend until smooth and pour
into chilled red wine glass. Sprinkle
with ground cinnamon.

LIMBO COCKTAIL

4 parts light rum (2 oz.)
1 part crème de bananes (½ oz.)
2 parts fresh orange juice (1 oz.)

Combine all ingredients with cracked ice in a cocktail shaker and shake well. Strain into chilled cocktail glass.

LIMEY

4 parts light rum (2 oz.)
2 parts lime liqueur (1 oz.)
1 part triple sec (½ oz.)
Fresh lime juice (1 tbsp.)
Lime twist

Combine all ingredients, except lime twist, in a blender with cracked ice. Blend until slushy and pour into chilled red wine glass. Garnish with lime slice.

LINSTEAD COCKTAIL

4 parts scotch (2 oz.)
Pernod (¼ tsp.)
4 parts pineapple juice (2 oz.)
Fresh lemon juice (¼ tsp.)
Bar sugar (½ tsp.)

Combine all ingredients in a cocktail shaker with cracked ice. Shake well and strain into chilled cocktail glass.

LITTLE DEVIL

4 parts gin (2 oz.)
3 parts light rum (1½ oz.)
2 parts triple sec (1 oz.)
2 parts fresh lemon juice (1 oz.)

Combine all ingredients with cracked ice in a cocktail shaker. Shake well and strain into chilled cocktail glass.

LITTLE DIX MIX

4 parts dark rum (2 oz.)
1 part crème de bananes (½ oz.)
1 part fresh lime juice (½ oz.)
Triple sec (1 tsp.)

Combine all ingredients with cracked ice in a cocktail shaker. Shake well and pour into chilled old-fashioned glass.

LITTLE PRINCE

4 parts sparkling apple cider
(2 oz.)
2 parts apricot nectar (1 oz.)
2 part fresh lemon juice (1 oz.)
Lemon twist

Combine all ingredients with cracked ice in a mixing glass. Shake well and pour into chilled old-fashioned glass. Garnish with lemon twist.

LITTLE PRINCESS

4 parts light rum (2 oz.)
2 parts sweet vermouth (1 oz.)

Combine ingredients with cracked ice in a mixing glass. Stir well and strain into chilled cocktail glass.

LOCH LOMOND

6 parts scotch (3 oz.)
1 part sugar syrup (½ oz.)
3 – 5 dashes Angostura bitters

Combine all ingredients with cracked ice in a cocktail shaker. Shake well and strain into chilled cocktail glass.

LOCOMOTIVE

6 oz. dry red wine
1 part maraschino liqueur
1 part triple sec (½ oz.)
1 part honey (½ oz.)
1 egg
Lemon slice
Ground cinnamon

Combine wine, liqueurs, and honey in a saucepan. Stir until honey is dissolved. Turn on burner and warm until hot, stirring often. Do not boil. Stir in a slightly beaten egg. Simmer and stir for about 1 minute. Pour into heated coffee mug and garnish with cinnamon and lemon slice.

LOLLIPOP

2 parts green Chartreuse
(1 oz.)
2 parts kirschwasser (1 oz.)
2 parts triple sec (1 oz.)
Maraschino liqueur (1 tsp.)

Combine all ingredients with cracked ice in a cocktail shaker. Shake well and strain into chilled cocktail glass.

LONDON COCKTAIL

6 parts gin (3 oz.)
Maraschino liqueur (½ tsp.)
5 dashes orange bitters
Bar sugar (½ tsp.)
Lemon twist

Combine all ingredients, except lemon, with cracked ice in a cocktail shaker. Shake well and strain into chilled cocktail glass. Garnish with lemon twist.

LONDON DOCK

6 parts dry red wine (3 oz.)
4 parts dark rum (2 oz.)
2 parts honey (1 oz.)
Lemon peel
Cinnamon stick
Freshly grated nutmeg
Boiling water

Dissolve honey with a little boiling water in the bottom of a heated coffee mug. Add remaining ingredients, except cinnamon and nutmeg, and fill with boiling water. Use cinnamon stick to stir and sprinkle with nutmeg.

LONDON FOG

2 parts white crème de menthe (1 oz.)
2 parts Pernod (1 oz.)
1 scoop vanilla ice cream

Combine ingredients with cracked ice in a blender. Blend for a few seconds at medium speed. Pour into chilled pousse-café glass.

LONDON FRENCH '75'

4 parts gin (2 oz.)
2 parts fresh lemon juice (½ oz.)
Bar sugar (½ tsp.)
Champagne or sparkling wine

Combine all ingredients, except champagne, with cracked ice in a cocktail shaker. Shake well and pour into chilled collins glass. Fill with cold champagne.

LONE TREE COCKTAIL

4 parts gin (2 oz.)
1 part sweet vermouth (½ oz.)
3 dashes orange bitters

Combine ingredients in a mixing glass with ice cubes. Stir well and strain into chilled cocktail glass.

LONG ISLAND ICED TEA

4 parts vodka (2 oz.)
2 parts gin (1 oz.)
2 parts white tequila (1 oz.)
2 parts white rum (1 oz.)
1 part white crème de menthe (½ oz.)
4 parts fresh lemon juice (2 oz.)
Bar sugar (1 tsp.)
Lime wedge
Cola

Combine all ingredients, except lime and cola, in a cocktail shaker with cracked ice. Shake well and strain into chilled collins glass over ice cubes. Fill with cola and stir gently. Garnish with lime wedge.

LONG ISLAND ICED TEA

LORD RODNEY

4 parts blended whiskey (2 oz.)
2 parts dark rum (1 oz.)
White crème de cacao (¼ tsp.)
Coconut syrup (1 tsp.)

Combine all ingredient with cracked
ice in a cocktail shaker. Shake well
and strain into chilled cocktail glass.

LOS ANGELES COCKTAIL

4 parts rye (2 oz.)
Sweet vermouth (¼ tsp.)
2 parts fresh lemon juice (1 oz.)
Bar sugar (1 tsp.)
1 whole egg

Combine ingredients with cracked ice
in a cocktail shaker. Shake vigorously
and strain into a chilled sour glass
over ice cubes.

LOUDSPEAKER

4 parts brandy (2 oz.)
3 parts gin (1½ oz.)
1 part triple sec (½ oz.)
2 parts fresh lemon juice (1 oz.)

Combine all ingredients with cracked
ice in a cocktail shaker. Shake well
and strain into chilled cocktail glass.

LOUISIANA PLANTER'S PUNCH

4 parts gold rum (2 oz.)
2 parts bourbon (1 oz.)
2 parts cognac (1 oz.)
Pernod (¼ tsp.)
5 dashes Peychaud's bitters
1 part sugar syrup (½ oz.)
2 parts fresh lemon juice (1 oz.)
Sparkling water
Lemon slice
Orange slice

Combine all ingredients, except
sparkling water and fruit, in a cocktail
shaker with cracked ice. Shake well
and strain into chilled highball glass
over ice cubes. Fill with sparkling
water and stir gently. Garnish with
fruit slices.

LOVE COCKTAIL

4 parts sloe gin (2 oz.)
Fresh lemon juice (½ tsp.)
Raspberry syrup (½ tsp.)
1 egg white

Combine ingredients with cracked ice
in a cocktail shaker. Shake vigorously
and strain into chilled cocktail glass.

LUGGER

4 parts brandy (2 oz.)
3 parts apple brandy (1½ oz.)
Apricot brandy (¼ tsp.)

Combine all ingredients in a cocktail
shaker with cracked ice. Shake well
and strain into chilled cocktail glass.

M

MADEIRA COCKTAIL

4 parts blended whiskey (2 oz.)
3 parts Madeira (1½ oz.)
Grenadine (1 tsp.)
Dash fresh lemon juice
Orange slice

Combine all ingredients, except
orange, with cracked ice in a cocktail
shaker. Shake well and strain over ice
into a chilled old-fashioned glass.
Garnish with orange slice.

MADRAS

4 parts vodka (2 oz.)
6 parts cranberry juice (3 oz.)
6 parts fresh orange juice (3 oz.)

Combine ingredients with cracked ice
in a mixing glass and stir. Strain over
ice cubes into a chilled highball glass.

MAHUKONA

4 parts light rum (2 oz.)
1 part white Curaçao (½ oz.)
1 part fresh lemon juice (½ oz.)
Orgeat (almond) syrup (½ tsp.)
5 dashes orange bitters
Pineapple spear

Combine all ingredients except
pineapple spear with cracked ice in a
blender. Blend until smooth and pour
into chilled highball glass. Garnish
with pineapple spear.

MAI KAI NO

4 parts light rum (2 oz.)
4 parts dark rum (2 oz.)
1 part 151-proof rum (½ oz.)
4 parts fresh lime juice (2 oz.)
2 parts passion fruit syrup (1 oz.)
1 part orgeat (almond) syrup (½ oz.)
Sparkling water
Pineapple spear

Combine all ingredients, except
sparkling water and pineapple spear,
with cracked ice in a cocktail shaker.
Shake well and pour into a chilled

collins glass over ice cubes. Fill with
sparkling water. Stir gently and
garnish with pineapple spear.

MAI TAI

4 parts dark rum (2 oz.)
4 parts light rum (2 oz.)
2 parts Curaçao (1 oz.)
2 parts fresh lime juice (1 oz.)
Grenadine (1 tbsp.)
Orgeat (almond) syrup (1 tbsp.)
Pineapple spear
(Orchid and paper umbrella optional)

Combine all ingredients with cracked
ice in a cocktail shaker and shake
well. Strain into a chilled highball
glass over ice cubes. Garnish with
pineapple and other decorations.

MAIDEN'S BLUSH

4 parts gin (2 oz.)
Triple sec (½ tsp.)
Grenadine (½ tsp.)
Fresh lemon juice (½ tsp.)

Combine all ingredients with cracked
ice in a cocktail shaker. Shake well
and strain into chilled cocktail glass.

MAIDEN'S PRAYER

4 parts gin (2 oz.)
2 parts Curaçao (1 oz.)
1 part fresh lemon juice (½ oz.)
Fresh orange juice (1 tbsp.)

Combine all ingredients with cracked
ice in a cocktail shaker and shake
well. Strain into chilled cocktail glass.

MAINBRACE

4 parts gin (2 oz.)
2 parts white Curaçao (1 oz.)
2 parts white grape juice (1 oz.)

Combine all ingredients with cracked
ice in a cocktail shaker and shake
well. Strain into chilled cocktail glass.

MAMIE TAYLOR

6 parts scotch (3 oz.)
2 parts fresh lime juice (1 oz.)
Ginger ale
Lime slice

Pour scotch and lime juice into a
chilled collins glass over ice cubes.
Fill with ginger ale and stir gently.
Garnish with lime slice.

MANDEVILLE

4 parts dark rum (2 oz.)
4 parts light rum (2 oz.)
Pernod (1 tbsp.)
Grenadine (½ tsp.)
Fresh lemon juice (1 tbsp.)
1 part cola (½ oz.)

Combine all ingredients with cracked
ice in a cocktail shaker. Shake well
and strain into a chilled old-fashioned
glass over ice cubes.

MANDY'S CURE

8 parts cranberry juice (4 oz.)
8 parts grapefruit juice (4 oz.)
2 parts fresh lime juice (1 oz.)
Lime slice

Stir juices in a mixing glass with
cracked ice. Pour into chilled collins
glass over ice cubes. Garnish with lime
slice.

MANGO DELIGHT

Ripe mango, chopped (¼ cup)
3 large fresh strawberries
2 parts fresh lime juice (1 oz.)
Lime slice

Combine all ingredients, except 1
strawberry and lime slice, in a blender
with cracked ice. Blend until slushy.
Pour into chilled wine glass and
garnish with strawberry and lime
slice.

MANHASSET

4 parts rye (2 oz.)
½ part dry vermouth (¼ oz.)
½ part sweet vermouth (½ oz.)
Fresh lemon juice (1 tbsp.)
Lemon twist

Combine all ingredients, except lemon
twist, with cracked ice in a cocktail
shaker. Shake well and strain into
chilled cocktail glass. Garnish with
lemon twist.

MANHASSET

MANHATTAN

6 parts rye (3 oz.)
2 parts sweet vermouth (1 oz.)
Dash Angostura bitters
Maraschino cherry

Combine all ingredients, except
cherry, with ice cubes in a mixing
glass. Stir well and strain into chilled
cocktail glass. Garnish with cherry.

MANHATTAN COOLER

8 parts dry red wine (½ cup or
4 oz.)
4 parts fresh lemon juice (2 oz.)
Gold rum (¼ tsp.)
Sugar syrup (1 tbsp.)

Combine all ingredients in mixing
glass with cracked ice. Stir well and
strain into chilled highball glass over
ice cubes.

MAN O'WAR

4 parts bourbon (2 oz.)
2 parts triple sec (1 oz.)
1 part sweet vermouth (½ oz.)
2 parts fresh lime juice (1 oz.)

Combine all ingredients with cracked
ice in a cocktail shaker. Shake well
and strain into chilled cocktail glass.

MARCONI WIRELESS

6 parts apple brandy (3 oz.)
1 part sweet vermouth (½ oz.)
3 – 5 dashes orange bitters

Combine ingredients with cracked ice
in a cocktail shaker. Shake well and
strain into cocktail glass.

MARGARITA

6 parts silver or gold tequila
(3 oz.)
2 parts triple sec (1 oz.)
4 parts fresh lime juice (2 oz.)
Coarse salt
Lime wedge

Rim a large cocktail glass by rubbing
the rim with the lime wedge and
dipping it into a saucer of coarse salt.
Combine remaining ingredients in a
cocktail shaker with cracked ice.
Shake well and strain into the chilled,
salted cocktail glass.

MARGIE'S MIMOSA

Chilled sparkling white grape
juice
Fresh orange juice

Fill half a chilled champagne flute
with orange juice. Pour grape juice to
the rim and stir gently.

MARGARITA (from Mesa Grill)

MARTINI WITH AN OLIVE (from Gallagher's Steak House)

MARTINI

6 parts gin (3 oz.)
Dry vermouth (¼ tsp. or less)
Cocktail olive

Combine gin and vermouth in a mixing glass with ice cubes. Stir well and pour into a chilled cocktail glass. Garnish with cocktail olive.

Note: One of the numerous variations on the Martini in this book combines the gin and vermouth with a splash of Dubonnet. Garnish with a twist of lemon instead of an olive.

MARY GARDEN COCKTAIL

4 parts Dubonnet rouge (2 oz.)
2 parts dry vermouth (1 oz.)

Combine ingredients with cracked ice in cocktail shaker and shake well. Strain into chilled cocktail glass.

PLEASE NOTE: Blue icons represent alcoholic drinks. Green icons represent non-alcoholic drinks.

MARTINI WITH DUBONNET AND A TWIST (from Hi-Life Bar & Grill)

MARY PICKFORD

4 parts light rum (2 oz.)
Maraschino liqueur (½ tsp.)
4 parts pineapple juice (2 oz.)
Grenadine (½ tsp.)

Combine ingredients with cracked ice
in a cocktail shaker. Shake well and
strain into chilled cocktail glass.

MATADOR

4 parts gold tequila (2 oz.)
1 part triple sec (½ oz.)
6 parts pineapple juice (3 oz.)
2 parts fresh lime juice (1 oz.)

Combine all ingredients with cracked
ice in a cocktail shaker. Shake well
and strain into chilled sour glass.

157

MATINEE

4 parts gin (2 oz.)
2 parts sweet vermouth (1 oz.)
1 part green Chartreuse (½ oz.)
1 part fresh orange juice (½ oz.)
Dash orange bitters

Combine all ingredients with cracked ice in a cocktail shaker and shake well. Strain into chilled cocktail glass.

MAURICE

4 parts gin (2 oz.)
1 part dry vermouth (½ oz.)
1 parts sweet vermouth (½ oz.)
2 parts fresh orange juice (1 oz.)
Dash Angostura bitters

Combine all ingredients with cracked ice in a cocktail shaker. Shake well and strain into chilled cocktail glass.

MC CLELLAND

4 parts sloe gin (2 oz.)
2 parts white Curaçao (1 oz.)
3 – 5 dashes orange bitters

Combine all ingredients with cracked ice in a cocktail shaker and shake well. Strain into chilled cocktail glass.

MELON BALL

4 parts vodka (2 oz.)
4 parts melon liqueur (2 oz.)
8 parts pineapple juice (½ cup or 4 oz.)
Slice of honeydew or cantaloupe

Combine all ingredients, except melon slice, with cracked ice in a mixing glass and stir. Strain over ice cubes into a chilled highball glass and garnish with melon.

MELON COCKTAIL

4 parts gin (2 oz.)
1 part maraschino liqueur (½ oz.)
1 part fresh lemon juice (½ oz.)
Maraschino cherry
Lemon twist

Combine all ingredients, except cherry and lemon twist, in a cocktail shaker with cracked ice. Shake well and strain into chilled cocktail glass. Garnish with cherry and lemon twist.

MELON MEDLEY

8 parts fresh orange juice (4 oz.)
8 parts cantaloupe, cubed (4 oz.)
1 part fresh lemon juice (½ oz.)

Combine ingredients with cracked ice in a blender. Blend until slushy and pour into chilled collins glass.

MERMAID'S SONG

4 parts orange juice (2 oz.)
2 parts passion fruit juice (1 oz.)
2 parts coconut milk (1 oz.)
2 parts pineapple juice (1 oz.)
1 part fresh lime juice (½ oz.)
Maraschino cherry

Combine all ingredients, except cherry, in a cocktail shaker with cracked ice. Shake well and strain into chilled red wine glass. Garnish with cherry.

MERRY WIDOW

4 parts gin (2 oz.)
2 parts dry vermouth (1 oz.)
1 part Pernod (½ oz.)
3 – 5 dashes Peychaud's bitters
Lemon twist

Combine all ingredients, except lemon twist, with cracked ice in a cocktail shaker. Shake well and strain into chilled cocktail glass. Garnish with lemon twist.

METROPOLITAN

MERRY WIDOW FIZZ

4 parts Dubonnet rouge (2 oz.)
4 parts fresh orange juice (2 oz.)
2 parts fresh lemon juice (1 oz.)
1 egg white
Sparkling water

Combine all ingredients, except egg
white, with cracked ice in a cocktail
shaker. Shake vigorously and strain
over ice cubes into a chilled collins
glass. Fill with sparkling water and stir
gently.

METROPOLITAN

4 parts brandy (2 oz.)
2 parts sweet vermouth (1 oz.)
Bar sugar (½ tsp.)
Dash Angostura bitters

Combine all ingredients with cracked
ice in a cocktail shake and shaker
well. Strain into chilled cocktail glass.

159

MEXICANA

4 parts silver tequila (2 oz.)
4 parts pineapple juice (2 oz.)
2 parts fresh lime juice (1 oz.)
Grenadine (¼ tsp.)

Combine all ingredients with cracked
ice in a cocktail shaker. Shake well
and strain over ice cubes into a chilled
highball glass.

MEXICAN COFFEE

4 parts gold tequila (2 oz.)
1 part coffee liqueur (½ oz.)
Hot black coffee
Whipped cream

Mix tequila and liqueur in a coffee
mug. Pour in hot coffee and stir
again. Top off with whipped cream.

MEXICOLA

4 parts white tequila (2 oz.)
Cola
Lime wedge

Pour tequila into a chilled collins
glass over ice cubes. Fill with cola and
squeeze lime over drink. Stir gently
and garnish with lime.

MIAMI

4 parts light rum (2 oz.)
2 parts peppermint schnapps
(1 oz.)
Fresh lime juice (¼ tsp.)

Combine all ingredients with cracked
ice in a cocktail shaker. Shake well
and strain into chilled cocktail glass.

MIAMI BEACH
COCKTAIL

4 parts scotch (2 oz.)
3 parts dry vermouth (1½ oz.)
4 parts grapefruit juice (2 oz.)

Combine all ingredients with cracked
ice in a cocktail shaker. Shake well
and strain into a chilled old-fashioned
glass over ice cubes.

MIDNIGHT COCKTAIL

4 parts apricot brandy (2 oz.)
Triple sec (1 tbsp.)
Fresh lemon juice (1 tbsp.)

Combine ingredients with cracked ice
in a cocktail shaker. Shake well and
strain into chilled cocktail glass.

MIDNIGHT SUN

4 parts aquavit (2 oz.)
2 parts grapefruit juice (1 oz.)
Grenadine (¼ tsp.)
Orange slice

Combine all ingredients, except
orange slice, with cracked ice in a
cocktail shaker. Shake well and strain
into chilled cocktail glass. Garnish
with orange slice.

MIKADO

6 parts brandy (3 oz.)
Crème de noyaux (¼ tsp.)
Triple sec (¼ tsp.)
Orgeat (almond) syrup (¼ tsp.)
3 – 5 dashes Angostura bitters

Combine all ingredients with cracked
ice in a cocktail shaker. Shake well
and strain into chilled cocktail glass.

MILK PUNCH

4 parts blended whiskey
14 parts milk (1 cup or 8 oz.)
Sugar syrup (1 tsp.)
Freshly grated nutmeg

Pour milk into chilled collins glass.
Stir in whiskey and sugar syrup.
Sprinkle nutmeg on top.

MILLIONAIRE

4 parts bourbon (2 oz.)
2 parts Pernod (1 oz.)
Triple sec (¼ tsp.)
Grenadine (¼ tsp.)
1 egg white

Combine all ingredients with cracked
ice in a cocktail shaker and shake
vigorously. Strain into chilled cocktail
glass.

MILLION-DOLLAR COCKTAIL

4 parts gin (2 oz.)
2 parts sweet vermouth (1 oz.)
2 parts pineapple juice (1 oz.)
Grenadine (1 tsp.)
1 egg white

Combine all ingredients with cracked
ice in a cocktail shaker. Shake
vigorously and strain into chilled
cocktail glass.

MIMOSA

Chilled champagne or sparkling
wine
Fresh orange juice

Half fill a chilled champagne flute
with orange juice. Add champagne to
the top and stir gently.

MINOR MADRAS

8 parts cranberry juice (4 oz.)
8 parts fresh orange juice (4 oz.)
2 parts fresh lemon juice (1 oz.)
Lime slice

Combine ingredients, except lime
slice, with cracked ice in a mixing
glass and stir. Pour over ice cubes into
a chilled collins glass. Garnish with
lime slice.

MIMOSA (from Tavern on the Green)

MINT COLLINS

6 parts gin (3 oz.)
2 parts fresh lemon juice (1 oz.)
Bar sugar (1 tsp.)
7 fresh mint leaves
Sparkling water
Lemon slice
Mint sprigs

Pour gin, lemon juice and sugar into
a chilled collins glass. Drop in the
mint leaves and crush them with a bar
spoon. Add ice cubes and fill with
sparkling water. Stir gently and
garnish with lemon slice and mint
sprigs.

MINT JULEP

6 parts bourbon (3 oz.)
Sugar syrup (1 tbsp.)
10 –15 large fresh mint leaves
Mint sprig

Muddle mint leaves with sugar syrup
in the bottom of a chilled highball
glass. Fill glass with shaved or crushed
ice and add bourbon. Garnish with
mint sprig.

MINT SUNRISE

3 parts scotch (1½ oz.)
1 part brandy (½ oz.)
1 part Curaçao (½ oz.)
Lemon slice
Mint sprig

Pour all ingredients, except for lemon
and mint, into a chilled highball glass
over ice cubes. Stir gently. Garnish
with lemon slice and mint sprig.

MISSISSIPPI MULE

4 parts gin (2 oz.)
1 part crème de cassis (½ oz.)
1 part fresh lemon juice (½ oz.)

Combine ingredients with cracked ice
in a cocktail shaker. Shake well and
pour into chilled old-fashioned glass.

MISTER PIP'S
ST. THOMAS SPECIAL

4 parts dark rum (2 oz.)
Passion fruit syrup (1 tbsp.)
Fresh orange juice
Freshly ground nutmeg

Stir rum and syrup with cracked ice in
a mixing glass. Strain into a chilled
collins glass over ice cubes. Fill with
orange juice and stir. Sprinkle nutmeg
on top.

MOCHA MINT

3 parts coffee liqueur
(1½ oz.)
3 parts white crème de cacao (1½ oz.)
3 parts white crème de menthe
(1½ oz.)

Combine ingredients with cracked ice
in a cocktail shaker. Shake well and
strain into chilled cocktail glass.

MOCHA SLUSH

4 parts coffee syrup (2 oz.)
2 parts chocolate syrup (1 oz.)
8 parts milk (4 oz.)
Chocolate shavings

Combine all ingredients, except
chocolate shavings, with cracked ice
in a blender. Blend until slushy and
pour into chilled wine glass. Sprinkle
chocolate on top.

MODERN COCKTAIL

5 parts scotch (2½ oz.)
Dark rum (1 tsp.)
Pernod (1 tsp.)
Fresh lemon juice (1 tsp.)
3 – 5 dashes orange bitters
Maraschino cherry

Combine all ingredients, except
cherry, with cracked ice in a cocktail
shaker. Shake well and pour into
chilled old-fashioned glass. Garnish
with cherry.

MOJITO

4 parts light rum (2 oz.)
2 parts fresh lime juice (1 oz.)
Bar sugar (1 tsp.)
5 – 7 fresh mint leaves
Dash Angostura bitters

Combine all ingredients with cracked
ice in a cocktail shaker and shake
well. Strain into chilled cocktail glass.

MOLDAU

4 parts gin (2 oz.)
2 parts slivovotz (1 oz.)
1 part fresh orange juice (½ oz.)
1 part fresh lemon juice (½ oz.)

Combine all ingredients with cracked
ice in a cocktail shaker. Shake well
and strain into chilled cocktail glass.

MOLL COCKTAIL

3 parts gin (1½ oz.)
2 parts sloe gin (1 oz.)
2 parts dry vermouth (1 oz.)
Dash Angostura bitters

Combine all ingredients with cracked
ice in a cocktail shaker. Shake well
and strain into chilled cocktail glass.

MONTANA

4 parts brandy (2 oz.)
2 parts ruby port (1 oz.)
2 parts dry vermouth (1 oz.)
Dash Angostura bitters

Combine ingredients with cracked ice
in a mixing glass. Stir well and strain
into chilled old-fashioned glass over
ice cubes.

MONTEZUMA

4 parts gold tequila (2 oz.)
2 parts Madeira (1 oz.)
1 egg yolk

Combine ingredients with cracked ice
in a blender and blend until smooth.
Pour into chilled cocktail glass.

MONTMARTE

4 parts gin (2 oz.)
1 part sweet vermouth (½ oz.)
1 part white Curaçao (½ oz.)

Combine ingredients with cracked ice
in a cocktail shaker and shake well.
Strain into chilled cocktail glass.

MOONLIGHT

4 parts apple brandy (2 oz.)
4 parts fresh lemon juice (2 oz.)
Bar sugar (½ tsp.)

Combine ingredients with cracked ice
in a cocktail shaker and shake well.
Strain into chilled old-fashioned glass
over ice cubes.

MOONSHOT

4 parts gin (2 oz.)
6 parts clam juice (3 oz.)
Dash Tabasco sauce

Combine all ingredients in a mixing glass with ice cubes and stir. Pour into chilled old-fashioned glass.

MORNING COCKTAIL

4 parts brandy (2 oz.)
2 parts dry vermouth (1 oz.)
White Curaçao (1 tsp.)
Maraschino liqueur (1 tsp.)
Pernod (1 tsp.)
3 – 5 dashes orange bitters
Maraschino cherry

Combine all ingredients, except cherry, with cracked ice in a cocktail shaker. Shake well and strain into a cocktail glass. Garnish with cherry.

MORNING GLORY FIZZ

6 parts scotch (3 oz.)
1 part Pernod (½ oz.)
2 parts fresh lemon juice (1 oz.)
Bar sugar (½ tsp.)
1 egg white
Dash Angostura bitters
Sparkling water

Combine all ingredients, except sparkling water, in a cocktail shaker with cracked ice. Shake well and strain over ice cubes into a chilled highball glass. Fill with sparkling water and stir gently.

MORNING JOY

4 parts gin (2 oz.)
3 parts crème de bananes (1½ oz.)
6 parts fresh orange juice (3 oz.)

Combine all ingredients with cracked ice in a cocktail shaker. Shake well and strain into chilled sour glass.

MORRO

4 parts gin (2 oz.)
2 parts dark rum (1 oz.)
1 part fresh lime juice (½ oz.)
1 part pineapple juice (½ oz.)
Bar sugar (½ tsp.)

Combine all ingredients with cracked ice in a cocktail shaker. Shake well and strain into a sugar-rimmed old-fashioned glass over ice cubes.

MOSCOW MULE

6 parts vodka (3 oz.)
Fresh lime juice (1 tbsp.)
Ginger beer
Lime wedge

Pour vodka and lime juice into a chilled beer mug over ice cubes. Fill with ginger beer and stir gently. Garnish with lime wedge.

MOTHER'S MILK

8 parts milk (4 oz.)
1 part honey (½ oz.)
Vanilla extract (¼ tsp.)
Freshly grated nutmeg

Combine all ingredients, except the nutmeg, in a cocktail shaker with cracked ice. Shake well. Strain into chilled old-fashioned glass and sprinkle with nutmeg.

MOULIN ROUGE

4 parts sloe gin (2 oz.)
1 part sweet vermouth (½ oz.)
3 – 5 dashes Angostura bitters

Combine all ingredients with cracked ice in a cocktail shaker. Shake well and strain into chilled cocktail glass.

MOUNTAIN COCKTAIL

4 parts blended whiskey (2 oz.)
1 part dry vermouth (½ oz.)
1 part sweet vermouth (½ oz.)
1 part fresh lemon juice (½ oz.)
1 egg white

Combine all ingredients with cracked ice in a cocktail shaker and shake vigorously. Strain into chilled cocktail glass.

MUDSLIDE

3 parts vodka (1½ oz.)
3 parts coffee liqueur (1½ oz.)
3 parts Irish cream liqueur (1½ oz.)

Combine all ingredients with cracked ice in a cocktail shaker. Shake well and strain into chilled cocktail glass.

MULE'S HIND LEG

4 parts apple brandy (2 oz.)
2 parts gin (1 oz.)
Apricot brandy (1 tbsp.)
Benedictine (1 tbsp.)
Maple syrup (1 tbsp.)

Combine all ingredients with cracked ice in a cocktail shaker. Shake well and strain over ice cubes into chilled old-fashioned glass.

NOTE: Mulled and hot-buttered drinks can be made in the microwave. Instead of a saucepan, put ingredients into the mug and microwave on high for 45 – 60 seconds.

MULLED CIDER

4 parts gold rum (2 oz.)
12 parts apple cider (6 oz.)
Honey (1 tsp.)
Cinnamon stick
Freshly grated nutmeg (to taste)
3 whole cloves
Lemon twist

Combine all ingredients in a sauce pan. Warm over medium heat, stirring occasionally. Do not boil. Pour into heated coffee mug.

MULLED CIDER WARMER

Apple cider (1 quart)
2 parts honey (1 oz.)
Ground allspice (¼ tsp.)
Cardamom seeds (5)
Freshly ground cinnamon (½ tsp.)
Ground ginger (¼ tsp.)
Freshly ground nutmeg (¼ tsp.)
8 whole cloves
Dried orange peel (1 tbsp.)
Cinnamon sticks

Combine all ingredients except cinnamon sticks in a saucepan. Heat and stir over high heat until the honey dissolves. Reduce heat and simmer for about 15 minutes or longer. Pour into warmed coffee mugs and garnish with cinnamon sticks. Serves 6.

MULLED CRANBERRY JUICE

12 parts cranberry juice (6 oz.)
2 lemon slices
3 whole cloves
Freshly grated nutmeg (¼ tsp.)
Honey to taste
Cinnamon stick

Combine all ingredients, except cinnamon stick, in a saucepan and heat over low flame until almost boiling. Stir well and pour into heated mug. Garnish with cinnamon stick.

MULLED WINE

12 parts dry red wine (6 oz.)
2 parts ruby port (1 oz.)
2 parts brandy (1 oz.)
Cinnamon stick
Freshly grated nutmeg (to taste)
3 whole cloves
Lemon twist

Combine all ingredients in a sauce pan. Warm over medium heat (do not boil) and pour into heated coffee mug.

MYRTLE BANK PUNCH

4 parts 151-proof rum (2 oz.)
2 parts maraschino liqueur (1 oz.)
3 parts fresh lime juice (1½ oz.)
Grenadine (1 tsp.)
Bar sugar (½ tsp.)

Combine all ingredients, except maraschino liqueur, in a blender with cracked ice. Blend until smooth and pour into chilled highball glass. Float liqueur on top.

N

NAPOLEON

4 parts gin (2 oz.)
1 part white Curaçao (½ oz.)
Dubonnet rouge (1 tsp.)
Amer Picon (1 tsp.)

Combine ingredients in mixing glass
with cracked ice and stir. Strain into
chilled cocktail glass.

NARAGANSETT

4 parts bourbon (2 oz.)
2 parts sweet vermouth (1 oz.)
Dash Pernod
Lemon twist

Stir liquid ingredients in a chilled old-
fashioned glass with ice cubes. Top
with lemon twist.

NAVY GROG

2 parts dark rum (1 oz.)
2 parts light rum (1 oz.)
2 parts 86-proof Demerara rum
(1 oz.)
1 part guava juice (½ oz.)
1 part fresh lime juice (½ oz.)
1 part pineapple juice (½ oz.)
1 part orgeat (almond) syrup (½ oz.)
Tamarind syrup (1 tbsp.)
Lime slice

Combine all ingredients, except lime
slice, with cracked ice in a blender.
Blend until slushy and pour into
chilled highball glass. Garnish with
lime slice.

NEGRONI

4 parts gin (2 oz.)
2 parts Campari (1 oz.)
1 part sweet vermouth (½ oz.)
Orange twist

Combine all ingredients, except
orange twist, in a cocktail shaker with
cracked ice. Shake well and strain into
chilled old-fashioned glass over ice
cubes. Garnish with orange twist.

NEGUS PUNCH

Ruby port (1 bottle –
750-ml.)
Zest of one whole lemon
8 sugar cubes
2 cinnamon sticks
1 whole nutmeg, crushed
7 whole cloves
Ground allspice (½ tsp.)
1 part fresh lemon juice (½ oz.)
Boiling water

Put lemon zest and sugar cubes in a
large warmed pitcher. Add enough
water to dissolve sugar. Add spices,
lemon juice and wine. Stir well and
add two cups of boiling water right
before serving. Serves 10 –12.

NETHERLANDS

4 parts brandy (2 oz.)
2 parts white Curaçao (1 oz.)
Dash orange bitters

Combine ingredients with cracked ice
in a cocktail shaker. Shake well and
strain into chilled old-fashioned glass
over ice cubes.

NEVADA COCKTAIL

4 parts dark rum (2 oz.)
4 parts grapefruit juice (2 oz.)
1 part fresh lime juice (½ oz.)
Bar sugar (½ tsp.)
Dash Angostura bitters

Combine ingredients with cracked ice
in a cocktail shaker. Shake well and
strain into chilled cocktail glass.

NEVINS

4 parts bourbon (2 oz.)
1 parts apricot brandy (½ oz.)
2 parts grapefruit juice (1 oz.)
1 part fresh lemon juice (½ oz.)
Dash Angostura bitters

Combine all ingredients with cracked
ice in a cocktail shaker. Shake well
and strain into chilled cocktail glass.

NEW ORLEANS BUCK

4 parts light rum (2 oz.)
2 parts fresh lime juice (1 oz.)
2 parts fresh orange juice (1 oz.)
Ginger ale
Lime slice

Combine all ingredients, except ginger ale and lime slice, with cracked ice in a cocktail shaker. Shake well and strain into a chilled collins glass over ice cubes. Fill with ginger ale and stir gently. Garnish with lime slice.

NEW ORLEANS COCKTAIL

4 parts bourbon (2 oz.)
1 part Pernod (½ oz.)
Dash Angostura bitters
Dash anisette
Dash orange bitters
Sugar syrup (½ tsp.)
Lemon twist

Combine all ingredients, except lemon twist, in a cocktail shaker with cracked ice. Shake well and pour into chilled old-fashioned glass. Garnish with lemon twist.

NEW ORLEANS GIN FIZZ

4 parts gin (2 oz.)
2 parts fresh lemon juice (1 oz.)
2 parts fresh lime juice (1 oz.)
Sugar syrup (1 tsp.)
1 part half-and-half (½ oz.)
1 egg white
Sparkling water
Lime slice

Combine all ingredients, except sparkling water and lime slice, in a cocktail shaker with cracked ice. Shake vigorously. Strain into a chilled collins glass over ice cubes. Fill with sparkling water and stir gently. Garnish with lime slice.

NEW YORK SOUR

NEW WORLD

6 parts blended whiskey (3 oz.)
2 parts fresh lime juice (1 oz.)
Grenadine (2 tsp.)
Lime twist

Combine all ingredients, except lime twist, in a cocktail shaker with cracked ice. Shake well and strain into chilled cocktail glass. Garnish with lime twist.

NEW YORK SOUR

4 parts blended whiskey (2 oz.)
3 parts fresh lemon juice (1½ oz.)
Bar sugar (1 tsp.)
Dry red wine (1 tbsp.)

Combine all ingredients, except wine, with cracked ice in a cocktail shaker. Shake well and strain into chilled sour glass. Float wine on top.

NEW YORKER COCKTAIL

4 parts blended whiskey (2 oz.)
2 parts fresh lemon juice (1 oz.)
Grenadine (½ tsp.)
Sugar syrup (1 tsp.)
Lemon twist

Combine all ingredients, except lemon twist, with cracked ice in a cocktail shaker. Shake well and strain into chilled cocktail glass. Garnish with lemon twist.

167

NEWBURY

4 parts gin (2 oz.)
3 parts sweet vermouth (1½ oz.)
Triple sec (¼ tsp.)
Lemon twist

Combine all ingredients, except lemon twist, with cracked ice in a cocktail shaker. Shake well and strain into chilled cocktail glass. Garnish with lemon twist.

NEWPORT COOLER

4 parts gin (2 oz.)
1 part brandy (½ oz.)
1 part peach liqueur (½ oz.)
Fresh lime juice (¼ tsp.)
Ginger ale

Pour all ingredients, except ginger ale, into a chilled collins glass over ice cubes. Fill with ginger ale and stir gently.

NIGHT CAP

4 parts light rum
Sugar syrup (1 tsp.)
Warm milk
Freshly grated nutmeg

Pour rum and syrup into a heated coffee mug. Fill mug with warm milk and stir. Sprinkle nutmeg on top.

NIGHTMARE

4 parts gin (2 oz.)
2 parts Madeira (1 oz.)
2 parts cherry brandy (1 oz.)
Fresh orange juice (1 tsp.)

Combine ingredients with cracked ice in a cocktail shaker. Shake well and strain into chilled cocktail glass.

168

NINETEEN

6 parts dry vermouth (3 oz.)
1 part gin (½ oz.)
1 part kirschwasser (½ oz.)
Pernod (¼ tsp.)
Sugar syrup (¼ tsp.)

Combine all ingredients with cracked ice in a cocktail shaker. Shake well and strain into chilled cocktail glass.

NINETEEN PICK-ME-UP

4 parts Pernod (2 oz.)
2 parts gin (1 oz.)
Sugar syrup (¼ tsp.)
3 – 5 dashes Angostura bitters
3 – 5 dashes orange bitters
Sparkling water

Combine all ingredients, except sparkling water, with cracked ice in a cocktail shaker. Shake well and strain over ice cubes into chilled highball glass. Fill with sparkling water and stir gently.

NINOTCHKA

4 parts vodka (2 oz.)
2 parts white crème de cacao (1 oz.)
1 part fresh lemon juice (½ oz.)

Combine all ingredients with cracked ice in a cocktail shaker. Shake well and strain into chilled cocktail glass.

NIGHT CAP

NIRVANA

4 parts dark rum (2 oz.)
1 part grenadine (½ oz.)
1 part tamarind syrup (½ oz.)
Sugar syrup (1 tsp.)
Grapefruit juice

Combine all ingredients, except grapefruit juice, with cracked ice in a cocktail shaker. Shake well and pour into a chilled collins glass over ice cubes. Fill with grapefruit juice and stir.

NORMANDY COCKTAIL

4 parts gin (2 oz.)
2 parts Calvados (1 oz.)
1 part apricot brandy (½ oz.)
Fresh lemon juice (¼ tsp.)

Combine all ingredients with cracked ice in a cocktail shaker and shake well. Strain into chilled cocktail glass.

NOVEMBER CIDER

6 parts apple cider (3 oz.)
6 parts fresh orange juice (3 oz.)
6 parts cold black tea (3 oz.)
3 parts fresh lemon juice (1½ oz.)
Lemon slice

Combine all ingredients in a mixing glass with ice cubes and stir well. Pour into chilled collins glass and garnish with lemon slice.

NUTCRACKER

4 parts crème de noisette
(2 oz.)
4 parts coconut amaretto (2 oz.)
4 parts half-and-half (2 oz.)

Combine all ingredients with cracked ice in a cocktail shaker. Shake well and strain into chilled cocktail glass.

NUTTY COLA

4 parts hazelnut or orgeat
(almond)syrup (2 oz.)
4 parts fresh lime juice (2 oz.)
Cola

Combine syrup and lime juice in a cocktail shaker and shake well. Pour into a chilled collins glass over ice cubes. Fill with cola and stir gently.

NUTTY COLADA

6 part amaretto (3 oz.)
2 parts gold rum (1 oz.)
2 parts coconut milk (1 oz.)
Coconut syrup (1 tbsp.)
4 parts pineapple juice (2 oz.)
Crème de noyaux (¼ tsp.)
Pineapple spear

Combine all ingredients, except pineapple spear, with cracked ice in a blender. Blend until slushy. Pour into chilled collins glass and garnish with pineapple spear.

O

OCHO RIOS

4 parts dark rum (2 oz.)
2 parts guava nectar (1 oz.)
2 parts fresh lime juice (1 oz.)
Falernum (1 tsp.)
2 parts half-and-half (1 oz.)

Combine ingredients with cracked ice in a blender. Blend at low speed until smooth. Pour into chilled champagne flute.

OH, HENRY!

4 parts blended whiskey (2 oz.)
1 part Benedictine (½ oz.)
Ginger ale
Lemon slice

Pour whiskey and Benedictine into a chilled old-fashioned glass over ice cubes. Fill with ginger ale and stir. Garnish with lemon slice.

OLD FASHIONED

4 parts blended whiskey, bourbon, or rye (2 oz.)
Sugar cube
Dash Angostura bitters
Water (1 tsp.)
Lemon twist

Place a sugar cube in the bottom of an old-fashioned glass. Add bitters and water. Muddle until sugar is dissolved. Add the whiskey and stir. Add lemon twist and ice cubes.

OLD PAL COCKTAIL

4 parts rye (2 oz.)
3 parts Campari (1½ oz.)
2 parts sweet vermouth (1 oz.)

Combine all ingredients with cracked ice in a cocktail shaker. Shake well and strain into chilled cocktail glass.

OLÉ

4 parts white tequila (2 oz.)
2 parts coffee liqueur (1 oz.)
Sugar syrup (1 tsp.)
Half-and-half (1 tbsp.)

Stir all ingredients, except half-and-half, in a mixing glass. Pour into a chilled cocktail glass over crushed ice. Float half-and-half on top.

OLYMPIC COCKTAIL

4 parts brandy (2 oz.)
3 parts white Curaçao (1½ oz.)
3 parts fresh orange juice (1½ oz.)
Orange twist

Combine all ingredients with cracked ice in a cocktail shaker and shake well. Strain into chilled cocktail glass and garnish with orange twist.

ONE IRELAND

4 parts Irish whiskey (2 oz.)
1 part green crème de menthe (1 oz.)
Small scoop vanilla ice cream

Combine ingredients in a blender. Blend until smooth and pour into chilled cocktail glass.

OPAL COCKTAIL

4 parts gin (2 oz.)
1 part triple sec (½ oz.)
2 parts fresh orange juice (1 oz.)
Bar sugar (¼ tsp.)

Combine all ingredients with cracked ice in a cocktail shaker. Shake well and strain into chilled cocktail glass.

OPENING COCKTAIL

4 parts Canadian whiskey (2 oz.)
2 parts sweet vermouth (1 oz.)
1 part grenadine (½ oz.)

Stir ingredients with cracked ice in a mixing glass. Strain into chilled cocktail glass.

OLD FASHIONED (from The Oak Bar)

OPERA

4 parts gin (2 oz.)
2 parts Dubonnet rouge (1 oz.)
1 part maraschino liqueur (½ oz.)

Stir ingredients with cracked ice in a
mixing glass. Strain into chilled
cocktail glass.

ORANGE BLOSSOM
COCKTAIL

4 parts gin (2 oz.)
4 parts fresh orange juice (2 oz.)
Orange slice

Combine all ingredients, except
orange slice, with cracked ice in a
cocktail shaker. Shake well and strain
into chilled cocktail glass. Garnish
with orange slice.

ORANGE BUCK

4 parts gin (2 oz.)
4 parts fresh orange juice (2 oz.)
2 parts fresh lime juice (1 oz.)
Ginger ale
Lime slice

Combine all ingredients, except ginger
ale and lime slice, with cracked ice in
a cocktail shaker. Shake well and
strain into a chilled collins glass over
ice cubes. Fill with ginger ale and stir
gently. Garnish with lime slice.

ORANGE JOEY

4 parts vanilla syrup (2 oz.)
8 parts fresh orange juice (4 oz.)
4 parts half-and-half (2 oz.)
Orange slice

Combine all ingredients, except
orange slice, in a blender with cracked
ice. Blend until smooth and pour into
chilled highball glass. Garnish with
orange slice.

ORANGE OASIS

4 parts gin (2 oz.)
2 parts cherry brandy (1 oz.)
8 parts fresh orange juice (½ cup
or 4 oz.)
Ginger ale

Combine all ingredients, except ginger
ale, with cracked ice in a cocktail
shaker. Strain over ice cubes into a
chilled highball glass. Fill with ginger
ale and stir gently.

ORIENTAL

4 parts blended whiskey
(2 oz.)
1 part sweet vermouth (½ oz.)
1 part white Curaçao (½ oz.)
2 parts fresh lime juice (1 oz.)

Combine all ingredients with cracked
ice in a cocktail shaker. Shake well
and strain into chilled cocktail glass.

OSTEND FIZZ

4 parts kirschwasser (2 oz.)
2 parts crème de cassis (1 oz.)
2 parts fresh lemon juice (1 oz.)
Sparkling water
Lemon slice

Combine all ingredients, except water
and lemon slice, with cracked ice in a
cocktail shaker. Shake well and pour
into chilled collins glass over ice
cubes. Fill with sparkling water and
stir gently. Garnish with lemon slice.

OUTRIGGER

4 parts gold rum (2 oz.)
1 part white Curaçao (½ oz.)
1 part apricot liqueur (½ oz.)
2 parts fresh lime juice (1 oz.)
Lime slice

Combine all ingredients, except lime
slice, in a cocktail shaker with cracked
ice and shake well. Strain into a
chilled old-fashioned glass over ice
cubes and garnish with lime slice.

P

PACIFIC PACIFIER

3 parts Cointreau (1½ oz.)
2 parts crème de bananes (1 oz.)
2 parts half-and-half (1 oz.)

Combine all ingredients with cracked
ice in a cocktail shaker. Shake well
and strain into chilled old-fashioned
glass over ice cubes.

PADDY COCKTAIL

4 parts Irish whiskey (2 oz.)
2 parts sweet vermouth (1 oz.)
3 – 5 dashes Angostura bitters

Combine all ingredients with cracked
ice in a cocktail shaker. Shake well
and strain into chilled cocktail glass.

PAGO PAGO

6 parts gold rum (3 oz.)
White crème de cacao (1 tsp.)
Green Chartreuse (1 tsp.)
2 parts fresh lime juice (1 oz.)
2 parts pineapple juice (1 oz.)

Combine all ingredients with cracked
ice in a cocktail shaker. Shake well
and pour into chilled old-fashioned
glass.

PAIN KILLER

6 parts dark rum (3 oz.)
2 parts pineapple juice (1 oz.)
2 parts orange juice (1 oz.)
1 part coconut cream (½ oz.)
2 – 3 dashes nutmeg
maraschino cherry

Combine all liquid ingredients with
cracked ice in a cocktail shaker. Shake
well and pour into a highball glass
over ice. Top off with nutmeg and
maraschino cherry.

PAISLEY MARTINI

6 parts gin (3 oz.)
Dry vermouth (½ tsp.)
Scotch (½ tsp.)

Combine all ingredients with ice cubes
in a mixing glass. Stir well and strain
into a chilled cocktail glass.

PALL MALL

4 parts gin (2 oz.)
1 part dry vermouth (½ oz.)
1 part sweet vermouth (½ oz.)
White crème de menthe (1 tsp.)
Dash orange bitters

Combine all ingredients in a mixing
glass with ice cubes. Stir well and
strain into chilled cocktail glass.

PALM BEACH
COCKTAIL

4 parts gin (2 oz.)
Sweet vermouth (1 tsp.)
4 parts grapefruit juice (2 oz.)

Combine ingredients with cracked ice
in a cocktail shaker. Shake well and
strain into chilled cocktail glass.

PALMER COCKTAIL

4 parts rye (2 oz.)
Fresh lemon juice (½ tsp.)
Dash Angostura bitters

Stir ingredients with ice cubes in a
mixing glass. Strain into chilled
cocktail glass.

PALMETTO COCKTAIL

4 parts light rum (2 oz.)
2 parts dry vermouth (1 oz.)
3 dashes Angostura bitters

Stir ingredients with ice cubes in a
mixing glass. Strain into chilled
cocktail glass.

PANAMA COCKTAIL

4 parts brandy (2 oz.)
3 parts white crème de cacao
(1½ oz.)
3 parts half-and-half (1½ oz.)

Combine ingredients with cracked ice
in a cocktail shaker. Shake well and
strain into chilled cocktail glass.

PANCHO VILLA

4 parts light rum (2 oz.)
2 parts gin (1 oz.)
2 parts apricot brandy (1 oz.)
Cherry brandy (1 tbsp.)
Pineapple juice (1 tbsp.)

Combine all ingredients with cracked
ice in a cocktail shaker. Shake well
and strain into chilled cocktail glass.

PANDA

2 parts apple brandy (1 oz.)
2 parts slivovitz (1 oz.)
2 parts gin (1 oz.)
2 parts fresh orange juice (1 oz.)
Dash sugar syrup

Combine all ingredients with cracked
ice in a cocktail shaker. Shake well
and strain into chilled cocktail glass.

PANTOMIME

6 parts dry vermouth (3 oz.)
3 – 5 dashes grenadine
3 – 5 dashes orgeat (almond) syrup
1 egg white

Combine ingredients in a blender with
cracked ice. Blend until smooth and
strain into chilled cocktail glass.

PAPAYA SMOOTHIE

1 banana, sliced
½ papaya, cubed
1 part honey (½ oz.)
12 parts cold fresh orange juice
(6 oz.)
Vanilla extract (¼ tsp.)

Combine all ingredients in a blender
and blend until smooth. Pour into
chilled collins glass.

PARADISE COCKTAIL

4 parts apricot brandy (2 oz.)
1 part gin (½ oz.)
3 parts fresh orange juice (1½ oz.)
Grenadine (½ tsp.)

Combine ingredients with cracked ice
in a cocktail shaker. Shake well and
strain into chilled cocktail glass.

PARISIAN

4 parts gin (2 oz.)
2 parts dry vermouth (1 oz.)
1 part crème de cassis (½ oz.)

Combine ingredients with cracked ice
in a cocktail shaker. Shake well and
strain into chilled cocktail glass.

PARK AVENUE

4 parts gin (2 oz.)
1 part sweet vermouth (½ oz.)
1 part pineapple juice (½ oz.)

Stir ingredients with cracked ice in a
mixing glass. Strain into chilled
cocktail glass.

PASSION CUP

4 parts vodka (2 oz.)
4 parts orange juice (2 oz.)
2 parts passion fruit juice (1 oz.)
1 part coconut milk (½ oz.)
1 part pineapple juice (½ oz.)
Maraschino cherry

Combine all ingredients, except
cherry, in a cocktail shaker with
cracked ice. Shake well and strain into
chilled red wine glass. Garnish with
cherry.

PASSIONATE
DAIQUIRI

4 parts light rum (2 oz.)
2 parts fresh lime juice (1 oz.)
1 part passion fruit syrup

Combine ingredients with cracked ice
in a cocktail shaker and shake well.
Strain into chilled cocktail glass.

PEACH BLOW FIZZ

6 parts gin (3 oz.)
2 parts fresh lemon juice (1 oz.)
2 parts half-and-half (1 oz.)
Sugar syrup (1 tsp.)
5 fresh strawberries, mashed
Sparkling water
Fresh peach wedge

Combine all ingredients, except sparkling water and peach, with cracked ice in a cocktail shaker. Shake well and pour into chilled highball glass. Fill with sparkling water and stir gently. Garnish with peach wedge.

PEACH BUCK

4 parts vodka (2 oz.)
2 parts peach brandy (1 oz.)
2 parts fresh lemon juice (1 oz.)
Ginger ale
Fresh peach slice

Combine all ingredients, except ginger ale and peach slice, with cracked ice in a cocktail shaker. Shake well and pour into chilled highball glass. Fill with ginger ale and stir gently. Garnish with peach slice.

PEACH DAIQUIRI

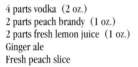

4 parts light rum (2 oz.)
2 parts fresh lime juice (1 oz.)
Bar sugar (½ tsp.)
½ fresh peach, peeled and diced

Combine ingredients with cracked ice in a blender. Blend until slushy and pour into chilled balloon wine glass.

PEACH FUZZ

4 parts fresh lemon juice
(2 oz.)
4 parts half-and-half (2 oz.)
Sugar syrup (1 tsp.)
5 fresh strawberries, mashed
Sparkling water
Fresh peach wedge

Combine all ingredients, except water and peach, with cracked ice in a cocktail shaker. Shake well and pour into chilled highball glass. Fill with sparkling water and stir gently. Garnish with peach wedge.

PEACH MARGARITA

4 parts silver tequila (2 oz.)
1 part peach liqueur (½ oz.)
Triple sec (1 tbsp.)
4 parts fresh lime juice (2 oz.)
Coarse salt
Lime wedge
Fresh peach slice

Rim a chilled cocktail glass with salt by rubbing the lime wedge along the tim and dipping it in a saucer of coarse salt. Combine remaining ingredients, except peach slice, with cracked ice in a cocktail shaker. Shake well and pour into salt-rimmed cocktail glass. Garnish with peach slice.

PEACHES AND CREAM

4 parts peach liqueur (2 oz.)
4 parts half-and-half (2 oz.)

Combine ingredients with cracked ice in a cocktail shaker. Shake well and strain into chilled old-fashioned glass over ice cubes

PEACHY CREAM

4 parts peach nectar (2 oz.)
4 parts half-and-half (2 oz.)

Combine ingredients with cracked ice in a cocktail shaker. Shake well and strain into chilled old-fashioned glass over ice cubes

PEACHY MELBA

6 parts peach nectar (3 oz.)
2 parts grenadine (1 oz.)
2 parts fresh lemon juice (1 oz.)
2 parts fresh lime juice (1 oz.)
Peach slice

Combine all ingredients, except peach slice, with cracked ice in a cocktail shaker. Shake well and pour into chilled old-fashioned glass. Garnish with peach.

PEGGY COCKTAIL

4 parts gin (2 oz.)
1 part sweet vermouth (½ oz.)
Dubonnet rouge (¼ tsp.)
Pernod (¼ tsp.)

Combine all ingredients with cracked
ice in a cocktail shaker and shake
well. Strain into chilled cocktail glass.

PEGU CLUB COCKTAIL

4 parts gin (2 oz.)
2 parts white Curaçao (1 oz.)
Fresh lime juice (1 tbsp.)
Dash Angostura bitters
Dash orange bitters

Combine all ingredients with cracked
ice in a cocktail shaker. Shake well
and strain into chilled cocktail glass.

PENDENNIS CLUB
COCKTAIL

4 parts gin (2 oz.)
2 parts apricot brandy (1 oz.)
2 parts fresh lime juice (1 oz.)
Sugar syrup (1 tsp.)
3 – 5 dashes Peychaud's bitters

Combine all ingredients with cracked
ice in a cocktail shaker. Shake well
and strain into chilled cocktail glass.

PEPPER POT

8 parts pineapple juice (4 oz.)
2 parts orgeat (almond) syrup
(1 oz.)
2 parts fresh lemon juice (1 oz.)
Tabasco sauce (3 – 5 dashes)
Cayenne pepper to taste
Curry powder

Combine all ingredients, except the
curry powder, in a cocktail shaker with
cracked ice. Shake well and pour into
chilled highball glass. Sprinkle curry
powder on top.

PLEASE NOTE: Blue icons represent
alcoholic drinks. Green icons represent
non-alcoholic drinks.

PEPPERMINT PATTY

PEPPERMINT PATTY

4 parts white crème de cacao
(2 oz.)
4 parts white crème de menthe (2 oz.)
2 parts half-and-half (1 oz.)

Combine all ingredients with cracked
ice in a cocktail shaker and shake
well. Pour into chilled old-fashioned
glass.

PERFECT MANHATTAN

6 parts rye (3 oz.)
1 part dry vermouth (½ oz.)
1 part sweet vermouth (½ oz.)
Maraschino cherry

Combine all ingredients, except cherry,
in a cocktail shaker with cracked ice.
Shake well and strain into chilled
cocktail glass. Garnish with cherry.

PERFECT MARTINI

6 parts gin (3 oz.)
Dry vermouth (½ tsp.)
Sweet vermouth (½ tsp.)
Cocktail olive

Combine liquid ingredients with ice
cubes in a mixing glass and stir well.
Strain into chilled cocktail glass and
garnish with olive.

PERNOD COCKTAIL

4 part Pernod (2 oz.)
1 part water (½ oz.)
Sugar syrup (¼ tsp.)
3 – 5 dashes Angostura bitters

Fill an old-fashioned glass with crushed ice, sugar syrup, bitters and water. Stir well and add Pernod. Stir again.

PERNOD FLIP

4 parts Pernod (2 oz.)
3 parts half-and-half (1½ oz.)
1 part orgeat (almond) syrup (½ oz.)
1 egg
Freshly ground nutmeg

Combine all ingredients, except nutmeg, in a blender with cracked ice. Blend until smooth and pour into chilled wine glass. Sprinkle with nutmeg.

PERNOD FRAPPE

6 parts pernod (3 oz.)
1 part anisette (½ oz.)
2 parts half-and-half (1 oz.)
1 egg white

Combine ingredients with cracked ice in a cocktail shaker. Shake vigorously and strain into chilled wine glass.

PEYTON PLACE

3 parts sloe gin (1½ oz.)
2 parts gin (1 oz.)
5 parts grapefruit juice
1 part sugar syrup (½ oz.)
Club soda

Mix all ingredients, except soda, with cracked ice in a cocktail shaker. Pour into chilled collins glass. Fill with club soda. Stir gently.

PEYTON PLACE

PHOEBE SNOW

4 parts Dubonnet rouge (2 oz.)
4 parts Pernod (2 oz.)

Combine all ingredients with cracked
ice in a cocktail shaker. Shake well
and strain into chilled cocktail glass.

PICCADILLY COCKTAIL

4 parts gin (2 oz.)
2 parts dry vermouth (1 oz.)
Pernod (¼ tsp.)
Dash grenadine

Stir ingredients with ice in a mixing
glass and strain into chilled cocktail
glass.

PICON

4 parts Amer Picon (2 oz.)
4 parts sweet vermouth (2 oz.)

Combine ingredients with cracked ice
in a cocktail shaker. Shake well and
strain into chilled cocktail glass.

PICON FIZZ

4 parts Amer Picon (2 oz.)
1 part grenadine (½ oz.)
1 part brandy (½ oz.)
Sparkling water

Pour Amer Picon and grenadine into
a chilled highball glass over ice cubes
and stir well. Fill with sparkling water
and stir gently. Float brandy on top.

PILOT BOAT

4 parts dark rum (2 oz.)
2 parts crème de bananes
(1 oz.)
4 parts fresh lime juice (2 oz.)

Combine ingredients with cracked ice
in a cocktail shaker. Shake well and
strain into chilled cocktail glass.

PIMM'S CUP

4 parts Pimm's Cup No. 1 (2 oz.)
Cointreau (1 tsp.)
4 parts fresh lime juice (2 oz.)
Sugar syrup (1 tsp.)
Lemon-lime soda
2 thin cucumber slices
Fresh mint sprig
Lime slice

Combine sugar syrup and lime juice
in a chilled collins glass. Fill with ice
cubes. Add Pimm's and cointreau. Fill
with lemon-lime soda and stir gently.
Garnish with cucumber, mint and
lime slice.

PHOEBE SNOW

179

PIMM'S CUP

PIÑA

4 parts gold tequila (2 oz.)
6 parts fresh pineapple juice (3 oz.)
2 parts fresh lime juice (1 oz.)
Honey (1 tsp.)
Lime slice

Combine all ingredients, except lime
slice, with cracked ice in a cocktail
shaker. Shake well and pour into
chilled old-fashioned glass. Garnish
with lime slice.

PIÑA COLADA FOR FRIENDS

16 parts light rum (1 cup or 8 oz.)
4 parts dark rum (2 oz.)
10 parts coconut cream (5 oz.)
20 parts. pineapple juice (10 oz.)
4 parts half-and-half (2 oz.)
4 pineapple spears

Combine all ingredients, except
pineapple spears, in a blender with
cracked ice. Blend until smooth.
Pour into chilled collins glasses and
garnish with pineapple spears.
Serves 4.

PIÑA COLADA

4 parts light rum (2 oz.)
2 parts dark rum (1 oz.)
6 parts pineapple juice (3 oz.)
4 parts coconut cream (2 oz.)
Pineapple spear

Combine all ingredients, except
pineapple spear, with cracked ice in a
blender. Blend until smooth and pour
into chilled collins glass. Garnish with
pineapple spear.

PIÑATA

4 parts gold tequila (2 oz.)
2 parts crème de bananes (1 oz.)
3 parts fresh lime juice (1½ oz.)

Combine all ingredients with cracked
ice in a cocktail shaker. Shake well
and strain into chilled cocktail glass.

PINEAPPLE COOLER

6 parts chilled white wine (3 oz.)
6 parts pineapple juice (3 oz.)
1 part fresh lemon juice (½ oz.)
Bar sugar (1 tsp.)
Sparkling water
Lemon twist

Combine all ingredients, except lemon
twist and sparkling water, in a cocktail
shaker with cracked ice. Shake well
and strain into a chilled collins glass
over ice cubes. Fill with sparkling
water and stir gently. Garnish with
lemon twist.

PIÑA COLADA

PINEAPPLE DAIQUIRI

4 parts light rum (2 oz.)
1 part triple sec (½ oz.)
6 parts pineapple juice (3 oz.)
1 part fresh lime juice (½ oz.)
Pineapple spear

Combine all ingredients, except
pineapple spear, with cracked ice in a
blender. Blend until slushy and pour
into chilled wine glass.

PINEAPPLE FIZZ

4 parts light rum (2 oz.)
6 parts pineapple juice (3 oz.)
Sugar syrup (1 tsp.)
Sparkling water

Combine all ingredients, except
sparkling water, with cracked ice in a
cocktail shaker and shake well. Pour
into chilled collins glass over ice
cubes. Fill with sparkling water and
stir gently.

PINEAPPLE LEMONADE

4 parts vodka (2 oz.)
6 parts pineapple juice (3 oz.)
Fresh lemonade

Pour vodka and pineapple juice into a chilled collins glass over ice cubes. Fill with lemonade and stir.

PINEAPPLE SPARKLER

8 parts pineapple juice (4 oz.)
1 part sugar syrup (½ oz.)
Sparkling water
Lime slice

Combine ingredients, except sparkling water and lime slice, with cracked ice in a cocktail shaker and shake well. Pour into chilled collins glass over ice cubes. Fill with sparkling water and stir gently. Garnish with lime slice.

PINK ALMOND

4 parts blended whiskey (2 oz.)
2 parts amaretto (1 oz)
1 part crème de noyaux (½ oz.)
1 part kirschwasser (½ oz.)
2 parts fresh lemon juice (1 oz.)
Lemon slice

Combine all ingredients, except lemon slice, with cracked ice in a cocktail shaker. Shake well and pour into a chilled sour glass. Garnish with lemon slice

PINK CREOLE

4 parts light rum (2 oz.)
1 part fresh lime juice (½ oz.)
Grenadine (1 tsp.)
Half-and-half (1 tsp.)
Black cherry soaked in rum

Combine all ingredients, except cherry, in a cocktail shaker with cracked ice. Shake well and strain into chilled cocktail glass. Garnish with cherry.

PINK LADY

4 parts gin (2 oz.)
Grenadine (1 tsp.)
Half-and-half (1 tsp.)
Fresh lemon juice (1 tsp.)
1 egg white

Combine all ingredients with cracked ice in a cocktail shaker. Shake vigorously and strain into chilled cocktail glass.

PINK LEMONADE

4 parts vodka (2 oz.)
2 parts maraschino liqueur
Fresh lemonade

Pour vodka and liqueur into a chilled collins glass over ice cubes. Fill with lemonade and stir.

PINK PANTHER

4 parts vodka (2 oz.)
2 parts dry vermouth (1 oz.)
1 part crème de cassis (½ oz.)
2 parts orange juice (1 oz.)
½ egg white

Combine all ingredients with cracked ice in a cocktail shaker. Shake vigorously. Strain into chilled cocktail glass.

PINK PUSSYCAT

4 parts gin (2 oz.)
Pineapple juice
Dash grenadine
Pineapple spear

Pour gin into a chilled highball glass over ice cubes. Fill with pineapple juice and add a dash of grenadine. Stir gently and garnish with pineapple spear.

PINK ROSE

4 parts gin (2 oz.)
Fresh lemon juice (1 tsp.)
Half-and-half (1 tsp.)
Grenadine (¼ tsp.)
1 egg white

Combine all ingredients with cracked ice in a cocktail shaker. Shake well and strain into chilled cocktail glass.

PINK SQUIRREL

2 parts dark crème de cacao
(1 oz.)
2 parts crème de noyaux (1 oz.)
2 parts half-and-half (1 oz.)

Combine all ingredients with cracked
ice in a cocktail shaker. Shake well
and strain into chilled cocktail glass.

PINK VERANDA

2 parts gold rum (1 oz.)
2 parts dark rum (1 oz.)
4 parts cranberry juice (2 oz.)
1 part fresh lime juice (½ oz.)
Sugar syrup (1 tsp.)
½ egg white

Combine all ingredients with cracked
ice in a cocktail shaker. Shake
vigorously and pour into chilled old-
fashioned glass.

PIRATE'S JULEP

6 parts gold rum (3 oz.)
White Curaçao (1 tsp.)
Orgeat (almond) syrup (1 tsp.)
3 – 5 dashes Peychaud's bitters
10 mint leaves
Fresh mint sprig

Muddle mint leaves in a chilled highball glass with orgeat (almond) syrup.
Add bitters, fill glass with crushed
ice and pour in rum. Stir until glass
frosts. Float Curaçao on top and
garnish with mint sprig.

PLANTATION PUNCH

4 parts dark rum (2 oz.)
2 parts Southern Comfort (1 oz.)
2 parts fresh lemon juice (1 oz.)
Ruby port (1 tsp.)
Brown sugar (1 tsp.)
Sparkling water
Lemon slice
Orange slice

Combine all ingredients, except port,
water and fruit, with cracked ice in a
cocktail shaker. Shake well and pour
into chilled collins glass. Fill almost to
the rim with sparkling water and float
port on top. Garnish with fruit.

PLANTER'S COCKTAIL

4 parts dark rum (2 oz.)
2 parts fresh lemon juice (1 oz.)
Sugar syrup (1 tsp.)

Combine ingredients with cracked ice
in a cocktail shaker and shake well.
Strain into chilled cocktail glass.

PLANTER'S PUNCH

4 parts dark rum (2 oz.)
4 parts light rum (2 oz.)
2 parts fresh lime juice (1 oz.)
2 parts fresh lemon juice (1 oz.)
Triple sec (¼ tsp.)
Dash grenadine
Bar sugar (1 tsp.)
Sparkling water
Lime slice
Maraschino cherry
Orange slice
Pineapple spear

Combine all ingredients, except sparkling water and fruit, with cracked ice
in a cocktail shaker. Shake well and
strain into a chilled collins glass over
ice cubes. Fill with sparkling water
and stir gently. Garnish with fruit.

PLANTER'S PUNCH

183

PLUM FIZZ

PLAZA COCKTAIL

2 parts dry vermouth (1 oz.)
2 parts sweet vermouth (1 oz.)
2 parts gin (1 oz.)

Combine all ingredients with ice cubes in a mixing glass and stir. Strain into chilled cocktail glass.

PLUGGY'S FAVORITE

4 parts gin (2 oz.)
4 parts Pernod (2 oz.)
4 parts water (2 oz.)

Combine all ingredients with cracked ice in a cocktail shaker. Shake well and strain into chilled old-fashioned glass over ice cubes.

PLUM FIZZ

4 parts slivovitz (plum brandy)
(2 oz.)
1 part lime juice (½ oz.)
Sugar syrup (1 tsp.)
Club soda
Plum slice

Mix all ingredients, except for club
soda and plum, in a cocktail shaker.
Shake well. Pour into chilled highball
glass. Add more ice if necessary and
fill with cold club soda. Garnish with
plum slice.

POKER COCKTAIL

6 parts light rum (3 oz.)
2 parts sweet vermouth (1 oz.)

Combine ingredients with cracked ice
in a cocktail shaker. Shake well and
strain into chilled cocktail glass.

POLISH SIDECAR

4 parts gin (2 oz.)
2 parts blackberry brandy (1 oz.)
2 parts fresh lemon juice (1 oz.)
Fresh blackberries

Combine all ingredients, except
berries, with cracked ice in a cocktail
shaker. Shake well and strain into
chilled cocktail glass. Garnish with
blackberries.

POLLYANNA

6 parts gin (3 oz.)
1 part sweet vermouth (½ oz.)
Grenadine (½ tsp.)
3 orange slices
3 pineapple slices

Muddle fruit slices with all ingredients
in a mortar and pestle. Pour
ingredients into a cocktail shaker with
cracked ice. Shake well and strain into
chilled cocktail glass.

POLISH SIDECAR

POLO DREAM

4 parts bourbon (2 oz.)
2 parts fresh orange juice (1 oz.)
1 part orgeat (almond) syrup (½ oz.)

Combine ingredients with cracked ice
in a cocktail shaker. Shake well and
strain into chilled cocktail glass.

POLONAISE

4 parts brandy (2 oz.)
1 part blackberry brandy (½ oz.)
1 part dry sherry (½ oz.)
3 dashes fresh lemon juice
Dash orange bitters

Combine ingredients with cracked ice
in a cocktail shaker. Shake well and
strain into a chilled old-fashioned
glass over ice cubes.

POLYNESIAN COCKTAIL

4 parts vodka (2 oz.)
2 parts cherry brandy (1 oz.)
1 part fresh lime juice (½ oz.)
1 part fresh lemon juice (½ oz.)
Lime wedge
Bar sugar

Rim a chilled cocktail glass with
sugar by rubbing the rim of the glass
with the lime wedge and dipping it in
the sugar. Discard the lime. Combine
remaining ingredients with cracked
ice in a cocktail shaker and shake
well. Strain into the cocktail glass.

185

POLYNESIAN PEPPER POT

4 parts vodka (2 oz.)
2 parts gold rum (1 oz.)
8 parts pineapple juice (½ cup or 4 oz.)
1 part orgeat (almond) syrup (½ oz.)
Fresh lemon juice (1 tsp.)
3 – 5 dashes Tabasco sauce
Cayenne pepper (¼ tsp. or to taste)
Curry powder

Combine all ingredients, except the curry powder, in a cocktail shaker with cracked ice. Shake well and pour into chilled highball glass. Sprinkle curry powder on top.

POLYNESIAN SOUR

4 parts light rum (2 oz.)
1 part guava nectar (½ oz.)
1 part fresh lemon juice (½ oz.)
1 part fresh orange juice (½ oz.)

Combine all ingredients with cracked ice in a blender. Blend until smooth and pour into chilled cocktail glass.

POLYNESIAN SWEET AND SOUR

4 parts guava nectar (2 oz.)
4 parts fresh lemon juice (2 oz.)
2 parts fresh orange juice (1 oz.)

Combine all ingredients with cracked ice in a blender. Blend until smooth and pour into chilled cocktail glass.

POMPANO

4 parts gin (2 oz.)
2 parts dry vermouth (1 oz.)
4 parts grapefruit juice (2 oz.)
Dash orange bitters

Combine all ingredients with cracked ice in a cocktail shaker. Shake well and strain into chilled cocktail glass.

POOP DECK COCKTAIL

4 parts brandy (2 oz.)
2 parts ruby port (1 oz.)
1 part blackberry brandy (½ oz.)

Combine ingredients with cracked ice in a cocktail shaker. Shake well and strain into chilled cocktail glass.

PORT ANTONIO

2 parts gold rum (1 oz.)
2 parts dark rum (1 oz.)
1 part coffee liqueur (½ oz.)
1 part fresh lime juice (½ oz.)
Falernum (1 tsp.)
Lime slice

Combine all ingredients, except lime slice, with cracked ice in a cocktail shaker. Shake well and pour into chilled old-fashioned glass. Garnish with lime slice.

PORT MILK PUNCH

6 parts ruby port (3 oz.)
16 parts milk (1 cup or 8 oz.)
Sugar syrup (1 tsp.)
Freshly grated nutmeg

Combine all ingredients, except nutmeg, with cracked ice in a cocktail shaker. Shake well and strain into chilled collins glass. Sprinkle with nutmeg.

PORT WINE COBBLER

6 parts ruby port (3 oz.)
Bar sugar (1 tsp.)
4 parts sparkling water (2 oz.)
Orange slice
Maraschino cherry

Dissolve sugar in sparkling water in the bottom of a chilled red wine glass. Fill with shaved ice and add port. Stir and garnish with fruit.

PORT WINE COCKTAIL

6 parts ruby port (3 oz.)
Brandy (1 tsp.)

Stir ingredients with ice cubes in a mixing glass. Strain into chilled cocktail glass.

PORT WINE FLIP

4 parts ruby port (2 oz.)
Sugar syrup (1 tsp.)
Half-and-half (1 tbsp.)
1 whole egg
Freshly grated nutmeg

Combine all ingredients, except
nutmeg, with cracked ice in a cocktail
shaker. Shake vigorously and strain
into chilled sour glass. Sprinkle
nutmeg on top.

PORT WINE SANGAREE

6 parts ruby port (3 oz.)
Brandy (1 tbsp.)
Bar sugar (½ tsp.)
Water (1 tsp.)
Sparkling water

Dissolve sugar in water in the bottom
of a chilled highball glass. Add the
port and fill glass with ice cubes. Fill
with sparkling water almost to the top.
Stir gently and float brandy on top.

POST-MODERN
LEMONADE

4 parts sloe gin (2 oz.)
4 parts dry sherry (2 oz.)
2 parts aquavit (1 oz.)
6 parts fresh lemon juice (3 oz.)
Slivovitz (1 tbsp.)
2 parts sugar syrup (1 oz.)
Sparkling water
Lemon twist

Combine all ingredients, except lemon
twist and sparkling water, with cracked
ice in a cocktail shaker. Shake well
and strain over ice cubes into chilled
collins glass. Stir gently and garnish
with lemon twist.

POUSSE-CAFÉ

1 part grenadine (½ oz.)
1 part white crème de cacao (½ oz.)
1 part maraschino liqueur (½ oz.)
1 part white Curaçao (½ oz.)
1 part green crème de menthe (½ oz.)
1 part brandy (½ oz.)

Pour ingredients in the order given,
slowly and carefully into a pousse-café
glass so each ingredient forms a
separate layer.

POUSSE L'AMOUR

1 part maraschino liqueur
(½ oz.)
1 egg yolk
1 part Benedictine (½ oz.)
1 part cognac (½ oz.)

Pour ingredients, in the order given,
slowly and carefully into a pousse-café
glass so each ingredient forms a
separate layer.

PRADO

4 parts silver tequila (2 oz.)
2 parts fresh lime juice (1 oz.)
Maraschino liqueur (1 tbsp.)
Grenadine (1 tsp.)
1 egg white
Lime slice

Combine all ingredients in a cocktail
shaker with cracked ice. Shake
vigorously and strain into a chilled
sour glass. Garnish with lime slice.

PRAIRIE OYSTER

4 parts brandy (2 oz.)
1 part red wine vinegar (½ oz.)
1 part Worcestershire sauce (½ oz.)
Tomato catsup (1 tsp.)
Dash Tabasco sauce
Cayenne pepper to taste
1 egg yolk

Combine all ingredients, except egg
yolk and cayenne, with cracked ice in
a cocktail shaker. Strain into chilled
old-fashioned glass. Float unbroken
egg yolk on top and sprinkle with
cayenne. Swallow in one swig without
breaking the yolk.

PREAKNESS
COCKTAIL

4 parts blended whiskey (2 oz.)
2 parts sweet vermouth (1 oz.)
Benedictine (1 tsp.)
Dash Angostura bitters
Lemon twist

Combine all ingredients, except lemon
twist, with cracked ice in a cocktail
shaker. Shake well and strain into
chilled cocktail glass. Garnish with
lemon twist.

187

PRESBYTERIAN

6 parts bourbon (3 oz.)
Ginger ale
Sparkling water

Pour bourbon over ice cubes into a
chilled highball glass. Add equal parts
ginger ale and sparkling water. Stir
gently.

PRESIDENTE COCKTAIL

4 parts light rum (2 oz.)
1 part dry vermouth (½ oz.)
1 part triple sec (½ oz.)
Dash grenadine
Lemon twist

Combine all ingredients, except lemon
twist, with cracked ice in a cocktail
shaker. Shake well and strain into
chilled cocktail glass. Garnish with
lemon twist.

PRESTO COCKTAIL

4 parts brandy (2 oz.)
2 parts sweet vermouth (1 oz.)
Pernod (1 tsp.)
1 part fresh orange juice (1 oz.)

Combine all ingredients with cracked ice in a cocktail shaker. Shake well and strain into chilled cocktail glass.

PRINCE EDWARD

4 parts scotch (2 oz.)
1 part Lillet blanc (½ oz.)
1 part Drambuie (½ oz.)
Orange slice

Combine all ingredients, except orange slice, with cracked ice in a cocktail shaker. Shake well and pour into chilled old-fashioned glass. Garnish with orange slice.

PRINCE OF WALES

2 parts brandy (1 oz.)
2 parts Madeira (1 oz.)
1 part white Curaçao (½ oz.)
3 – 5 dashes Angostura bitters
Champagne or sparkling wine
Orange slice

Combine all ingredients, except champagne and orange slice, with cracked ice in a cocktail shaker. Shake well and strain into chilled red wine glass. Fill with champagne and stir gently. Garnish with orange slice.

PRINCE'S SMILE

4 parts gin (2 oz.)
2 parts apple brandy (1 oz.)
2 parts apricot brandy (1 oz.)
Fresh lemon juice (1 tsp.)

Combine all ingredients with cracked ice in a cocktail shaker. Shake well and strain into chilled cocktail glass.

PRINCESS MARY'S PRIDE

4 parts apple brandy (2 oz.)
2 parts Dubonnet rouge (1 oz.)
1 part dry vermouth (½ oz.)

Combine ingredients with cracked ice in a cocktail shaker. Shake well and strain into chilled cocktail glass.

PRINCETON COCKTAIL

6 parts gin (3 oz.)
2 parts ruby port (1 oz.)
3 – 5 dashes Angostura bitters
Lemon twist

Combine all ingredients with cracked ice in a cocktail shaker and shake well. Strain into chilled cocktail glass and garnish with lemon twist.

PUERTO APPLE

4 parts apple brandy (2 oz.)
2 parts light rum (1 oz.)
1 part fresh lime juice (½ oz.)
1 part orgeat (almond) syrup (½ oz.)
Lime slice

Combine all ingredients, except lime slice, with cracked ice in a cocktail shaker. Shake well and strain into a chilled old-fashioned glass over ice cubes. Garnish with lime slice.

PURPLE PASSION

4 parts vodka (2 oz.)
8 parts purple grape juice
(½ cup or 4 oz.)
8 parts grapefruit juice (½ cup or 4 oz.)

Combine ingredients with cracked ice in a cocktail shaker. Shake well and strain into a chilled collins glass over ice cubes.

PURPLE PEOPLE EATER

8 parts purple grape juice (4 oz.)
1 part fresh lime juice (½ oz.)
Sparkling water
Lime slice

Combine juices in a cocktail shaker with cracked ice and shake well. Pour over ice cubes into a chilled collins glass. Fill with sparkling water and stir gently. Garnish with lime slice.

QUAKER COCKTAIL

5 parts brandy (2½ oz)
3 parts light rum (1½ oz.)
1 part fresh lemon juice (½ oz.)
1 part raspberry syrup (½ oz.)
Lemon twist

Combine all ingredients, except lemon twist, with cracked ice in a cocktail shaker. Shake well and strain into chilled cocktail glass. Garnish with lemon twist.

QUARTER DECK COCKTAIL

4 parts dark rum (2 oz.)
2 parts cream sherry (1 oz.)
Fresh lime juice (1 tbsp.)

Combine all ingredients with cracked ice in a cocktail shaker and shake well. Strain into chilled cocktail glass.

QUÉBEC COCKTAIL

6 parts Canadian whisky
(3 oz.)
2 parts Amer Picon (1 oz.)
2 parts dry vermouth (1 oz.)
1 part maraschino liqueur (½ oz.)

Combine all ingredients with cracked ice in a cocktail shaker and shake well. Strain into chilled cocktail glass.

QUEEN ELIZABETH

6 parts gin (3 oz.)
1 part dry vermouth (½ oz.)
Benedictine (2 tsp.)

Combine ingredients with ice cubes in a mixing glass and stir well. Strain into chilled cocktail glass.

QUEEN ELIZABETH WINE

4 parts Benedictine (2 oz.)
2 parts dry vermouth (1 oz.)
2 parts fresh lemon juice (1 oz.)
Lemon twist

Combine all ingredients, except lemon twist, with ice cubes in a mixing glass. Stir well and strain into chilled cocktail glass. Garnish with lemon twist.

QUICK PICK

Iced tea, unsweetened
4 parts peppermint syrup (2 oz.)
Lime wedge
Fresh mint sprig

Pour syrup and iced tea into a chilled collins glass filled with ice cubes. Squeeze the lime wedge over drink and drop in. Stir and garnish with mint sprig.

QUIET PASSION

8 parts white grape juice (4 oz.)
8 parts grapefruit juice (4 oz.)
2 parts passion fruit juice (1 oz.)

Combine ingredients with cracked ice in a cocktail shaker. Shake well and strain into a chilled collins glass over ice cubes.

R

RACQUET CLUB COCKTAIL

4 parts gin (2 oz.)
1½ parts dry vermouth (¾ oz.)
Dash orange bitters

Combine all ingredients in a mixing glass with ice cubes. Stir well and strain into chilled cocktail glass.

RAMOS FIZZ

6 parts gin (3 oz.)
1 part fresh lemon juice (½ oz.)
1 part fresh lime juice (½ oz.)
Bar sugar (1 tsp.)
Half-and-half (1 tsp.)
3 – 5 dashes orange flower water
1 egg white
Sparkling water

Combine all ingredients, except egg white and sparkling water, with cracked ice in a cocktail shaker. Shake vigorously and pour into chilled collins glass. Fill with sparkling water and egg white and stir gently.

RAMPART STREET PARADE

4 parts light rum (2 oz.)
2 parts crème de bananes (1 oz.)
1 part Southern Comfort (½ oz.)
2 parts fresh lime juice

Combine all ingredients with cracked ice in a cocktail shaker. Shake well and strain into chilled cocktail glass.

RATTLESNAKE

4 parts blended whiskey (2 oz.)
1 part fresh lemon juice (½ oz.)
Sugar syrup (1 tsp.)
1 egg white
Pernod (¼ tsp.)

Combine all ingredients with cracked ice in a cocktail shaker. Shake vigorously and pour into chilled old-fashioned glass.

RED APPLE

4 parts apple brandy (2 oz.)
4 parts grapefruit juice (2 oz.)
3 – 5 dashes grenadine

Combine all ingredients with cracked ice in a cocktail shaker. Shake well and strain into chilled cocktail glass.

RED APPLE SUNSET

4 parts apple juice (2 oz.)
4 parts grapefruit juice (2 oz.)
Grenadine (3 – 5 dashes)

Combine all ingredients with cracked ice in a cocktail shaker. Shake well and strain into chilled cocktail glass.

RED CLOUD

4 parts gin (2 oz.)
2 parts apricot liqueur (1 oz.)
2 parts fresh lemon juice (1 oz.)
Grenadine (1 tsp.)
Dash Angostura bitters

Combine all ingredients with cracked ice in a cocktail shaker. Shake well and strain into chilled cocktail glass.

RED LION

4 parts gin (2 oz.)
3 parts orange liqueur (1½ oz.)
1 part fresh lemon juice (½ oz.)
1 part fresh orange juice (½ oz.)
Grenadine (½ tsp.)

Combine ingredients with cracked ice in a cocktail shaker. Shake well and strain into chilled cocktail glass.

RED SNAPPER

4 parts vodka (2 oz.)
6 parts tomato juice (3 oz.)
3 – 5 dashes Worcestershire sauce
Salt to taste
Freshly ground black pepper to taste
Cayenne pepper to taste
Dash lemon juice
Celery rib

Combine all ingredients, except
vodka, tomato juice and celery, in a
cocktail shaker. Shake well. Add ice
cubes, vodka and tomato juice and
shake again. Pour into chilled
highball glass; garnish with celery rib.

REFORM COCKTAIL

4 parts fino sherry (2 oz.)
2 parts sweet vermouth (1 oz.)
3 – 5 dashes Angostura bitters

Combine ingredients with ice cubes in
a mixing glass. Stir well and strain
into chilled cocktail glass.

REFRIGERATOR TEA

Loose tea of your choice
(4 heaping tsp.)
10 –15 crushed fresh mint leaves
(optional)
60 parts water (30 oz.)
Sugar to taste

Combine tea and water in a glass jar
and cover. Refrigerate overnight.
Strain into chilled collins glasses filled
with ice cubes and sweeten to taste.

REGENT'S PUNCH

Sweet white wine (Riesling, Sauterne,
etc.) (1 bottle – 750-ml.)
Madeira (2 bottles – 750-ml. each)
Triple sec (1 bottle – 750-ml.)
Cognac (1 bottle – 750-ml.)
Champagne or sparkling wine
(3 bottles – 750-ml.)
Dark rum (1 pint or 16 oz.)
Strong black iced tea (1 pint or 16 oz.)
Fresh lemon juice (1 cup or 8 oz.)
Orange juice (3 cups or 24 oz.)
Bar sugar (¼ cup)
Sparkling water (2 quarts or 2 liters)

Chill ingredients for at least two
hours. Pour all ingredients, except
champagne and sparkling water, into
a very large punch bowl and stir. Add
one cake of ice. Before serving, add
champagne and sparkling water. Stir
gently. Serves 80.

REMSEN COOLER

6 parts scotch (3 oz.)
Sugar syrup (1 tsp.)
Sparkling water
Lemon twist

Pour scotch and syrup into a chilled
collins glass filled with ice cubes. Fill
with sparkling water and stir gently.
Garnish with lemon twist.

RENAISSANCE

4 parts gin (2 oz.)
1 part fino sherry (½ oz.)
1 part half-and-half (½ oz.)
Freshly grated nutmeg

Combine all ingredients, except
nutmeg, with cracked ice in a cocktail
shaker. Shake well and strain into
chilled old-fashioned glass over ice
cubes. Sprinkle nutmeg on top.

RENDEZ-VOUS

4 parts gin (2 oz.)
2 parts kirschwasser (1 oz.)
1 part Campari (½ oz.)
Lemon twist

Combine all ingredients, except lemon
twist, with cracked ice in a cocktail
shaker. Shake well and strain into
chilled cocktail glass. Garnish with
lemon twist.

RESOLUTE COCKTAIL

4 parts gin (2 oz.)
2 parts apricot brandy (1 oz.)
1 part fresh lemon juice (½ oz.)

Combine ingredients with cracked ice
in a cocktail shaker. Shake well and
strain into chilled cocktail glass.

RHETT BUTLER

4 parts Southern Comfort
(2 oz.)
1 part fresh lime juice (½ oz.)
1 part white Curaçao (½ oz.)
Fresh lemon juice (1 tsp.)
Lemon twist

Combine all ingredients, except lemon
twist, with cracked ice in a cocktail
shaker. Shake well and strain into
chilled cocktail glass. Garnish with
lemon twist.

ROAD RUNNER

4 parts gin (2 oz.)
1 part dry vermouth (½ oz.)
Grenadine (1 tsp.)
Pernod (¼ tsp.)

Combine all ingredients with cracked
ice in a cocktail shaker. Shake well
and strain into chilled cocktail glass.

ROB ROY

6 parts scotch (3 oz.)
2 parts sweet vermouth (1 oz.)
Dash Angostura bitters
Maraschino cherry

Combine all ingredients, except
cherry, with ice cubes in a mixing
glass. Stir well and strain into chilled
cocktail glass. Garnish with cherry.

ROBSON COCKTAIL

4 parts dark rum (2 oz.)
1 part fresh lemon juice (½ oz.)
1 part fresh orange juice (½ oz.)
Grenadine (1 tbsp.)

Combine all ingredients with cracked
ice in a cocktail shaker and shake
well. Strain into chilled cocktail glass.

193

ROCK AND RYE COOLER

4 parts vodka (2 oz.)
3 parts rock and rye (1½ oz.)
2 parts fresh lime juice (1 oz.)
Bitter lemon soda
Lime slice

Combine all ingredients, except soda and lime slice, with cracked ice in a cocktail shaker. Strain into a chilled collins glass over ice cubes and fill with bitter lemon soda. Stir gently and garnish with lime slice.

ROCKY GREEN DRAGON

4 parts gin (2 oz.)
2 parts green Chartreuse (1 oz.)
1 part cognac (½ oz.)

Combine ingredients in a cocktail shaker with cracked ice. Shake well and strain into chilled cocktail glass.

ROLLS ROYCE

6 parts gin (3 oz.)
2 parts dry vermouth (1 oz.)
2 parts sweet vermouth (1 oz.)
Benedictine (¼ tsp.)

Combine all ingredients with ice cubes in a mixing glass. Stir well and strain into chilled cocktail glass.

ROMAŇ COOLER

4 parts gin (2 oz.)
2 parts Punt e Mes (1 oz.)
1 part fresh lemon juice (½ oz.)
Sugar syrup (1 tsp.)
Sweet vermouth (½ tsp.)
Sparking water
Orange twist

Combine all ingredients, except sparkling water and orange twist, with cracked ice in a cocktail shaker. Strain into a chilled highball glass over ice cubes. Fill with sparkling water and stir gently. Garnish with orange twist.

ROMAN SNOWBALL

6 parts white Sambuca (3 oz.)
5 coffee beans

Pour Sambuca into a champagne flute half-filled with crushed ice. Add coffee beans and serve with a straw. Chew the beans after they have been steeping for a while.

ROSE COCKTAIL

4 parts gin (2 oz.)
2 parts apricot brandy (1 oz.)
2 parts dry vermouth (1 oz.)
Grenadine (1 tsp.)
Fresh lemon juice (1 tsp.)
Lemon wedge
Bar sugar

Rim a chilled cocktail glass with sugar by moistening the rim with the lemon wedge and dipping it into a saucer with bar sugar. Discard the lemon wedge. Combine remaining ingredients with cracked ice in a cocktail shaker and shake well. Strain into thesugar-rimmed glass.

ROSE HALL NIGHTCAP

4 parts cognac (2 oz.)
2 parts Pernod (1 oz.)
Dark crème de cacao (1 tbsp.)
4 parts half-and-half (2 oz.)

Combine all ingredients, except crème de cacao, in a cocktail shaker with cracked ice. Shake well and strain into chilled cocktail glass.

ROSELYN COCKTAIL

4 parts gin (2 oz.)
2 parts dry vermouth (1 oz.)
Grenadine (1 tsp.)
Lemon twist

Combine all ingredients, except lemon twist, with ice cubes in a mixing glass. Stir well and strain into chilled cocktail glass. Garnish with lemon twist.

PLEASE NOTE: Blue icons represent alcoholic drinks. Green icons represent non-alcoholic drinks.

ROSITA

4 parts white tequila (2 oz.)
4 parts Campari (2 oz.)
1 part dry vermouth (½ oz.)
1 part sweet vermouth (½ oz.)
Lemon twist

Combine all ingredients, except lemon
twist, in a mixing glass with cracked
ice. Stir well and pour into chilled old-
fashioned glass. Garnish with lemon
twist.

ROSY DAWN

2 parts fresh lemon juice
(1 oz.)
2 parts fresh lime juice (1 oz.)
4 parts fresh orange juice (2 oz.)
1 part coconut cream (½ oz.)
Grenadine (1 tsp.)
Orgeat (almond) syrup (1 tsp.)

Combine all ingredients with cracked
ice in a blender and blend until
smooth. Pour into a chilled cocktail
glass.

ROYAL GIN FIZZ

4 parts gin (2 oz.)
2 parts fresh lemon juice (1 oz.)
Bar sugar (1 tsp.)
1 whole egg
Sparkling water

Combine all ingredients, except
sparkling water, with cracked ice in a
cocktail shaker. Shake vigorously and
strain into a chilled highball glass
over ice cubes. Fill with sparkling
water and stir gently.

ROYAL MATADOR

8 parts gold tequila (4 oz.)
3 parts Framboise (1½ oz.)
Amaretto (1 tbsp.)
4 parts fresh lime juice (2 oz.)
One whole, ripe pineapple

Cut the top off the pineapple and save
it. Scoop out the pineapple, being
careful not to damage the shell. Put
pineapple chunks in blender, and
liquify. Strain the pineapple juice and
put it back in the blender. Add
remaining ingredients and cracked
ice,blend until slushy, and pour into
pineapple shell. Add more ice if

necessary. Replace pineapple "lid"
and serve with straws. Serves 2.

ROYAL ROOST

4 parts bourbon (2 oz.)
2 part Dubonnet rouge (1 oz.)
White Curaçao (¼ tsp.)
Pernod (¼ tsp.)
Dash Peychaud's bitters
Lemon twist
Orange slice
Pineapple spear

Combine all ingredients, except fruit,
with cracked ice in a mixing glass.
Stir and strain into chilled old-
fashioned glass over ice cubes.
Garnish with fruit.

ROYAL SMILE
COCKTAIL

4 parts apple brandy (2 oz.)
2 parts gin (1 oz.)
2 parts fresh lemon juice (1 oz.)
Grenadine (1 tsp.)

Combine ingredients with ice cubes in
a mixing glass and stir. Strain into
chilled cocktail glass.

RUBY FIZZ

6 parts sloe gin (3 oz.)
3 parts fresh lemon juice (1½ oz.)
Grenadine (1 tbsp.)
Sugar syrup (1 tsp.)
1 egg white
Sparkling water

Combine all ingredients, except
sparkling water, with cracked ice in a
cocktail shaker. Shake well and strain
into chilled highball glass over ice
cubes. Fill with sparkling water and
stir gently.

RUM BUCK

4 parts light rum (2 oz.)
2 parts fresh lime juice (1 oz.)
Ginger ale
Lime slice

Combine rum and lime juice with
cracked ice in a cocktail shaker. Shake
well and pour into chilled collins
glass. Fill with ginger ale and stir
gently. Garnish with lime slice.

RUM COBBLER

4 parts light rum (2 oz.)
4 parts sparkling water (2 oz.)
Bar sugar (1 tsp.)
Pineapple spear
Lime slice
Orange slice

Dissolve sugar in sparkling water in the bottom of a chilled wine glass. Fill glass with crushed ice and add rum. Stir and garnish with fruits.

RUM COLLINS

6 parts light rum (3 oz.)
3 parts fresh lime juice (1½ oz.)
Bar sugar (1 tsp.)
Sparkling water
Lemon slice
Maraschino cherry

Combine all ingredients, except sparkling water and fruit, with cracked ice in a cocktail shaker. Shake well and strain into chilled collins glass over ice cubes. Fill with sparkling water and stir gently. Garnish with fruit.

RUM COOLER

6 parts light rum (3 oz.)
Sugar syrup (1 tsp.)
Ginger ale
Orange twist

Pour rum and sugar syrup into a chilled collins glass. Fill with ice cubes and ginger ale. Stir gently and garnish with orange twist.

RUM DAISY

4 parts gold rum (2 oz.)
2 parts fresh lemon juice (2 oz.)
Bar sugar (1 tsp.)
Grenadine (½ tsp.)
Maraschino cherry
Orange slice

Combine all ingredients, except fruit, with cracked ice in a cocktail shaker. Shake well and strain into chilled old-fashioned glass over ice cubes. Garnish with fruit.

RUM DUBONNET

4 parts light rum (2 oz.)
1 part Dubonnet rouge (½ oz.)
1 part fresh lemon juice (½ oz.)

Combine ingredients with cracked ice in a cocktail shaker. Shake well and strain into chilled cocktail glass.

RUM FIX

4 parts gold rum (2 oz.)
2 parts fresh lemon juice (1 oz.)
1 part water (½ oz.)
Bar sugar (1 tsp.)
Maraschino cherry
Lemon slice

Combine sugar, lemon juice and water in a cocktail shaker with cracked ice. Shake well and strain into a chilled highball glass filled with crushed ice. Add rum and stir well. Garnish with fruit.

RUM MARTINI

6 parts light rum (3 oz.)
Dry vermouth (½ tsp.)
Dash orange bitters

Combine ingredients with ice cubes in a mixing glass. Stir well and strain into chilled cocktail glass.

RUM OLD FASHIONED

4 parts light rum (2 oz.)
151-proof Demerara rum (1 tbsp.)
Sugar syrup (½ tsp.)
Dash Angostura bitters
Lime twist

Put bitters and syrup in chilled old-fashioned glass. Stir and add ice cubes. Add light rum and stir again. Float Demerara rum on top and garnish with lime twist.

RUM PUNCH

6 parts dark rum (3 oz.)
2 parts fresh lime juice (1 oz.)
Brown sugar (2 tbsp.)
Bar sugar (1 tbsp.)
Grenadine (1 tsp.)

Combine all ingredients with cracked ice in a blender. Blend until smooth and pour into chilled collins glass.

RUM SCREWDRIVER

4 parts dark rum (2 oz.)
Fresh orange juice

Pour rum into chilled highball glass over ice cubes. Fill with orange juice and stir.

RUM SOUR

4 parts light rum (2 oz.)
2 parts fresh lemon juice (1 oz.)
Bar sugar (1 tsp.)
Lemon slice
Maraschino cherry

Combine all ingredients, except fruit, with cracked ice in a cocktail shaker. Shake well and strain into chilled sour glass. Garnish with fruit.

RUM SWIZZLE

4 parts dark rum (2 oz.)
3 parts fresh lime juice (1½ oz.)
2 dashes Angostura bitters
Bar sugar (1 tsp.)
Sparkling water

Combine all ingredients, except sparkling water, in a cocktail shaker with cracked ice. Strain over ice cubes into chilled collins glass. Fill with sparkling water and stir gently. Serve with a swizzle stick.

RUMFUSTIAN

16 parts ale (1 cup or 8 oz.)
4 parts gin (2 oz.)
4 parts fino sherry (2 oz.)
Sugar (1 tsp.)
2 egg yolks
Lemon twist
Cinnamon stick
5 whole cloves
Dash allspice
Freshly grated nutmeg

Beat eggs and sugar in a bowl. Set aside. In a saucepan, combine all remaining ingredients, except nutmeg, and heat until almost at a boil. Add egg mixture, stirring constantly with a wire whisk for about 45 seconds. Serve in heated mug and sprinkle with nutmeg.

RUSSIAN BEAR

4 parts vodka (2 oz.)
2 parts dark crème de cacao (1 oz.)
1 part half-and-half (½ oz.)

Combine all ingredients with cracked ice in a cocktail shaker. Shake well and strain into a chilled cocktail glass.

RUSSIAN COCKTAIL

4 parts vodka (2 oz.)
3 parts gin (1½ oz.)
3 parts white crème de cacao (1½ oz.)

Combine ingredients with cracked ice in a cocktail shaker. Shake well and strain into chilled cocktail glass.

RUSSIAN COFFEE

4 parts coffee liqueur (2 oz.)
2 parts vodka (1 oz.)
3 parts half-and-half (1½ oz.)

Combine all ingredients in a blender with cracked ice. Blend until smooth and pour into chilled brandy snifter.

RUSSIAN QUAALUDE

4 parts vodka (2 oz.)
2 parts Frangelico (1 oz.)
2 parts Irish cream liqueur (1 oz.)

Combine ingredients with cracked ice in a cocktail shaker. Shake well and pour into chilled old-fashioned glass.

RUSSIAN ROSE

6 parts vodka (3 oz.)
1 part grenadine (½ oz.)
Dash orange bitters

Combine all ingredients with cracked ice in a cocktail shaker. Shake well and strain into chilled cocktail glass.

RUSTY NAIL

4 parts scotch (2 oz.)
2 parts Drambuie (1 oz.)

Pour ingredients into a chilled old-fashioned glass over ice cubes and stir.

RYE FLIP

4 parts rye (2 oz.)
Sugar syrup (1 tsp.)
1 whole egg
Freshly ground nutmeg

Combine all ingredients, except nutmeg, with cracked ice in a cocktail shaker. Shake vigorously and strain into chilled wine glass. Sprinkle nutmeg on top.

RYE WHISKEY COCKTAIL

6 parts rye (3 oz.)
Bar sugar (1 tsp.)
Dash Angostura bitters
Maraschino cherry

Combine all ingredients, except cherry, with cracked ice in a cocktail shaker. Shake well and strain into chilled cocktail glass. Garnish with cherry.

S.F. SOUR

4 parts blended whiskey (2 oz.)
2 parts Benedictine (1 oz.)
Fresh lemon juice (1 tsp.)
Fresh lime juice (1 tsp.)
Dash grenadine
Orange slice

Combine all ingredients, except
orange slice, in a cocktail shaker with
cracked ice. Strain into chilled sour
glass and garnish with orange slice.

SADIE SMASH

6 parts bourbon (3 oz.)
2 parts sparkling water (1 oz.)
Bar sugar (1 tsp.)
4 fresh mint sprigs
Orange slice
Maraschino cherry

Muddle the mint sprigs with sugar
and sparkling water in the bottom of a
chilled old-fashioned glass. Fill the
glass with ice cubes and add bourbon.
Stir and garnish with fruits.

SAFE SEX ON THE BEACH

4 parts peach nectar (2 oz.)
6 parts cranberry juice (3 oz.)
6 parts pineapple juice (3 oz.)
Maraschino cherry

Pour all ingredients, except cherry,
into a chilled collins glass filled with
ice cubes and stir well. Garnish with
cherry.

SAKETINI

6 parts gin (3 oz.)
1 part sake (½ oz.)
Lemon twist

Combine all ingredients, except lemon
twist, with cracked ice in a cocktail
shaker. Shake well and strain int
chilled cocktail glass. Garnish with
lemon twist.

SALLY'S SUMMER COOLER

6 parts peppermint schnapps (3 oz.)
2 parts fresh lime juice (1 oz.)
Sparkling water
Lime slice

Pour schnapps and lime juice into
chilled collins glass over ice cubes. Fill
with sparkling water and stir gently.
Garnish with lime slice.

SALTY DOG

4 parts vodka (2 oz.)
Grapefruit juice
Coarse salt
Granulated sugar
Lime wedge

Mix salt and sugar together in a
saucer. Moisten rim of chilled old-
fashioned glass with lime wedge. Dip
the rim into the salt/sugar mixture.
Discard lime. Fill glass with ice cubes
and pour in vodka and grapefruit
juice. Stir.

SALTY DOG

SALTY PUPPY

Grapefruit juice
Coarse salt
Granulated sugar
Lime wedge

Mix salt and sugar together in a
saucer. Moisten rim of chilled old-
fashioned glass with lime wedge. Dip
the rim into the salt-sugar mixture.
Discard lime. Fill glass with ice cubes
and grapefruit juice. Stir well.

SAN FRANCISCO
COCKTAIL

3 parts dry vermouth (1½ oz.)
3 parts sweet vermouth (1½ oz.)
3 parts sloe gin (1½ oz.)
3 – 5 dashes Angostura bitters
3 – 5 dashes orange bitters
Maraschino cherry

Combine all ingredients, except
cherry, with cracked ice in a cocktail
shaker. Shake well and strain into
chilled cocktail glass.

SAN JUAN

4 parts light rum (2 oz.)
Brandy (1 tbsp.)
3 parts grapefruit juice (1½ oz.)
Coconut milk (1 tbsp.)
Fresh lime juice (1 tbsp.)

Combine all ingredients, except
brandy, with cracked ice in a blender.
Blend until smooth and pour into
chilled wine glass. Float brandy
on top.

SAN JUAN
CAPISTRANO

4 parts grapefruit juice (2 oz.)
2 parts coconut milk (1 oz.)
2 parts fresh lime juice (1 oz.)
Lime twist

Combine all ingredients with cracked
ice in a blender. Blend until smooth
and pour into chilled wine glass.
Garnish with lime twist.

SAN SEBASTIAN

4 parts gin (2 oz.)
1 part light rum (½ oz.)
1 part triple sec (½ oz.)
1 part fresh lemon juice (½ oz.)
1 part grapefruit juice (½ oz.)

Combine all ingredients with cracked
ice in a cocktail shaker. Shake well
and strain into chilled cocktail glass.

SANCTUARY

4 parts Dubonnet rouge (2 oz.)
2 parts Amer Picon (1 oz.)
2 parts triple sec (1 oz.)
Lemon twist

Combine all ingredients, except lemon
twist, with cracked ice in a cocktail
shaker and shake well. Strain into
chilled cocktail glass and garnish with
lemon twist.

SANGRIA

Dry red wine
(2 bottles – 750-ml. each)
8 parts triple sec (4 oz.)
6 parts brandy (3 oz.)
6 parts fresh orange juice (3 oz.)
4 parts fresh lemon juice (2 oz.)
4 parts fresh lime juice (2 oz.)
Sugar syrup (½ cup or 4 oz.)
Lemon slices
Lime slices
Orange slices

Chill all ingredients for at least one
hour. Pour into punch bowl and stir.
Add a large cake of ice and float fruit
slices on top. Serves 20.

SANGRITA

32 parts tomato juice
(1 pint or 16 oz.)
16 parts fresh orange juice (1 cup or
8 oz.)
6 parts fresh lime juice (3 oz.)
½ jalapeno pepper, seeded and
chopped fine
Tabasco sauce (1 tbsp.)
Worcestershire sauce (2 tsp.)
White pepper (¼ tsp.)
Celery salt to taste
4 parts silver tequila per person
(2 oz.)

SANGRIA (from Bolo)

Pour all ingredients, except tequila, in a large pitcher. Chill for at least one hour (the longer you chill this, the spicier it gets). When ready to serve, strain into a fresh pitcher. Pour the tequila into one shot glass; the sangrita into another. Drink the tequila in one swallow and chase it with a shot of sangrita. Serves 14.

SANGRITA SECA

32 parts tomato juice (16 oz.)
16 parts cup fresh orange juice (8 oz.)
6 parts fresh lime juice (3 oz.)
1 jalapeño pepper, seeded and chopped fine
1 part Tabasco sauce (½ oz.)
Worcestershire sauce (2 tsp.)
White pepper (½ tsp.)
Celery salt to taste

Pour all ingredients into a large pitcher. Chill for at least one hour (the longer you chill this, the spicier it gets). When ready to serve, strain into a fresh pitcher. Serve over ice in chilled highball glasses. Serves 6 – 8.

201

SARATOGA COCKTAIL

SANTIAGO COCKTAIL

4 parts light rum (2 oz.)
4 parts fresh lime juice (2 oz.)
Dash grenadine
Sugar syrup (½ tsp.)

Combine ingredients with cracked ice in a cocktail shaker. Shake well and strain into chilled cocktail glass.

SARATOGA COCKTAIL

6 parts brandy (3 oz.)
Maraschino liqueur (½ tsp.)
Fresh lemon juice (1 tsp.)
Pineapple juice (1 tbsp.)

Combine all ingredients with cracked ice in a cocktail shaker. Shake well and strain into chilled cocktail glass.

SAUCY SUE-SUE

4 parts apple brandy (2 oz.)
2 parts apricot brandy (1 oz.)
Pernod (¼ tsp.)
Orange twist

Combine all ingredients, except orange twist, with cracked ice in a cocktail shaker. Shake well and strain into chilled cocktail glass. Garnish with orange twist.

SAUZALIKY

4 parts gold tequila (2 oz.)
Fresh orange juice (½ cup or 4 oz.)
Fresh lime juice (½ tsp.)
½ banana, sliced

Combine all ingredients with cracked ice in a blender and blend until smooth. Pour into chilled wine glass.

SAVOY HOTEL

1½ parts dark crème de cacao (¾ oz.)
1½ parts Benedictine (¾ oz.)
1½ part cognac (¾ oz.)

Pour ingredients, in order given, slowly and carefully into a chilled pousse-café glass so that each ingredient forms a separate layer.

SAXON COCKTAIL

4 parts light rum (2 oz.)
2 parts fresh lime juice (1 oz.)
Grenadine (¼ tsp.)
Orange twist

Combine all ingredients, except orange twist, with cracked ice in a cocktail shaker. Shake well and strain into chilled cocktail glass. Garnish with orange twist.

SAZERAC

6 parts bourbon or rye (3 oz.)
Pernod (½ tsp.)
Bar sugar (½ tsp.)
2 dashes Angostura or Peychaud's bitters
Water (1 tsp.)
Lemon twist

Pour the Pernod into chilled old-fashioned glass and swirl around until inside of the glass is coated. Add the sugar, water and bitters. Muddle until the sugar is dissolved. Fill with ice cubes and add bourbon. Stir well and drop the lemon twist into thedrink.

SCARLETT O'HARA

4 parts Southern Comfort (2 oz.)
4 parts cranberry juice (2 oz.)
2 parts fresh lime juice (1 oz.)

Combine all ingredients with cracked ice in a cocktail shaker and shake well. Strain into chilled cocktail glass.

SCARLETT O'HARA

SCORPION

SCORPION

4 parts gold rum (2 oz.)
2 parts brandy (1 oz.)
1 part orgeat (almond) syrup (½ oz.)
3 parts fresh lemon juice (1½ oz.)
4 parts fresh orange juice (1½ oz.)
Orange slice
Lemon slice

Combine all ingredients, except fruit, with cracked ice in a blender. Blend until smooth and pour into chilled wine glass. Garnish with fruit.

SCOTCH COBBLER

4 parts scotch (2 oz.)
1 part honey (½ oz.)
1 part white Curaçao (½ oz.)
Fresh mint sprig

Combine all ingredients, except mint, with cracked ice in a cocktail shaker. Shake well and strain into chilled old-fashioned glass over ice cubes. Garnish with mint sprig.

SCOTCH COOLER

6 parts scotch (3 oz.)
1 part white crème de menthe (½ oz.)
Sparkling water

Pour scotch and crème de menthe into chilled highball glass over ice cubes. Fill with sparkling water and stir gently.

SCOTCH HOLIDAY SOUR

4 parts scotch (2 oz.)
2 parts cherry Heering (1 oz.)
2 parts fresh lemon juice (1 oz.)
1 part sweet vermouth (½ oz.)
Lemon slice

Combine all ingredients with cracked ice in a cocktail shaker. Shake well and strain into chilled sour glass. Garnish with lemon slice.

SCOTCH MIST

6 parts scotch (3 oz.)
Lemon twist

Pour scotch into a chilled old-fashioned glass filled with crushed ice. Garnish with lemon twist.

SCOTCH SOUR

SCOTCH ORANGE FIX

4 parts scotch (2 oz.)
Triple sec (1 tbsp.)
2 parts fresh lemon juice (1 oz.)
Bar sugar (½ tsp.)
Orange twist

Combine all ingredients, except triple
sec and orange twist, in a cocktail
shaker with cracked ice. Shake well
and strain into chilled highball glass
over ice cubes. Drop orange twist in
drink and float triple sec on top.

SCOTCH SANGAREE

4 parts scotch (2 oz.)
Honey (1 tsp.)
Lemon twist
Sparkling water
Freshly grated nutmeg

Muddle the honey with a little
sparkling water in the bottom of a
chilled highball glass until the honey
is dissolved. Add the scotch, lemon
twist and ice cubes. Fill with sparkling
water and stir gently. Sprinkle nutmeg
on top.

SCOTCH SMASH

6 parts scotch (3 oz.)
Honey (1 tbsp.)
8 fresh mint leaves
Dash orange bitters
Fresh mint sprig

Muddle mint leaves with honey in the
bottom of a chilled highball glass. Fill
the glass with crushed ice and add the
scotch. Stir well and top off with
bitters and mint sprig.

SCOTCH SOUR

4 parts scotch (2 oz.)
2 parts fresh lemon juice (2 oz.)
Sugar syrup (1 tsp.)
Maraschino cherry
Orange slice

Combine liquid ingredients with
cracked ice in a cocktail shaker. Shake
well and strain into chilled cocktail
glass. Garnish with fruit.

SCREWDRIVER

SCREWDRIVER

4 parts vodka
Fresh orange juice
Orange slice

Pour vodka and orange juice into
chilled highball glass over ice cubes.
Stir and garnish with orange slice.

SEA BREEZE

4 parts vodka (2 oz.)
4 parts cranberry juice (2 oz.)
Grapefruit juice

Pour vodka and cranberry juice into a
chilled highball glass filled with ice
cubes. Fill with grapefruit juice and
stir.

SEABOARD

4 parts blended whiskey (2 oz.)
2 parts gin (1 oz.)
1 part fresh lemon juice (½ oz.)
Bar sugar (1 tsp.)
Fresh mint sprig

Combine all ingredients, except mint,
with cracked ice in a cocktail shaker.
Shake well and strain into a chilled
old-fashioned glass over ice cubes.
Garnish with mint sprig.

SEA BREEZE

SECRET

4 parts scotch (2 oz.)
White crème de menthe (½ tsp.)
Sparkling water

Combine scotch and liqueur with
cracked ice in a cocktail shaker and
shake well. Strain into chilled
highball glass over ice cubes and fill
with sparkling water. Stir gently.

SELF-STARTER

4 parts gin (2 oz.)
2 parts Lillet blanc (1 oz.)
1 part apricot brandy (½ oz.)
Pernod (¼ tsp.)

Combine all ingredients with cracked
ice in a cocktail shaker and shake
well. Strain into chilled cocktail glass.

SEPTEMBER MORN

6 parts light rum (3 oz.)
2 parts fresh lime juice (1 oz.)
Grenadine (1 tsp.)
1 egg white

Combine ingredients with cracked ice in a cocktail shaker. Shake vigorously and strain into chilled cocktail glass.

SERPENT'S TOOTH

4 parts Irish whiskey (2 oz.)
2 parts sweet vermouth (1 oz.)
1 part Jagermeister (½ oz.)
3 parts fresh lemon juice (1½ oz.)
3 – 5 dashes Angostura bitters
Lemon twist

Combine all ingredients, except lemon twist, with cracked ice in a cocktail shaker. Shake well and pour into chilled old-fashioned glass. Garnish with lemon twist.

7 & 7

4 parts Seagram's 7-Crown blended whiskey (2 oz.)
7-Up

Pour whiskey into a chilled highball glass over ice cubes. Fill with 7-Up and stir gently.

SEVENTH HEAVEN

4 parts gin (2 oz.)
1 part maraschino liqueur (½ oz.)
1 part grapefruit juice (½ oz.)
Fresh mint sprig

Combine all ingredients, except mint sprig, with cracked ice in a cocktail shaker and shake well. Strain into chilled cocktail glass and garnish with mint sprig.

SEVILLA

4 parts light rum (2 oz.)
4 parts ruby port (2 oz.)
Sugar (½ tsp.)
1 whole egg

Combine ingredients with cracked ice and shake vigorously. Strain into chilled wine glass.

SEVILLE

4 parts gin (2 oz.)
1 part fino sherry (½ oz.)
1 part fresh lemon juice (½ oz.)
1 part fresh orange juice (½ oz.)
Sugar syrup (1 tbsp.)

Combine all ingredients with cracked ice in a cocktail shaker. Shake well and pour into chilled old-fashioned glass.

SEX ON THE BEACH

4 parts vodka (2 oz.)
3 parts peach schnapps (1½ oz.)
6 parts cranberry juice (3 oz.)
6 parts pineapple juice (3 oz.)
Maraschino cherry

Pour all ingredients, except cherry, into a chilled highball glass filled with ice cubes and stir well. Garnish with cherry.

SHADY LADY

4 parts silver tequila (2 oz.)
2 parts melon liqueur (1 oz.)
Grapefruit juice

Stir tequila and liqueur with ice cubes in a chilled highball glass. Fill with grapefruit juice and stir again.

SHAMROCK

4 parts Irish whiskey (2 oz.)
1 part dry vermouth (½ oz.)
1 part green crème de menthe (½ oz.)
Green Chartreuse (1 tsp.)

Combine all ingredients with cracked ice in a cocktail shaker. Shake well and strain into chilled cocktail glass.

SHANDY GAFF

Beer
Ginger ale

Pour equal parts simultaneously into a chilled collins glass.

SHARK ATTACK (from Lucy's)

SHANGHAI COCKTAIL

4 parts dark rum (2 oz.)
1 part Pernod (½ oz.)
2 parts fresh lemon juice (1 oz.)
Grenadine (¼ tsp.)

Combine all ingredients with cracked
ice in a cocktail shaker and shake
well. Strain into chilled cocktail glass.

SHARK ATTACK

6 parts vodka (3 oz.)
3 parts lemonade (1½ oz.)
2 dashes grenadine

In a collins glass over ice cubes, pour
in ingredients and stir.

SHARK'S TOOTH

SHARK BITE

4 parts dark rum (2 oz.)
6 parts fresh orange juice
(3 oz.)
2 parts fresh lemon juice (1 oz.)
2 parts grenadine (1 oz.)

Combine all ingredients with cracked ice in a blender. Blend until smooth and pour into chilled wine glass.

SHARK'S TOOTH

4 parts 151-proof rum (2 oz.)
2 parts fresh lime juice (1 oz.)
2 parts fresh lemon juice (1 oz.)
Dash grenadine
Sugar syrup (¼ tsp.)
Sparkling water
Lime wedge

Combine all ingredients, except sparkling water and lime, with cracked icein a cocktail shaker. Shake well and pour into chilled highball glass. Fill with sparkling water and garnish with lime wedge.

SHARKY PUNCH

4 parts apple brandy (2 oz.)
2 parts rye (1 oz.)
Bar sugar (½ tsp.)
Sparkling water

Combine all ingredients, except sparkling water, with cracked ice in a cocktail shaker. Shake well and pour into chilled old-fashioned glass. Fill with sparkling water and stir gently.

SHERRY AND EGG

Manzanilla sherry
1 whole egg

Carefully break one egg into a chilled wine glass so the yolk does not rupture. Fill with sherry.

SHERRY COBBLER

8 parts Amontillado sherry
(½ cup or 4 oz.)
White Curaçao (¼ tsp.)
Sugar syrup (¼ tsp.)
Lemon twist
Pineapple spear

Fill a wine glass with crushed ice and add the Curaçao and syrup. Stir well until a frost appears on the glass. Add the sherry and stir again. Garnish with lemon twist and pineapple spear.

SHERRY COCKTAIL

6 parts Amontillado sherry
(3 oz.)
3 dashes Angostura bitters
Orange twist

Stir ingredients with ice cubes in a mixing glass. Strain into chilled cocktail glass and garnish with orange twist.

SHERRY EGGNOG

6 parts cream sherry (3 oz.)
Bar sugar (½ tsp.)
1 whole egg
Milk
Freshly grated nutmeg

Combine all ingredients, except milk
and nutmeg, with cracked ice in a
cocktail shaker. Shake vigorously.
Strain into chilled collins glass, fill
with milk and stir well. Sprinkle
nutmeg on top.

SHERRY FLIP

4 parts fino sherry (2 oz.)
Bar sugar (1 tsp.)
1 part half-and-half (½ oz.)
1 whole egg
Freshly grated nutmeg

Combine all ingredients, except
nutmeg, with cracked ice in a cocktail
shaker. Shake vigorously and strain
into chilled sour glass. Sprinkle
nutmeg on top.

SHERRY SANGAREE

4 parts fino sherry (2 oz.)
Ruby port (1 tbsp.)
Bar sugar (½ tsp.)
Water (1 tsp.)
2 parts sparkling water (1 oz.)

In the bottom of a chilled old-
fashioned glass, dissolve sugar in
water, add sherry and stir. Fill glass
with ice cubes and sparkling water.
Float port on top.

SHERRY TWIST

4 parts cream sherry (2 oz.)
2 parts brandy (1 oz.)
1 part dry vermouth (½ oz.)
1 part white Curaçao (½ oz.)
Fresh lemon juice (1 tsp.)
Orange twist

Combine all ingredients, except
orange twist, with cracked ice in a
cocktail shaker. Shake well and strain
into chilled cocktail glass. Garnish
with orange twist.

SHIRLEY TEMPLE

2 parts fresh lemon juice
(2 oz.)
1 part sugar syrup (½ oz.)
1 part grenadine (½ oz.)
Ginger ale
Maraschino cherry
Orange slice

Combine all ingredients, except fruit
and ginger ale, with cracked ice in a
cocktail shaker. Shake well and strain
into chilled old-fashioned glass over
ice cubes. Fill with ginger ale and stir
gently. Garnish with fruit.

SHRINER COCKTAIL

4 parts brandy (2 oz.)
2 parts sloe gin (1 oz.)
3 dashes Angostura bitters
Bar sugar (¼ tsp.)
Lemon twist

Combine all ingredients, except lemon
twist, with cracked ice in a cocktail
shaker. Shake well and strain into
chilled cocktail glass. Garnish with
lemon twist.

SIDECAR

4 parts brandy (2 oz.)
2 parts triple sec (1 oz.)
2 parts fresh lemon juice (1 oz.)

Combine all ingredients with cracked
ice in a cocktail shaker. Shake well
and strain into chilled cocktail glass.

SILK STOCKINGS

4 parts silver tequila (2 oz.)
2 parts white crème de cacao
(1 oz.)
4 parts half-and-half (2 oz.)
Dash grenadine
Ground cinnamon

Combine all ingredients, except
cinnamon, with cracked ice in a
cocktail shaker. Shake well and strain
into chilled cocktail glass. Sprinkle
with cinnamon.

SILVER BULLET

4 parts gin (2 oz.)
2 parts Jagermeister (1 oz.)
1 part fresh lemon juice

Combine all ingredients with cracked ice in a cocktail shaker. Shake well and strain into chilled cocktail glass.

SILVER COCKTAIL

4 parts gin (2 oz.)
2 parts dry vermouth (1 oz.)
Maraschino liqueur (1 tsp.)
3 dashes orange bitters
Lemon twist

Combine all ingredients, except lemon twist, with cracked ice in a cocktail shaker. Shake well and strain into chilled cocktail glass. Garnish with lemon twist.

SILVER FIZZ

6 parts gin (3 oz.)
3 parts fresh lemon juice (1½ oz.)
Bar sugar (1 tsp.)
1 egg white
Sparkling water

Combine all ingredients, except sparkling water, with cracked ice in a cocktail shaker. Shake well and strain into chilled highball glass over ice cubes. Fill with sparkling water and stir gently.

SILVER KING COCKTAIL

4 parts gin (2 oz.)
2 parts fresh lemon juice (1 oz.)
Sugar syrup (1 tsp.)
1 egg white
Dash Angostura bitters

Combine all ingredients with cracked ice in a cocktail shaker and shake vigorously. Strain into chilled cocktail glass.

SILVER STALLION

4 parts gin (2 oz.)
2 parts fresh lime juice (1 oz.)
Scoop vanilla ice cream
Sparkling water

Combine all ingredients, except sparkling water, in a blender with cracked ice. Blend briefly until thick and smooth and pour into chilled highball glass. Fill with sparkling water.

SILVER STREAK

6 parts gin (3 oz.)
3 parts Jagermeister (1½ oz.)

Combine ingredients with cracked ice in a cocktail shaker and shake well. Strain into chilled cocktail glass.

SINGAPORE SLING

6 parts gin (3 oz.)
2 parts cherry brandy (1 oz.)
2 parts fresh lemon juice (1 oz.)
Bar sugar (1 tsp.)
Sparkling water
Maraschino cherry
Orange slice

Combine all ingredients, except sparkling water, brandy and fruit, with cracked ice in a cocktail shaker. Shake well and strain into chilled collins glass over ice cubes. Fill with sparkling water and float brandy on top. Garnish with fruit.

SINGAPORE SLING

211

SINK OR SWIM

4 parts brandy (2 oz.)
1 part sweet vermouth (½ oz.)
3 – 5 dashes Angostura bitters

Combine ingredients with cracked ice
in a cocktail shaker. Shake well and
strain into chilled cocktail glass.

SIR WALTER RALEIGH COCKTAIL

4 parts dark rum (2 oz.)
3 parts brandy (1½ oz.)
1 part grenadine (½ oz.)
1 part white Curaçao (½ oz.)
1 part fresh lemon juice (½ oz.)

Combine ingredients with cracked ice
in a cocktail shaker and shake well.
Strain into chilled cocktail glass.

SLEDGEHAMMER

2 parts apple brandy (1 oz.)
2 parts brandy (1 oz.)
2 parts gold rum (1 oz.)
Pernod (¼ tsp.)

Combine ingredients with cracked ice
in a cocktail shaker. Shake well and
strain into chilled cocktail glass.

SLEEPING BULL

8 parts beef bouillon (4 oz.)
8 parts tomato juice (4 oz.)
Tabasco sauce to taste
Worcestershire sauce (¼ tsp.)
1 part fresh lime juice (½ oz.)
Celery salt to taste
Freshly ground pepper to taste

Combine all ingredients in a
saucepan. Heat well, stirring
occasionally, but do not boil. Pour
into heated coffee mug.

SLEEPY HEAD

6 parts brandy (3 oz.)
5 mint leaves
Ginger ale
Orange twist

Lightly muddle mint leaves with
brandy in the bottom of a chilled

highball glass. Fill with ice cubes and
ginger ale. Stir gently and garnish
with orange twist.

SLIPPERY NIPPLE

4 parts white Sambuca (2 oz.)
2 parts Irish cream liqueur
(1 oz.)
Dash grenadine

Pour Sambuca into chilled cocktail
glass. Float Irish cream on top and
drop grenadine on top in the center of
the drink.

SLOE GIN COCKTAIL

6 parts sloe gin (3 oz.)
Dry vermouth (1 tsp.)
2 dashes Angostura bitters

Stir ingredients with ice cubes in a
mixing glass and strain into chilled
cocktail glass.

SLOE GIN FIZZ

4 parts sloe gin (2 oz.)
3 parts fresh lemon juice (1½ oz.)
Sugar syrup (1 tsp.)
Sparkling water
Lemon slice

Combine all ingredients, except sparkling water and lemon slice, with
cracked ice in a cocktail shaker. Shake
well and strain into a chilled highball
glass over ice cubes. Fill with sparkling water, stir gently and garnish
with lemon slice.

SLOE GIN FLIP

4 parts sloe gin (2 oz.)
2 parts half-and-half (1 oz.)
Bar sugar (½ tsp.)
1 whole egg
Freshly grated nutmeg

Combine all ingredients, except
nutmeg, with cracked ice in a cocktail
shaker. Shake vigorously and strain
into chilled sour glass. Sprinkle with
nutmeg.

SLOE SCREW (from The Royalton)

SLOE GIN RICKEY

4 parts sloe gin (2 oz.)
2 parts fresh lime juice (1 oz.)
Sparkling water
Lime slice

Pour sloe gin and lime juice into a
chilled highball glass over ice cubes.
Fill with sparkling water and stir
gently. Garnish with lime slice.

SLOE SCREW

4 parts sloe gin (2 oz.)
Fresh orange juice

Pour sloe gin into a chilled highball
glass over ice cubes. Fill with orange
juice and stir.

PLEASE NOTE: Blue icons represent
alcoholic drinks. Green icons represent
non-alcoholic drinks.

SLOE TEQUILA

4 parts silver tequila (2 oz.)
2 parts sloe gin (1 oz.)
1 part fresh lime juice (½ oz.)
Cucumber slice

Combine all ingredients, except cucumber, with cracked ice in a blender. Blend until slushy and pour into chilled old-fashioned glass. Add more ice if necessary and garnish with cucumber.

SLOE VERMOUTH

4 parts dry vermouth (2 oz.)
2 parts sloe gin (1 oz.)
1 part fresh lemon juice (½ oz.)

Combine all ingredients with cracked ice in a cocktail shaker. Shake well and strain into chilled cocktail glass.

SLOPPY JOE'S COCKTAIL

4 parts light rum (2 oz.)
3 parts dry vermouth (1½ oz.)
Grenadine (½ tsp.)
Triple sec (½ tsp.)
3 parts fresh lime juice (1½ oz.)

Combine all ingredients with cracked ice in a cocktail shaker. Shake well and strain into chilled cocktail glass.

SLOPPY RUDY'S COCKTAIL

4 parts brandy (2 oz.)
3 parts ruby port (1½ oz.)
Grenadine (½ tsp.)
Triple sec (½ tsp.)
3 parts pineapple juice (1½ oz.)

Combine all ingredients with cracked ice in a cocktail shaker. Shake well and strain into chilled cocktail glass.

SLOW COMFORTABLE SCREW

4 parts vodka (2 oz.)
2 parts Southern comfort (1 oz.)
1 part sloe gin (½ oz.)
Fresh orange juice

Combine all ingredients, except orange juice, in a cocktail shaker with cracked ice. Strain into a chilled highball glass over ice cubes and fill with orange juice. Stir well.

SMILER COCKTAIL

2 parts dry vermouth (1 oz.)
2 parts sweet vermouth (1 oz.)
2 parts gin (1 oz.)
Dash Angostura bitters
Fresh orange juice (½ tsp.)

Combine all ingredients with cracked ice in a cocktail shaker. Shake well and strain into chilled cocktail glass.

SMOKIN' TEXAS MARY

6 parts vodka (3 oz.)
1 part fresh lime juice (1 oz.)
1 part barbecue sauce (1 oz.)
Tabasco sauce to taste
3 – 5 dashes Worcestershire sauce
Freshly ground pepper
Tomato juice
Pickled jalapeno pepper
Lime slice

Combine all ingredients, except tomato juice, jalapeno and lime slice, in a cocktail shaker with cracked ice. Shake well and pour into chilled highball glass. Fill with tomato juice and stir. Garnish with jalapeno and lime slice.

SNEAKY PETE

4 parts silver tequila or mescal (2 oz.)
2 parts white crème de menthe (1 oz.)
2 parts fresh lime juice (1 oz.)
2 parts pineapple juice (1 oz.)
Lime slice

Combine all ingredients, except lime slice, with cracked ice in a cocktail shaker. Shake well and strain into chilled cocktail shaker. Garnish with lime slice.

SNOWBALL

4 parts gin (2 oz.)
2 parts Pernod (1 oz.)
1 part half-and-half (½ oz.)

Combine ingredients with cracked ice in a cocktail shaker. Shake well and strain into chilled cocktail glass.

SOMBRERO

SOBER STRAWBERRY COLADA

2 parts coconut cream (1 oz.)
10 parts pineapple juice (5 oz.)
6 fresh strawberries
Pineapple spear

Combine all ingredients, except
pineapple spear and one strawberry, in
a blender with cracked ice. Blend until
smooth and pour into chilled highball
glass. Garnish with pineapple and
remaining strawberry.

SOMBRERO

4 parts coffee liqueur (2 oz.)
2 parts half-and-half (1 oz.)

Pour liqueur into chilled old-
fashioned glass over ice cubes. Float
half-and-half on top.

SOUL KISS

4 parts bourbon (2 oz.)
2 parts dry vermouth (1 oz.)
1 part Dubonnet rouge (½ oz.)
1 part fresh orange juice (½ oz.)

Combine ingredients with cracked ice in a cocktail shaker. Shake well and strain into chilled cocktail glass.

SOUTH PACIFIC

4 parts brandy (2 oz.)
2 parts vodka (1 oz.)
6 parts pineapple juice (3 oz.)
2 parts fresh lemon juice (1 oz.)
Grenadine (¼ tsp.)

Combine ingredients with cracked ice in a cocktail shaker. Shake well and strain into chilled sour glass.

216

SOUTHERN BRIDE

6 parts gin (3 oz.)
Maraschino liqueur (1 tsp.)
4 parts grapefruit juice (2 oz.)

Combine ingredients with cracked ice in a cocktail shaker. Shake well and strain into chilled cocktail glass.

SOUTHERN GIN COCKTAIL

6 parts gin (3 oz.)
1 part triple sec (½ oz.)
3 dashes orange bitters
Lemon twist

Combine all ingredients, except lemon twist, with ice cubes in a mixing glass. Stir well and strain into chilled cocktail glass. Garnish with lemon twist.

SOUTHERN GINGER

4 parts 100-proof bourbon (2 oz.)
1 part ginger brandy (½ oz.)
1 part fresh lemon juice (½ oz.)
Ginger ale
Lemon twist

Combine all ingredients, except ginger ale and lemon twist, with cracked ice in a cocktail shaker and pour into chilled highball glass. Fill with ginger ale and stir gently. Garnish with lemon twist.

SOUTHSIDE COCKTAIL

6 parts gin (3 oz.)
3 parts fresh lemon juice (1½ oz.)
Bar sugar (1 tsp.)
Fresh mint sprig

Combine all ingredients, except mint, with cracked ice in a cocktail shaker. Shake well and strain into chilled cocktail glass. Garnish with mint.

SOVIET COCKTAIL

6 parts vodka (3 oz.)
2 parts Manzanilla sherry (1 oz.)
1 part dry vermouth (½ oz.)
Lemon twist

Combine all ingredients, except lemon twist, with cracked ice in a cocktail shaker. Shake well and pour into chilled old-fashioned glass over ice cubes. Garnish with lemon twist.

SOYER AU CHAMPAGNE

Cognac (¼ tsp.)
Maraschino liqueur (¼ tsp.)
Triple sec (¼ tsp.)
Vanilla ice cream (2 heaping tbsp.)
Champagne or sparkling water
Maraschino cherry

Mix ice cream with cognac and liqueurs in a chilled wine glass. Fill with champagne and stir gently. Garnish with cherry.

SPANISH MOSS

6 parts white tequila (3 oz.)
2 parts coffee liqueur (1 oz.)
1 part green crème de menthe (½ oz.)

Combine ingredients with cracked ice in a cocktail shaker. Strain into chilled old fashioned glass over ice cubes.

SPANISH TOWN COCKTAIL

6 parts light rum (3 oz.)
1 part triple sec (½ oz.)

Combine ingredients in a mixing glass with ice cubes and stir. Strain into chilled cocktail glass.

SPARKLING PEACH MELBA

Frozen raspberries (¼ cup)
8 parts peach nectar (4 oz.)
Sparkling water

Puree the raspberries and strain out
the seeds. Combine with peachnectar
in a cocktail shaker and shake well.
Pour into chilled collins glass and fill
with sparkling water. Stir gently.

SPECIAL ROUGH

4 parts apple brandy (2 oz.)
3 parts brandy (1½ oz.)
Pernod (1 tsp.)

Combine ingredients with ice cubes in
a mixing glass. Stir well and strain
into chilled cocktail glass.

SPENCER COCKTAIL

4 parts gin (2 oz.)
2 parts apricot brandy (1 oz.)
Fresh orange juice (½ tsp.)
Dash Angostura bitters
Maraschino cherry
Orange twist

Combine all ingredients, except fruit,
with cracked ice in a cocktail shaker.
Shake well and strain into chilled
cocktail glass. Garnish with cherry
and orange twist.

SPICED ICED COFFEE

64 parts strong hot black
coffee (32 oz.)
Cinnamon sticks, 4
Whole cloves, 12
Ground nutmeg (½ tsp.)
Ground ginger (½ tsp.)
Peels of 2 lemons and 2 oranges cut
into thin strips
4 sugar cubes

In a heat proof pitcher, mash together
the cinnamon, cloves, fruit peel and
sugar. Add hot coffee, stir and chill in
refrigerator. Serve over ice in chilled
highball glasses. Serves 6 – 8.

SPRITZER

6 parts red or white wine
(3 oz.)
Sparkling water
Lemon twist

Pour wine into chilled wine glass over
ice cubes. Fill with sparkling water
and garnish with lemon twist.

ST. MARK'S PLACE LEMONADE

4 parts fresh lemon juice (2 oz.)
4 parts fresh lime juice (2 oz.)
Bar sugar (1 tsp.)
Passion fruit syrup (2 tsp.)
Sparkling water
Orange slice

Combine juices, sugar, and syrup in a
cocktail shaker with cracked ice.
Shake well. Strain into a chilled
highball glass almost filled with ice
cubes. Top off with sparkling water.
Stir gently and garnish with orange
slice.

ST. PETERSBURG

6 parts vodka (3 oz.)
Orange bitters (½ tsp.)
Orange slice

Pour vodka and bitters into a mixing
glass with cracked ice. Stir well and
strain into chilled old-fashioned glass
over ice cubes. Garnish with orange
slice.

STANLEY SPRITZER

4 parts fresh lime juice (2 oz.)
4 parts fresh orange juice (2 oz.)
Ginger ale
Lime slice

Combine all ingredients, except ginger
ale and lime slice, with cracked ice in
a cocktail shaker. Shake well and
strain into a chilled collins glass over
ice cubes. Fill with ginger ale and stir
gently. Garnish with lime slice.

STAR COCKTAIL

4 parts apple brandy (2 oz.)
2 parts sweet vermouth (1 oz.)
Dash Angostura bitters
Lemon twist

Combine all ingredients, except for lemon twist, with cracked ice in a cocktail shaker. Shake well and strain into chilled cocktail glass. Garnish with lemon twist.

STAR DAISY

4 parts gin (2 oz.)
3 parts apple brandy (1½ oz.)
3 parts fresh lemon juice (1½ oz.)
Triple sec (½ tsp.)
Sugar syrup (1 tsp.)

Combine ingredients with cracked ice in a cocktail shaker. Shake well and strain into chilled wine glass.

STARS AND STRIPES

1½ parts cherry Heering
(¾ oz.)
1½ parts half-and-half (¾ oz.)
1½ parts blue Curaçao (¾ oz.)

Pour ingredients carefully, in order
given, into chilled pousse café glass,
so that each ingredient forms a
separate layer.

STEAMING BULL

4 parts white tequila (2 oz.)
6 parts beef bouillon (3 oz.)
6 parts tomato juice (3 oz.)
Tabasco sauce to taste
Worcestershire sauce (¼ tsp.)
1 part fresh lime juice (½ oz.)
Celery salt to taste
Freshly ground pepper to taste

Combine all ingredients, except
tequila, in a saucepan. Heat well but
do not boil. Pour tequila into heated
coffee mug and fill with bouillon
mixture. Stir.

STILETTO

4 parts bourbon (2 oz.)
1 parts amaretto (½ oz.)
2 parts fresh lemon juice (1 oz.)

Combine ingredients with cracked ice
in a cocktail shaker. Shake well and
strain into a chilled old-fashioned
glass over ice cubes.

STINGER

4 parts brandy (2 oz.)
2 parts white crème de menthe (1 oz.)

Combine ingredients with cracked ice
in a cocktail shaker. Shake well and
pour into chilled old-fashioned glass.

STIRRUP CUP

4 parts brandy (2 oz.)
3 parts cherry brandy (1½ oz.)
3 parts fresh lemon juice (1½ oz.)
Bar sugar (1 tsp.)

Combine ingredients with cracked ice
in a cocktail shaker. Shake well and
strain into chilled old-fashioned glass
over ice cubes.

STINGER

STONE FENCE

4 parts scotch (2 oz.)
Dash Angostura bitters
Sparkling apple cider

Pour scotch and bitters into a chilled
highball glass over ice cubes. Fill with
cider and stir.

STRAIGHT LAW COCKTAIL

6 parts amontillado sherry (3 oz.)
2 parts gin (1 oz.)

Combine ingredients with ice cubes in
a mixing glass and stir. Strain into
chilled cocktail glass.

STRAWBERRY COLADA

6 parts gold rum (3 oz.)
2 parts coconut cream (1 oz.)
8 parts pineapple juice (4 oz.)
6 fresh strawberries
Pineapple spear

Combine all ingredients, except
pineapple spear and one strawberry, in
a blender with cracked ice. Blend until
smooth and pour into chilled collins
glass. Garnish with pineapple and
remaining strawberry.

STRAWBERRY COLADA

STRAWBERRY DAIQUIRI

4 parts light rum (2 oz.)
2 parts fresh lime juice (1 oz.)
Sugar syrup (1 tsp.)
7 large fresh strawberries (if it's not
the season, frozen are fine)

Combine all ingredients, except for
one strawberry, with cracked ice in a
blender. Blend until smooth and pour
into chilled cocktail glass. Garnish
with remaining strawberry.

STRAWBERRY MARGARITA

4 parts silver tequila (2 oz.)
Triple sec (1 tbsp.)
1 part strawberry syrup (½ oz.)
4 parts fresh lime juice (2 oz.)
Fresh strawberry
Coarse salt
Lime wedge

Rim a chilled cocktail glass with
coarse salt by rubbing the lime wedge
along the rim and dipping it into a
saucer of coarse salt. Combine the remaining ingredients with cracked ice
in a cocktail shaker and shake well.
Strain into a chilled cocktail glass and
garnish with fresh strawberry.

221

STRAWBERRY/ BANANA KEFIR

1 banana, sliced
Fresh strawberries (1 cup)
2 parts honey (1 oz.)
16 parts vanilla yogurt (8 oz.)
16 parts apple juice (8 oz.)

Combine all ingredients, except apple juice, in a blender and blend until smooth. Slowly pour apple juice while continuing to blend at low speed until desired liquid consistency is achieved. Chill in a pitcher and serve in chilled highball glasses garnished with fresh strawberries. Serves 4.

Note: Using the honey/yogurt/juice combinations, you may create other fruit kefirs.

SUBMARINO

STREGA FLIP

4 parts Strega (2 oz.)
2 parts brandy (1 oz.)
2 parts fresh lemon juice (1 oz.)
3 parts fresh orange juice (1½ oz.)
1 part sugar syrup (½ oz.)
1 whole egg
Freshly grated nutmeg

Combine all ingredients, except nutmeg, with cracked ice in a blender. Blend until smooth and pour into chilled highball glass. Sprinkle with nutmeg.

STREGA SOUR

4 parts gin (2 oz.)
2 parts Strega (1 oz.)
2 parts fresh lemon juice (1 oz.)
Lemon slice

Combine all ingredients, except lemon slice, in a cocktail shaker with cracked ice. Shake well and strain into chilled sour glass. Garnish with lemon slice.

SUBMARINO

4 parts white tequila (2 oz.)
Beer

Fill chilled mug ¾ full with beer. Pour tequila into shot glass. Drop the shot glass into the beer.

SUBWAY COOLER

4 parts cherry cider (2 oz.)
8 parts fresh orange juice (4 oz.)
Ginger ale
Maraschino cherry

Combine ingredients, except ginger ale, with cracked ice in a cocktail shaker. Strain over ice cubes into a chilled highball glass. Fill with ginger ale and stir gently. Garnish with cherry.

SUFFERING BASTARD

4 parts gin (2 oz.)
3 parts brandy (1½ oz.)
1 part fresh lime juice (½ oz.)
Sugar syrup (1 tsp.)
Angostura bitters (1 tbsp.)
Ginger beer
Cucumber slice
Mint sprig
Lime slice

Pour bitters into chilled collins glass and swirl around until the inside of the glass is coated. Discard the excess. Fill glass with ice cubes and add gin, brandy, lime juice, and sugar syrup. Stir well and fill with ginger beer. Stir gently and garnish with cucumber slice, lime slice, and mint sprig.

SUFFERING BASTARD

SUISSESSE COCKTAIL

4 parts Pernod (2 oz.)
1 part half-and-half (½ oz.)
1 egg white

Combine ingredients with cracked ice in a cocktail shaker. Shake vigorously and strain into chilled cocktail glass.

SUN TEA

Loose tea of your
choice (2 tbsp.)
60 parts water (30 oz.)
Peel of one lemon
Sugar to taste
Lemon wedges

Combine tea, water and lemon peel in a glass jar and cover. Set in direct sunlight for at least 4 hours. Strain into pitcher and chill. Serve over ice cubes in collins glasses garnished with lemon wedges and sugar to taste.

SWAMP WATER

SWEET AND SOUR BOURBON

4 parts bourbon (2 oz.)
2 parts fresh lemon juice (1 oz.)
6 parts fresh orange juice (3 oz.)
Dash salt
Bar sugar (¼ tsp.)
Maraschino cherry

Combine all ingredients, except cherry, with cracked ice in a cocktail shaker. Shake well and strain into chilled sour glass. Garnish with cherry.

SWEET JANE

4 parts fresh orange juice (2 oz.)
4 parts fresh lime juice (2 oz.)
2 parts coconut cream (1 oz.)
1 part orgeat (almond) syrup (1 oz.)

Combine all ingredients with cracked ice in a blender. Blend at low speed until smooth. Pour into chilled balloon wine glass.

SWEET MARTINI

6 parts gin (3 oz.)
1 part sweet vermouth (½ oz.)
Dash orange bitters
Orange twist

Pour all ingredients, except orange twist, with ice cubes in a mixing glass. Stir well and strain into chilled cocktail glass. Garnish with orange twist.

SUNDOWNER

4 parts gold rum (2 oz.)
2 parts fresh lime juice (1 oz.)
Maraschino liqueur (¼ tsp.)
White Curaçao (¼ tsp.)
Tonic water
Lime slice

Combine all ingredients, except tonic and lime slice, with cracked ice in a cocktail shaker. Strain into chilled highball glass over ice cubes and fill with tonic water. Stir gently and garnish with lime slice.

SWAMP WATER

4 parts dark rum (2 oz.)
1 part blue Curaçao (½ oz.)
3 parts fresh orange juice (1½ oz.)
1 part fresh lemon juice (½ oz.)

Combine all ingredients with cracked ice in a cocktail shaker. Shake well and strain into chilled old-fashioned glass over ice cubes.

T

TAHITI CLUB

6 parts gold rum (3 oz.)
1 part maraschino liqueur (½ oz.)
2 parts pineapple juice (1 oz.)
1 part fresh lemon juice (½ oz.)
1 part fresh lime juice (½ oz.)
Orange slice

Combine all ingredients, except
orange slice, with cracked ice in a
cocktail shaker. Pour into chilled old-
fashioned glass and garnish with
orange slice.

TAHOE JULIUS

4 parts vodka (2 oz.)
8 parts fresh orange juice (4 oz.)
2 parts half-and-half (1 oz.)
Sugar syrup (1 tsp.)
1 whole egg

Combine all ingredients in a blender
and blend until smooth. Pour into
chilled wine glass.

TAILSPIN

4 parts gin (2 oz.)
3 parts green Chartreuse
(1½ oz.)
3 parts sweet vermouth (1½ oz.)
Dash orange bitters
Lemon twist
Maraschino cherry

Pour all ingredients, except cherry
and lemon twist, into a mixing glass
with ice cubes. Stir well and strain
into chilled cocktail glass. Garnish
with lemon twist and cherry.

TAMARINDO

4 parts tamarind syrup (2 oz.)
2 parts grenadine (1 oz.)
Grapefruit juice

Combine all ingredients, except
grapefruit juice, with cracked ice in
a cocktail shaker. Shake well and
pour into a chilled collins glass over
ice cubes. Fill with grapefruit juice
and stir.

TANGO COCKTAIL

4 parts gin (2 oz.)
2 parts dry vermouth (1 oz.)
2 parts sweet vermouth (1 oz.)
1 part triple sec (½ oz.)

Combine ingredients with cracked ice
in a cocktail shaker. Shake well and
strain into chilled cocktail glass.

TEA SANDWICH

8 parts unsweetened pineapple
juice (4 oz.)
8 parts cucumber, peeled, seeded and
chopped (4 oz.)
4 sprigs watercress
1 sprig fresh mint
1 sprig parsley
Fresh lime juice (½ tsp.)

Combine ingredients in a blender with
cracked ice and blend until smooth.
Pour into chilled collins glass.

TEMPTATION COCKTAIL

4 parts blended whiskey (2 oz.)
1 part Cointreau (½ oz.)
1 part Dubonnet rouge (½ oz.)
Pernod (1 tsp.)
Lemon twist

Combine all ingredients, except lemon
twist, with cracked ice in a cocktail
shaker. Shake well and strain into
chilled cocktail glass. Garnish with
lemon twist.

TEMPTER COCKTAIL

4 parts ruby port (2 oz.)
3 parts apricot brandy (1½ oz.)

Pour ingredients into a mixing glass
and stir with ice cubes. Strain into
chilled cocktail glass.

TEN-GALLON COCKTAIL

2 parts gin (1 oz.)
2 parts coffee liqueur (1 oz.)
2 parts sweet vermouth (1 oz.)
Egg yolk

Mix all ingredients in blender or cocktail shaker. Pour into chilled old-fashioned glass.

TENNESSEE

4 parts rye (2 oz.)
2 parts maraschino liqueur
(1 oz.)
2 parts fresh lemon juice (1 oz.)

Combine all ingredients with cracked ice in a cocktail shaker. Shake well and strain into chilled cocktail glass.

TEQUILA COCKTAIL

6 parts gold tequila (3 oz.)
2 parts fresh lime juice (1 oz.)
Grenadine (¼ tsp.)
Dash Angostura bitters

Combine all ingredients in a cocktail shaker with cracked ice. Shake well and strain into chilled cocktail glass.

TEQUILA COLLINS

4 parts silver tequila (2 oz.)
2 parts fresh lemon juice (1 oz.)
Sugar syrup (1 tsp.)
Sparkling water
Maraschino cherry

Pour tequila into a chilled collins glass over ice cubes. Add lemon juice and syrup. Stir well and add sparkling water. Stir gently and garnish with cherry.

TEQUILA FIZZ

6 parts white tequila (3 oz.)
2 parts fresh lime juice (1 oz.)
2 parts grenadine (1 oz.)
1 egg white
Ginger ale

Combine all ingredients, except ginger ale, with cracked ice in a cocktail shaker. Shake vigorously. Strain into chilled collins glass over ice cubes and fill with ginger ale. Stir gently.

TEQUILA GHOST

4 parts silver tequila (2 oz.)
2 parts Pernod (1 oz.)
1 part fresh lemon juice (½ oz.)

Combine ingredients with cracked ice in a cocktail shaker. Shake well and strain into chilled cocktail glass.

TEQUILA GIMLET

6 parts silver tequila (3 oz.)
2 parts Rose's lime juice (1 oz.)
Lime slice

Pour tequila and lime juice into an old-fashioned glass filled with ice cubes. Stir and garnish with lime wedge.

TEQUILA MANHATTAN

6 parts gold tequila (3 oz.)
2 parts sweet vermouth (1 oz.)
Fresh lime juice (1 tsp.)
Maraschino cherry
Orange slice

Combine all ingredients, except fruit, with cracked ice in a cocktail shaker. Shake well and strain into a chilled old-fashioned glass over ice cubes. Garnish with fruit.

TEQUILA MOCKINGBIRD

TEQUILA MARIA

4 parts white tequila (2 oz.)
8 parts tomato juice (4 oz.)
1 part fresh lime juice (½ oz.)
White horseradish (1 tsp.)
Tabasco sauce to taste
3 – 5 dashes Worcestershire sauce
Ground black pepper to taste
Celery salt to taste
Pinch of cilantro
Lime wedge

Combine all ingredients, except lime wedge, with cracked ice in a mixing glass. Pour into chilled old-fashioned glass and garnish with lime wedge.

TEQUILA MOCKINGBIRD

4 parts silver tequila (2 oz.)
2 parts white crème de menthe (1 oz.)
2 parts fresh lime juice (1 oz.)

Combine all ingredients with cracked ice in a cocktail shaker. Shake well and strain into chilled cocktail glass.

TEQUILA OLD-FASHIONED

4 parts gold tequila (2 oz.)
Bar sugar (1 tsp.)
3 – 5 dashes Angostura bitters
Sparkling water
Maraschino cherry

Combine sugar, water and bitters in the bottom of a chilled old-fashioned glass. Fill glass with ice cubes and add tequila. Stir well and garnish with cherry.

TEQUILA SHOT

4 parts tequila of your choice (2 oz.)
Lemon wedge
Salt

Pour tequila into shot glass. Moisten hand between thumb and forefinger and put salt on it. Lick the salt, down the shot, and suck on the lemon.

TEQUILA SOUR

4 parts white tequila (2 oz.)
3 parts fresh lemon juice (1½ oz.)
Bar sugar (1 tsp.)
Lemon slice
Maraschino cherry

Combine all ingredients, except fruit, with cracked ice in a cocktail shaker. Shake well and strain into chilled sour glass. Garnish with fruit.

TEQUILA STINGER

4 parts gold tequila (2 oz.)
2 parts white crème de menthe (1 oz.)

Combine ingredients with cracked ice in a cocktail shaker. Shake well and strain into chilled cocktail glass.

228

TEQUILA SUNRISE

4 parts silver tequila (2 oz.)
Fresh orange juice
2 parts grenadine (1 oz.)

Pour tequila into chilled highball glass over ice cubes. Fill glass with orange juice, leaving a little room on top and stir. Slowly pour in grenadine.

TEQUINI

6 parts silver tequila (3 oz.)
1 part dry vermouth (½ oz.)
Dash Angostura bitters
Lemon twist

Stir all ingredients, except lemon twist, with ice cubes in a mixing glass. Strain into chilled cocktail glass and garnish with lemon twist.

TEQUONIC

4 parts silver tequila (2 oz.)
3 parts fresh lime juice (1½ oz.)
Tonic water
Lime wedge

Pour tequila into chilled highball
glass over ice cubes. Add juice and stir.
Fill with tonic water and garnish with
lime wedge.

TEXAS VIRGIN

2 parts fresh lime juice (1 oz.)
2 parts barbecue sauce (1 oz.)
Tabasco sauce to taste
Worcestershire sauce (3 – 5 dashes)
Freshly ground pepper
Tomato juice
1 pickled jalapeño pepper
Lime slice

Combine all ingredients, except
tomato juice, jalapeno, and lime slice,
in a cocktail shaker with cracked ice.
Shake well and pour into chilled
highball glass. Fill with tomato juice
and stir. Garnish with jalapeno and
lime slice.

THANKSGIVING
SPECIAL COCKTAIL

4 parts gin (2 oz.)
3 parts apricot brandy (1½ oz.)
2 parts dry vermouth (1 oz.)
1 part fresh lemon juice (½ oz.)
Maraschino cherry

Combine all ingredients, except
cherry, with cracked ice in a cocktail
shaker. Shake well and strain into
chilled cocktail glass. Garnish with
cherry.

THIRD DEGREE
COCKTAIL

6 parts gin (3 oz.)
2 parts dry vermouth (1 oz.)
1 part Pernod (½ oz.)

Pour ingredients into mixing glass
with ice cubes. Stir and strain into
chilled cocktail glass.

THIRD RAIL
COCKTAIL

4 parts apple brandy (2 oz.)
4 parts brandy (2 oz.)
1 part light rum (½ oz.)
Pernod (¼ tsp.)

Combine all ingredients with cracked
ice in a cocktail shaker. Shake well
and strain into chilled cocktail glass.

THISTLE COCKTAIL

4 parts scotch (2 oz.)
3 parts sweet vermouth
(1½ oz.)
3 dashes Angostura bitters

Combine ingredients with ice cubes in
a mixing glass. Stir and strain into
chilled cocktail glass.

THREE MILLER
COCKTAIL

4 parts light rum (2 oz.)
2 parts brandy (1 oz.)
1 part grenadine (½ oz.)
1 part fresh lemon juice (½ oz.)

Combine ingredients with ice in a
cocktail shaker. Shake well and strain
into chilled cocktail glass.

THREE STRIPES
COCKTAIL

4 parts gin (2 oz.)
2 parts dry vermouth (1 oz.)
2 parts fresh orange juice (1 oz.)

Combine all ingredients with cracked
ice in a cocktail shaker and shake
well. Strain into chilled cocktail glass.

THUNDER COCKTAIL

4 parts brandy (2 oz.)
Bar sugar (1 tsp.)
Cayenne pepper (¼ tsp.)
1 egg yolk

Combine ingredients with cracked ice
in a cocktail shaker. Shake vigorously
and pour into chilled cocktail glass.

THIRD RAIL

THUNDERCLAP

4 parts blended whiskey
(2 oz.)
2 parts brandy (1 oz.)
2 parts gin (1 oz.)

Combine ingredients with cracked ice
in a cocktail shaker. Shake well and
strain into chilled cocktail glass.

TIDBIT

4 parts gin (2 oz.)
1 part fino sherry (½ oz.)
1 scoop vanilla ice cream

Put all ingredients in a blender and
blend until smooth. Pour into chilled
highball glass.

TIGER TAIL

4 parts Pernod (2 oz.)
8 parts fresh orange juice
(4 oz.)
Cointreau (¼ tsp.)
Lime wedge

Combine all ingredients, except lime
wedge, with cracked ice in a blender.
Blend until smooth and pour into
chilled wine glass. Garnish with lime
wedge.

TIGER'S MILK

4 parts gold rum (2 oz.)
3 parts cognac (1½ oz.)
10 parts milk (5 oz.)
Sugar syrup (1 tsp.)
Ground cinnamon

Combine all ingredients, except
cinnamon, with cracked ice in a
blender. Blend until smooth and pour
into chilled wine glass. Sprinkle
cinnamon on top.

231

TINTORETTO

4 parts Poire William
(2 oz.)
Pureed ripe Anjou pear (¼ cup)
Champagne or sparkling wine

Puree pear in food processor or food
mill and pour into chilled wine glass.
Add the brandy and top off with
champagne. Stir gently.

TIPPERARY
COCKTAIL

4 parts Irish whiskey (2 oz.)
2 parts green Chartreuse (1 oz.)
1 part sweet vermouth (½ oz.)

Combine all ingredients with cracked
ice in a cocktail shaker. Shake well
and strain into chilled cocktail glass.

TOASTED ALMOND

4 parts coffee liqueur (2 oz.)
3 parts amaretto (1½ oz.)
4 parts half-and-half (2 oz.)

Combine ingredients with cracked ice
in a cocktail shaker. Shake well and
strain into chilled old-fashioned glass
over ice cubes.

TOM AND JERRY

4 parts light rum (2 oz.)
2 parts brandy (1 oz.)
12 parts hot milk (6 oz.)
1 whole egg, separated
Freshly ground nutmeg

Beat the white and the yolk of the egg
separately. Mix them together in a
coffee mug glass. Add the sugar and
beat the egg mixture again. Pour in
the rum and brandy. Add the hot milk
and stir gently. Sprinkle with nutmeg.

TOM COLLINS

6 parts gin (3 oz.)
4 parts fresh lemon juice (2 oz.)
1 part sugar syrup (½ oz.)
Sparkling water
Maraschino cherry
Orange slice

Combine all ingredients, except fruit
and sparkling water, in a chilled
collins glass filled with ice cubes. Fill
with sparkling water and stir gently.
Garnish with fruit.

TOMATO
COCKTAIL

32 parts tomato juice
(16 oz.)
2 parts red wine vinegar (1 oz.)
Salt (½ tsp.)
Paprika (⅛ tsp.)
Basil (½ tsp.)
Freshly ground pepper (½ tsp.)
1 whole cucumber, peeled and pureed
4 lime wedges

Combine all ingredients, except lime
wedges, in a glass pitcher and stir well.
Chill and serve over ice cubes in
highball glasses garnished with lime
wedges.

TOREADOR

4 parts white tequila
(2 oz.)
2 parts dark crème de cacao (1 oz.)
2 parts half-and-half (1 oz.)
Whipped cream
Cocoa powder

Combine all ingredients, except
whipped cream and cocoa, with
cracked ice in a blender. Blend until
smooth and pour into chilled wine
glass. Top with whipped cream and
sprinkle cocoa on top.

TORPEDO

4 parts apple brandy (2 oz.)
2 parts brandy (1 oz.)
Gin (¼ tsp.)

Combine ingredients in a cocktail
shaker with cracked ice. Shake well
and strain into chilled cocktail glass.

TORRIDORA COCKTAIL

4 parts light rum (2 oz.)
151-proof rum (1 tbsp.)
2 parts coffee liqueur (1 oz.)
1 parts half-and-half (½ oz.)

Combine all ingredients, except 151-rum, with cracked ice in a cocktail shaker. Shake well and strain into chilled cocktail glass. Float 151-rum on top.

TOVARISCH COCKTAIL

6 parts vodka (3 oz.)
3 parts Jagermeister (1½ oz.)
2 parts fresh lime juice (1 oz.)

Combine ingredients with cracked ice in a cocktail shaker. Shake well and strain into chilled cocktail glass.

TRADE WINDS

4 parts gold rum (2 oz.)
2 parts slivovitz (1 oz.)
2 parts fresh lime juice (1 oz.)
1 part Falernum (½ oz.)

Combine all ingredients with cracked ice in a cocktail shaker. Shake well and strain into chilled cocktail glass.

TRILBY COCKTAIL

6 parts bourbon (3 oz.)
2 parts sweet vermouth (1 oz.)
3 dashes Angostura bitters

Combine all ingredients with cracked ice in a cocktail shaker. Shake well and strain into chilled cocktail glass.

TROIS RIVIERES

4 parts Canadian whisky (2 oz.)
1 part Dubonnet rouge (½ oz.)
Cointreau (1 tbsp.)
Orange twist

Combine all ingredients, except orange twist, in a cocktail shaker with cracked ice. Shake well and strain into chilled cocktail glass. Garnish with orange twist.

TROLLEY COOLER

6 parts bourbon (3 oz.)
Cranberry juice
Grapefruit juice

Pour bourbon into a chilled collins glass filled with ice cubes. Add equal parts of each juice. Stir well.

TROPICAL COCKTAIL

4 parts white crème de cacao (2 oz.)
3 parts maraschino liqueur (1½ oz.)
2 parts dry vermouth (1½ oz.)
Dash Angostura bitters

Combine all ingredients with cracked ice in a cocktail shaker. Shake well and strain into chilled cocktail glass.

TROPICAL STORM

4 parts pineapple juice (2 oz.)
4 parts fresh lime juice (2 oz.)
2 parts passion fruit syrup (1 oz.)
Orgeat (almond) syrup (½ tsp.)
Pineapple spear

Combine all ingredients, except pineapple spear, with cracked ice in a cocktail shaker. Shake well. Pour into chilled old-fashioned glass. Garnish with pineapple spear.

TULIP COCKTAIL

4 parts apple brandy (2 oz.)
3 parts sweet vermouth (1½ oz.)
1 part apricot brandy (½ oz.)
1 parts fresh lemon juice (½ oz.)

Combine ingredients with cracked ice in a cocktail shaker. Shake well and strain into chilled cocktail glass.

TURF COCKTAIL

4 parts gin (2 oz.)
2 parts dry vermouth (1 oz.)
1 part pernod (½ oz.)
1 part fresh lemon juice (½ oz.)
3 dashes Angostura bitters

Combine ingredients with cracked ice in a cocktail shaker. Shake well and strain into chilled cocktail glass.

TUTTI-FRUTTI

6 parts gin (3 oz.)
2 parts amaretto (1 oz.)
2 parts cherry liqueur (1 oz.)
Chopped fresh apples (2 oz.)
Chopped fresh pears (2 oz.)
Chopped fresh peaches (2 oz.)

Combine all ingredients in a blender
with cracked ice. Blend until smooth
and pour into chilled highball glass.
Note: if you must used canned fruit,
use the kind that is packed in its own
juice with no added sugar.

TUXEDO COCKTAIL

4 parts gin (2 oz.)
3 parts dry vermouth (1½ oz.)
Maraschino liqueur (½ tsp.)
3 dashes orange bitters
Maraschino cherry

Combine all ingredients, except
cherry, with ice cubes in a mixing
glass. Stir and strain into chilled
cocktail glass. Garnish with cherry.

TWIN HILLS

4 parts bourbon (2 oz.)
1 part Benedictine (½ oz.)
1 parts fresh lemon juice (½ oz.)
1 part fresh lime juice (½ oz.)
Sugar syrup (1 tsp.)
Lemon slice
Lime slice

Combine all ingredients, except fruit,
with cracked ice in a cocktail shaker.
Strain into chilled sour glass and
garnish with fruit.

TWIN SIX COCKTAIL

4 parts gin (2 oz.)
2 parts sweet vermouth (1 oz.)
Dash grenadine
1 egg white

Combine ingredients with cracked ice
in a cocktail shaker. Shake vigorously
and strain into chilled cocktail glass.

U, V

ULANDA COCKTAIL

4 parts gin (2 oz.)
2 parts triple sec (1 oz.)
Pernod (1 tsp.)

Combine ingredients with ice cubes in a mixing glass and stir. Strain into chilled cocktail glass.

UNDER THE BOARDWALK

4 parts fresh lemon juice (2 oz.)
Bar sugar (½ tsp.)
½ fresh peach, peeled and diced
Fresh raspberries
Sparkling water

Combine all ingredients, except the raspberries and water, in a blender with cracked ice. Blend until slushy and pour into chilled highball glass. Fill with sparkling water and stir gently. Garnish with fresh raspberries.

UNION JACK

4 parts gin (2 oz.)
2 parts sloe gin (1 oz.)
Grenadine (1 tsp.)

Combine ingredients with cracked ice in a cocktail shaker. Shake well and strain into chilled cocktail glass.

UNION LEAGUE CLUB

4 parts gin (2 oz.)
2 parts ruby port (1 oz.)
3 – 5 dashes orange bitters
Orange twist

Combine all ingredients, except orange twist, with cracked ice in a cocktail shaker. Shake well and strain into chilled cocktail glass. Garnish with orange twist.

VALENCIA COCKTAIL

4 parts gin (2 oz.)
2 parts amontillado sherry (1 oz.)
Lemon twist

Combine ingredients, except lemon twist, in mixing glass with ice cubes. Stir and strain into chilled cocktail glass. Garnish with lemon twist.

VANDERBILT COCKTAIL

4 parts brandy (2 oz.)
2 parts cherry brandy (1 oz.)
Bar sugar (½ tsp.)
3 dashes Angostura bitters

Combine ingredients with cracked ice in a cocktail shaker. Shake well and strain into chilled cocktail glass.

VANITY FAIR

4 parts apple brandy (2 oz.)
2 parts kirschwasser (1 oz.)
1 part maraschino liqueur (½ oz.)
Amaretto (1 tbsp.)

Combine all ingredients, except amaretto, with cracked ice in a cocktail shaker. Strain into chilled cocktail glass and float amaretto on top.

VELVET HAMMER

6 parts vodka (3 oz.)
2 parts dark crème de cacao (1 oz.)
2 parts half-and-half (1 oz.)

Combine ingredients with cracked ice in a cocktail shaker. Shake well and strain into chilled cocktail glass.

VELVET KISS

4 parts gin (2 oz.)
1 part crème de bananes
(½ oz.)
2 parts pineapple juice (1 oz.)
2 parts half-and half (1 oz.)
Dash grenadine

Combine ingredients with cracked ice
in a cocktail shaker. Shake well and
strain into chilled cocktail glass.

VERMOUTH CASSIS

4 parts dry vermouth (2 oz.)
2 parts crème de cassis
Sparkling water

Pour vermouth and cassis into chilled
highball glass over ice cubes and stir.
Fill with sparkling water and stir
gently.

VERMOUTH COCKTAIL

3 parts dry vermouth (1½ oz.)
3 parts sweet vermouth (1½ oz.)
Dash Angostura bitters
Maraschino cherry

Combine all ingredients, except
cherry, with ice cubes in a mixing
glass. Stir and strain into chilled
cocktail glass. Garnish with cherry.

VERONA COCKTAIL

4 parts gin (2 oz.)
2 parts amaretto (1 oz.)
1 part sweet vermouth (½ oz.)
Fresh lemon juice (¼ tsp.)
Orange slice

Combine all ingredients, except
orange, with cracked ice in a cocktail
shaker. Shake well and strain into
chilled old-fashioned glass over ice
cubes. Garnish with orange slice.

VIA VENETO

4 parts brandy (2 oz.)
2 parts white Sambuca (1 oz.)
2 parts fresh lemon juice (1 oz.)
Bar sugar (½ tsp.)
1 egg white

Combine all ingredients with cracked ice in a cocktail shaker. Shake vigorously and pour into chilled old-fashioned glass.

VICTOR

4 parts gin (2 oz.)
2 parts brandy (1 oz.)
1 part sweet vermouth (½ oz.)

Combine ingredients with cracked ice in a cocktail shaker. Shake well and strain into chilled cocktail glass.

VICTORY

4 parts Pernod (2 oz.)
2 parts grenadine (1 oz.)
Sparkling water

Combine all ingredients, except sparkling water, in a cocktail shaker with cracked ice. Pour into chilled highball glass and fill with sparkling water. Stir gently.

VIRGIN ISLAND

6 parts pineapple juice (3 oz.)
2 parts coconut cream (1 oz.)
2 parts fresh lime juice (1 oz.)
Orgeat (almond) syrup (½ tsp.)
Pineapple spear

Combine all ingredients, except pineapple spear, in a blender with cracked ice. Blend until slushy and pour into chilled highball glass. Garnish with pineapple spear.

VIRGIN MARY

8 parts tomato juice (4 oz.)
2 parts fresh lime juice (1 oz.)
White horseradish (¼ tsp.)
Tabasco sauce (3 – 5 dashes)
Worcestershire sauce (3 – 5 dashes)
Freshly ground pepper to taste
Salt to taste
Lime wedge

Combine all ingredients, except lime wedge, with cracked ice in a cocktail shaker. Shake well and pour into chilled highball glass. Garnish with lime wedge.

VIVA VILLA

4 parts silver tequila (2 oz.)
4 parts fresh lime juice (2 oz.)
Bar sugar (1 tsp.)
Lime wedge
Coarse salt

Rim a chilled old-fashioned glass with salt by moistening the rim of the glass with the lime wedge and dipping the glass into the salt. Discard the lime. Combine remaining ingredients with cracked ice in a cocktail shaker. Shake well and strain into chilled old-fashioned glass over ice cubes.

VODKA AND TONIC

6 parts vodka (3 oz.)
Tonic water
Lime wedge

Pour vodka into a chilled collins glass over ice cubes. Fill with tonic and stir gently. Garnish with lime wedge.

VODKA COLLINS

6 parts vodka (3 oz.)
4 parts fresh lemon juice (2 oz.)
1 part sugar syrup (½ oz.)
Sparkling water
Maraschino cherry
Orange slice

Combine all ingredients, except fruit and sparkling water, in a chilled collins glass filled with ice cubes. Fill with sparkling water and stir gently. Garnish with fruit.

VODKA COOLER

4 parts vodka (2 oz.)
Bar sugar (½ tsp.)
Sparkling water
Lemon peel

Mix vodka with sugar in the bottom of a chilled collins glass. Add ice cubes and fill with sparkling water. Stir gently and garnish with lemon peel.

VODKA DAISY

6 parts vodka (3 oz.)
2 parts fresh lemon juice (1 oz.)
Grenadine (1 tbsp.)
Sugar syrup (1 tsp.)
Sparkling water
Orange slice

Combine all ingredients, except
orange slice and sparkling water, in a
cocktail shaker with cracked ice.
Shake well. Pour into chilled highball
glass. Top off with sparkling water, stir
gently, and garnish with orange slice.

VODKA GIMLET

6 parts vodka (3 oz.)
2 parts Rose's lime juice (1 oz.)
Lime slice

Pour vodka and lime juice into an
old-fashioned glass filled with ice
cubes. Stir and garnish with lime
wedge.

VODKA GRASSHOPPER

4 parts vodka (2 oz.)
4 parts green crème de menthe (2 oz.)
4 parts white crème de cacao (2 oz.)

Combine all ingredients with cracked
ice in a cocktail shaker and shake
well. Strain into chilled cocktail glass.

VODKA MARTINI

6 parts iced vodka (3 oz.)
Dry vermouth (⅛ – ¼ tsp.)
Cocktail olive

Combine vodka and vermouth with
cracked ice in a mixing glass. Stir well
and strain into chilled cocktail glass.
Garnish with olive.

VODKA SLING

4 parts vodka (2 oz.)
1 part fresh lemon juice (1 oz.)
Water (1 tsp.)
Bar sugar (1 tsp.)
Orange twist

In the bottom of a mixing glass,
dissolve sugar in water and lemon
juice. Add vodka and stir. Pour over ice
cubes into a chilled old-fashioned
glass and garnish with orange twist.

VODKA SOUR

4 parts vodka (2 oz.)
3 parts fresh lemon juice (1½ oz.)
Bar sugar (1 tsp.)
Lemon slice
Maraschino cherry

Combine all ingredients, except fruit,
with cracked ice in a cocktail shaker.
Shake well and strain into chilled sour
glass. Garnish with fruit.

VODKA STINGER

4 parts vodka (2 oz.)
2 parts white crème de menthe
(1 oz.)

Combine ingredients with cracked ice
in a cocktail shaker. Shake well and
strain into chilled cocktail glass.

VOLGA BOATMAN

4 parts vodka (2 oz.)
2 parts kirschwasser (1 oz.)
2 parts fresh orange juice
Maraschino cherry

Combine all ingredients, except
cherry, with cracked ice in a cocktail
shaker. Strain into chilled cocktail
glass and garnish with cherry.

W

WAIKIKI BEACHCOMBER

4 parts vodka (2 oz.)
1 part raspberry liqueur (½ oz.)
2 parts fresh lime juice (1 oz.)
10 parts guava juice (5 oz.)

Combine all ingredients, except liqueur, with cracked ice in a cocktail shaker. Pour into chilled collins glass and float liqueur on top.

WALDORF COCKTAIL

4 parts bourbon (2 oz.)
2 parts Pernod (1 oz.)
1 part sweet vermouth (½ oz.)
Dash Angostura bitters

Combine all ingredients with cracked ice in a cocktail shaker. Shake well and strain into chilled cocktail glass.

WALKING ZOMBIE

4 parts fresh lime juice (2 oz.)
4 parts fresh orange juice (2 oz.)
4 parts pineapple juice (2 oz.)
4 parts guava nectar (2 oz.)
2 parts grenadine (1 oz.)
1 part orgeat (almond) syrup (½ oz.)
Fresh mint sprig
Pineapple spear

Combine all ingredients, except mint and pineapple spear, with cracked ice in a blender. Blend until smooth. Pour into chilled collins glass and garnish with pineapple and mint sprig.

WALTERS

6 parts scotch (3 oz.)
1 part fresh lemon juice (½ oz.)
1 part fresh orange juice (½ oz.)

Combine ingredients with cracked ice in a cocktail shaker. Shake well and strain into chilled cocktail glass.

WARD EIGHT

4 parts blended whiskey (2 oz.)
3 parts fresh lemon juice (1½ oz.)
Grenadine (1 tsp.)
Bar sugar (1 tsp.)

Combine ingredients with cracked ice in a cocktail shaker. Shake well and strain into chilled wine glass filled with cracked ice.

WARDAY'S COCKTAIL

3 parts gin (1½ oz.)
2 parts apple brandy (1 oz.)
2 parts sweet vermouth (1 oz.)
Yellow Chartreuse (1 tbsp.)

Combine all ingredients with cracked ice in a cocktail shaker. Shake well and strain into chilled cocktail glass.

WARSAW COCKTAIL

4 parts vodka (2 oz.)
2 parts blackberry brandy (1 oz.)
1 part dry vermouth (½ oz.)
Fresh lemon juice (1 tbsp.)

Combine ingredients with cracked ice in a cocktail shaker. Shake well and strain into chilled cocktail glass.

WASHINGTON COCKTAIL

4 parts dry vermouth (2 oz.)
2 parts brandy (1 oz.)
Sugar syrup (½ tsp.)
Dash Angostura bitters

Combine ingredients with cracked ice in a cocktail shaker. Shake well and strain into chilled cocktail glass.

WASSAIL BOWL

Ale (6 12-oz. bottles)
Cream sherry (1 cup or 8 oz.)
Bar sugar (½ cup)
Allspice (½ tsp.)
Ground cinnamon (1 tsp.)
Feshly ground nutmeg (2 tsp.)
Powdered ginger (¼ tsp.)
Lemon slice

In a large saucepan or stock pot, heat the sherry and one bottle of ale. Do not boil. Add sugar and spices and stir until dissolved. Add remaining ale and stir. Let stand at room temperature for about 3 hours. Pour into punch bowl and garnish with lemon slices. Serves 10.

WATERBURY COCKTAIL

4 parts brandy (2 oz.)
2 parts fresh lime juice (1 oz.)
Grenadine (1 tsp.)
Sugar syrup (1 tsp.)
1 egg white

Combine ingredients with cracked ice in a cocktail shaker. Shake vigorously and strain into chilled cocktail glass.

WEDDING BELLE COCKTAIL

4 parts gin (2 oz.)
3 parts Dubonnet rouge (1½ oz.)
1 part kirschwasser (½ oz.)
1 part fresh orange juice (½ oz.)

Combine ingredients with cracked ice in a cocktail shaker. Shake well and strain into chilled cocktail glass.

WEEP-NO-MORE

4 parts Dubonnet rouge (2 oz.)
3 parts brandy (1½ oz.)
Maraschino liqueur (1 tsp.)
2 parts fresh lime juice (1 oz.)

Combine ingredients with cracked ice in a cocktail shaker. Shake well and strain into chilled cocktail glass.

WEMBLY COCKTAIL

4 parts gin (2 oz.)
1 part dry vermouth (½ oz.)
Apricot brandy (1 tsp.)
Apple brandy (1 tsp.)

Combine all ingredients with cracked ice in a cocktail shaker. Shake well and strain into chilled cocktail glass.

WHIRLAWAY

4 parts bourbon (2 oz.)
2 parts triple sec (1 oz.)
3 – 5 dashes Angostura bitters
Sparkling water

Combine all ingredients, except sparkling water, with cracked ice in a cocktail shaker. Shake well and pour into chilled old fashioned glass. Top off with sparkling water.

WHISKEY COCKTAIL

6 parts blended whiskey (3 oz.)
Sugar syrup (1 tsp.)
Dash Angostura bitters

Combine ingredients with cracked ice in a cocktail shaker. Shake well and strain into chilled cocktail glass.

WHISKEY COLLINS

6 parts whiskey (3 oz.)
4 parts fresh lemon juice (2 oz.)
1 part sugar syrup (½ oz.)
Sparkling water
Maraschino cherry
Orange slice

Combine all ingredients, except fruit and sparkling water, in a chilled collins glass filled with ice cubes. Fill with sparkling water and stir gently. Garnish with fruit.

WHISKEY COOLER

4 parts blended whiskey (2 oz.)
Bar sugar (½ tsp.)
Sparkling water
Lemon peel

Mix whiskey with sugar in the bottom of a chilled collins glass. Add ice cubes and fill with sparkling water. Stir gently and garnish with lemon peel.

WHISKEY DAISY

6 parts whiskey (3 oz.)
2 parts fresh lemon juice (1 oz.)
Grenadine (1 tbsp.)
Sugar syrup (1 tsp.)
Sparkling water
Orange slice

Combine all ingredients, except
orange slice and sparkling water, in a
cocktail shaker with cracked ice.
Shake well. Pour into chilled highball
glass. Top off with sparkling water, stir
gently, and garnish with orange slice.

WHISKEY FIX

4 parts blended whiskey
(2 oz.)
2 parts fresh lemon juice (1 oz.)
Bar sugar (½ tsp.)
Orange twist

Combine all ingredients, orange twist,
in a cocktail shaker with cracked ice.
Shake well and strain into chilled
highball glass over ice cubes. Drop
orange twist in drink.

WHISKEY FLIP

4 parts blended whiskey (2 oz.)
2 parts half-and-half (1 oz.)
Bar sugar (½ tsp.)
1 whole egg
Freshly grated nutmeg

Combine all ingredients, except
nutmeg, with cracked ice in a cocktail
shaker. Shake vigorously and strain
into chilled sour glass. Sprinkle with
nutmeg.

WHISKEY MILK
PUNCH

6 parts blended whiskey (3 oz.)
1 cup milk (8 oz.)
Sugar syrup (1 tsp.)
Freshly grated nutmeg

Combine all ingredients, except
nutmeg, with cracked ice in a cocktail
shaker. Shake well and strain into
chilled collins glass. Sprinkle with
nutmeg.

WHISKEY RICKEY

4 parts whiskey (2 oz.)
2 parts fresh lime juice (1 oz.)
Sparkling water
Lime slice

Pour whiskey and lime juice into a
chilled highball glass over ice cubes.
Fill with sparkling water and stir
gently. Garnish with lime slice.

WHISKEY SANGAREE

4 parts blended whiskey
(2 oz.)
Ruby port (1 tbsp.)
Bar sugar (½ tsp.)
Water (1 tsp.)
2 parts sparkling water (1 oz.)

In the bottom of a chilled old-
fashioned glass, dissolve sugar in
water, add blended whiskey and stir.
Fill glass with ice cubes and sparkling
water. Float port on top.

WHISKEY SLING

4 parts blended whiskey
(2 oz.)
1 part fresh lemon juice (1 oz.)
Water (1 tsp.)
Bar sugar (1 tsp.)
Orange twist

In the bottom of a mixing glass,
dissolve sugar in water and lemon
juice. Add whiskey and stir. Pour over
ice cubes into a chilled old-fashioned
glass and garnish with orange twist.

WHISKEY SOUR

4 parts blended whiskey
(2 oz.)
2 parts fresh lemon juice (2 oz.)
Sugar syrup (1 tsp.)
Maraschino cherry
Orange slice

Combine liquid ingredients with
cracked ice in a cocktail shaker. Shake
well and strain into chilled cocktail
glass. Garnish with fruit.

WHISPERS OF THE FROST

2 parts ruby port (1 oz.)
2 parts fino sherry (1 oz.)
2 parts bourbon (1 oz.)
Sugar syrup (½ tsp.)
Lemon twist

Combine all ingredients with cracked ice in a cocktail shaker. Shake well and strain into chilled cocktail glass.

WHITE LILY

4 parts gin (2 oz.)
3 parts triple sec (1½ oz.)
3 parts light rum (1½ oz.)
Pernod (¼ tsp.)

Combine all ingredients with cracked ice in a cocktail shaker. Shake well and strain into chilled cocktail glass.

WHITE LION

4 parts dark rum (2 oz.)
2 part fresh lemon juice (1 oz.)
1 part orgeat (almond) syrup (½ oz.)
Raspberry syrup (¼ tsp.)

Combine all ingredients with cracked ice in a cocktail shaker. Shake well and strain into chilled cocktail glass.

WHITE ROSE

4 parts gin (2 oz.)
2 parts maraschino liqueur
(1 oz.)
4 parts fresh orange juice (2 oz.)
2 parts fresh lime juice (1 oz.)
Sugar syrup (1 tsp.)
1 egg white

Combine ingredients with cracked ice
in a cocktail shaker. Shake well and
strain into chilled cocktail glass.

WHITE RUSSIAN

4 parts vodka (2 oz.)
2 parts coffee liqueur (1 oz.)
2 parts half-and-half (1 oz.)

Combine ingredients with cracked ice
in a cocktail shaker. Shake well and
pour into chilled old-fashioned glass.

WHITE WAY COCKTAIL

4 parts gin (2 oz.)
2 parts white crème de menthe (1 oz.)

Combine ingredients with cracked ice
in a cocktail shaker. Shake well and
strain into chilled cocktail glass.

WHITE SPIDER

4 parts vodka (2 oz.)
2 parts white crème de menthe
(1 oz.)

Combine ingredients with cracked ice
in a cocktail shaker. Shake well and
strain into chilled cocktail glass.

WHY NOT?

4 parts gin (2 oz.)
2 parts apricot brandy (1 oz.)
2 parts dry vermouth (1 oz.)
Fresh lemon juice (¼ tsp.)

Combine ingredients with cracked ice
in a cocktail shaker and shake well.
Strain into chilled cocktail glass.

WOMAN WARRIOR

6 parts vodka (3 oz.)
2 parts blue Curaçao (1 oz.)
2 parts fresh lime juice

Combine ingredients with cracked ice
in a cocktail shaker. Shake well and
strain into chilled cocktail glass.

WONDERFUL TOWN

4 parts peppermint syrup
(2 oz.)
2 parts chocolate syrup (1 oz.)
Sparkling water
Fresh mint sprig

Mix syrups in the bottom of a chilled
highball glass. Fill glass with ice cubes
and top off with sparkling water. Stir
gently and garnish with mint.

Note: Use a thin chocolate syrup, such
as Fox's U-Bet

WOO-WOO

4 parts vodka (2 oz.)
4 parts peach schnapps (2 oz.)
8 parts cranberry juice (4 oz.)

Pour ingredients into chilled highball
glass over ice cubes. Stir.

WOODSTOCK

4 parts gin (2 oz.)
2 part fresh lemon juice (1 oz.)
Maple syrup (1 tbsp.)
Dash orange bitters

Combine ingredients with cracked ice
in a cocktail shaker. Shake well and
strain into chilled cocktail glass.

WOODWARD

4 parts scotch (2 oz.)
1 part dry vermouth (½ oz.)
1 part grapefruit juice (½ oz.)

Combine ingredients with cracked ice
in a cocktail shaker. Shake well and
strain into chilled cocktail glass.

X, Y, Z

X.Y.Z. COCKTAIL

4 parts light rum (2 oz.)
2 parts white Curaçao (1 oz.)
1 part fresh lemon juice (½ oz.)

Combine ingredients with cracked ice
in a cocktail shaker. Shake well and
strain into chilled cocktail glass.

XANADU

4 parts guava nectar (2 oz.)
4 parts fresh lime juice (2 oz.)
2 parts falernum (1 oz.)
2 parts half-and-half (1 oz.)

Combine ingredients with cracked ice
in a blender. Blend at low speed until
smooth. Pour into chilled champagne
flute.

XANTHIA

4 parts gin (2 oz.)
3 parts cherry brandy (1½ oz.)
3 parts yellow Chartreuse (1½ oz.)

Combine all ingredients with cracked
ice in a cocktail shaker. Shake well
and strain into chilled cocktail glass.

XERES COCKTAIL

6 parts manzanilla sherry
(3 oz.)
Dash orange bitters
Orange twist

Stir ingredients, except for orange
twist, with cracked ice in a mixing
glass and strain into cocktail glass.
Garnish with orange twist.

YALE COCKTAIL

4 parts gin (2 oz.)
1 part dry vermouth (½ oz.)
Maraschino liqueur (¼ tsp.)
3 – 5 dashes orange bitters

Combine all ingredients with cracked ice
in a cocktail shaker. Shake well and
strain into chilled cocktail glass.

YELLOW FINGERS

4 parts gin (2 oz.)
2 parts blackberry brandy
(1 oz.)
2 parts crème de bananes (1 oz.)
2 parts half-and-half (1 oz.)

Combine all ingredients with cracked
ice in a cocktail shaker. Shake well
and strain into chilled cocktail glass.

YELLOW PARROT

4 parts brandy (2 oz)
4 parts Pernod (2 oz.)
4 parts yellow Chartreuse (2 oz.)

Combine ingredients with cracked ice
in a cocktail shaker. Strain into
chilled cocktail glass.

YODEL

6 parts Fernet Branca (3 oz.)
8 parts fresh orange juice
(4 oz.)
Sparkling water

Pour liqueur and juice into chilled
highball glass over ice cubes. Stir and
fill with sparkling water.

YORSH

4 parts vodka
Beer

Fill a mug ¾ full with beer. Pour the
vodka into the beer and drink it.

ZAZA COCKTAIL

4 parts Dubonnet rouge
(2 oz.)
2 parts gin (1 oz.)
Dash orange bitters
Orange twist

Combine all ingredients, except
orange twist, with cracked ice in a
cocktail shaker. Shake well and strain
into chilled cocktail glass. Garnish
with orange twist.

ZOMBIE

ZOMBIE

4 parts dark rum (2 oz.)
4 parts light rum (2 oz.)
2 parts 151-proof rum (1 oz.)
2 parts triple sec (1 oz.)
Pernod (1 tsp.)
2 parts fresh lime juice (1 oz.)
2 parts fresh orange juice (1 oz.)
2 parts pineapple juice (1 oz.)
2 parts guava nectar (1 oz.)
Grenadine (1 tbsp.)
Orgeat (almond) syrup (1 tbsp.)
Fresh mint sprig
Pineapple spear

Combine all ingredients, except mint
and pineapple spear, with cracked ice
in a blender. Blend until smooth. Pour
into chilled collins glass and garnish
with pineapple and mint sprig.

ZESTY COOLER

2 parts fresh lime juice
(1 oz.)
Ginger beer
Lime wedge

Pour lime juice into a chilled beer
mug over ice cubes. Fill with ginger
beer and stir gently. Garnish with lime
wedge.

INDEX

Dubonnet, 36, 37, 41, 47, 57, 68, 69,
   97, 145, 156, 159, 166, 172, 177,
   179, 189, 195, 196, 200, 216,
   225, 233, 240, 244
Eggs, 39, 42, 63, 86, 95, 98, 110,
   127, 148, 150, 178, 187, 195,
   198, 207, 209, 210, 212, 222,
   225, 232, 241
Egg white, 29, 36, 40, 41, 42, 48, 49,
   59, 66, 69, 71, 76, 78, 82, 85, 89,
   96, 99, 102, 106, 117, 125, 136,
   140, 143, 145, 150, 161, 164,
   167, 175, 178, 182, 183, 187,
   191, 195, 207, 211, 223, 227,
   237, 240, 243
Egg yolk, 59, 83, 85, 91, 101, 107,
   118, 131, 147, 163, 187, 197,
   226, 230
Falernum, 72, 135, 141, 171, 186,
   233, 244
Fernet Branca, 244
Forbidden fruit, 50
Framboise, 195
Frangelico, 34, 106, 197
Fruit juice, 109
Galliano, 42, 59, 68, 110, 117, 118,
   122, 123, 137
Garlic, 110, 122
Gin, 29, 30, 31, 35, 36, 39, 40, 41,
   43, 45, 46, 47, 48, 49, 50, 53, 54,
   56, 58, 59, 65, 66, 67, 69, 75, 76,
   77, 78, 79, 80, 84, 85, 87, 88, 89,
   90, 93, 94, 95, 96, 97, 98, 100,
   102, 103, 104, 105, 106, 110,
   112, 113, 114, 115, 116, 117,
   118, 119, 120, 121, 122, 123,
   124, 125, 126, 127, 129, 130,
   131, 135, 136, 138, 139, 141,
   144, 145, 146, 148, 149, 150,
   151, 156, 158, 161, 162, 163,
   164, 165, 166, 167, 168, 169,
   170, 171, 172, 175, 176, 177,
   178, 179, 182, 184, 185, 186,
   189, 190, 191, 192, 193, 194,
   195, 197, 199, 200, 205, 206,
   207, 211, 214, 217, 218, 219,
   220, 222, 224, 225, 226, 230,
   231, 232, 233, 234, 235, 236,
   237, 239, 240, 242, 243, 244
Ginger ale, 36, 51, 69, 78, 113, 122,
   126, 127, 139, 140, 144, 146,
   152, 167, 168, 171, 172, 173,
   176, 188, 195, 196, 207, 210,
   212, 217, 218, 222, 227
Ginger, 165
Ginger beer, 51, 105, 135, 164, 222,
   245
Ginger brandy (see Brandy, ginger)
Ginger wine, 116
Grand Marnier, 42, 88, 119, 146
Grape juice, 120, 151, 155, 189
Grape juice, white, 102, 119, 190
Grapefruit juice, 29, 36, 40, 53, 85,
   87, 119, 128, 132, 152, 160, 166,
   170, 174, 178, 186, 189, 190,
   191, 199, 200, 205, 207, 217,
   225, 233, 243
Grappa, 110
Green chile, 122
Grenadine, 33, 34, 35, 36, 38, 47,
   49, 59, 61, 63, 64, 75, 78, 80, 82,
   85, 90, 92, 93, 94, 95, 96, 97, 98,
   99, 102, 103, 104, 106, 114, 123,
   124, 125, 134, 135, 139, 146,
   151, 152, 157, 160, 161, 165,
   167, 170, 171, 176, 176, 179,
   182, 187, 191, 193, 194, 196,
   197, 207, 209, 210, 212, 225,
   227, 229, 230, 237, 238, 239,
   241, 245
Guava juice, 166, 239
Guava nectar, 44, 171, 186, 239,
   244, 245
Half-and-half, 30, 31, 32, 35, 41, 42,
   43, 45, 53, 55, 61, 62, 63, 65, 69,
   70, 75, 76, 81, 83, 85, 86, 87, 90,
   103, 106, 117, 120, 125, 130,
   131, 135, 136, 144, 147, 167,
   170, 171, 172, 174, 175, 176,
   177, 178, 180, 182, 183, 187,
   191, 192, 194, 197, 210, 212,
   214, 215, 220, 223, 225, 232,
   233, 235, 236, 241, 243, 244
Hazelnut syrup, 125, 170
Honey, 36, 48, 61, 71, 117, 126, 128,
   129, 132, 148, 149, 164, 165,
   175, 180, 204, 205, 222
Horseradish, 29, 53, 67, 84, 237
Ice cream, vanilla, 118, 217, 231
Ice cream, 32, 149, 171, 211
Irish mist, 132, 133
Italian syrup, 134
Jagermeister, 31, 121, 207, 211, 233
Jalapeño pepper, 200, 201, 214, 230

Kahlua, 140

Kirsch (see also *Cherry Brandy*), 31

Kirschwasser (see also *Cherry Brandy*), 42, 51, 53, 57, 68, 80, 81, 94, 104, 121, 141, 142, 145, 148, 169, 173, 182, 192, 235, 238, 240

Kummel, 31

Lemon, 36, 40, 106, 165, 166, 200, 223,

Lemon juice, 30, 33, 36, 37, 38, 39, 40, 41, 45, 47, 48, 49, 50, 53, 55, 57, 59, 60, 61, 62, 63, 64, 65, 67, 68, 69, 71, 72, 73, 77, 78, 79, 80, 81, 82, 84, 85, 87, 88, 90, 92, 93, 94, 95, 96, 97, 98, 99, 103, 104, 105, 106, 107, 109, 110, 111, 112, 113, 114, 115, 116, 117, 118, 119, 120, 121, 123, 125, 126, 128, 129, 131, 132, 133, 134, 135, 136, 138, 139, 140, 141, 143, 144, 145, 146, 148, 149, 150, 151, 154, 158, 158, 160, 161, 162, 163, 164, 166, 167, 169,170, 173, 176, 177, 180, 182, 183, 185, 186, 187, 190, 191, 192, 193, 194, 195, 196, 197, 199, 200, 202, 203, 204, 205, 207, 208, 209, 210, 211, 212, 214, 216, 217, 218, 219, 220, 222, 224, 225, 226, 227, 228, 230, 232, 233, 234, 235, 236, 237, 238, 239, 240, 241, 242, 242, 244

Lemon sorbet, 78

Lemon street, 132

Lemon-lime soda, 36,179

Lemonade, 90, 125, 182, 208, 218

Lillet, 29, 90, 93, 121, 126, 189, 206

Limes, 40, 200

Lime juice, 29, 31, 32, 34, 35, 36, 38, 39, 40, 41, 42, 43, 44, 45, 46, 48, 49, 50, 53, 54, 55, 57, 59, 60, 64, 66, 67, 70, 71, 74, 75, 76, 78, 79, 81, 83, 84, 85, 88, 90, 93, 94, 95, 96, 99, 100, 101, 102, 103, 104, 105, 106, 107, 108, 109, 110, 114, 116, 117, 118,121, 122, 124, 126, 127, 130, 132, 134, 135, 136, 137, 138, 139, 140, 141, 142, 144, 146, 147, 148, 151, 152, 153, 154, 155, 157,

158, 160, 163, 164, 165, 166, 167, 170, 171, 172, 173, 174, 175, 176, 177, 179, 180, 181, 182, 183, 185, 186, 187, 189, 191, 193, 194, 195, 196, 197, 199, 200, 201, 202, 203, 207, 209, 211, 212, 213, 214, 218, 220, 221, 222, 224, 225, 226, 227, 230, 233, 234, 237, 239, 240, 241, 243, 244, 245

Lime juice, Rose's, 113, 227, 238

Lime liqueur, 148

Limeade, 67

Liqueur, apricot, 106, 117, 173, 191

Liqueur, banana, 42, 83

Liqueur, cherry, 35, 68, 76, 77, 81, 105, 130, 234

Liqueur, coconut, 41

Liqueur, coffee, 34, 48, 56, 58, 65, 70, 75, 85,87, 111, 118, 125, 134, 135, 140, 141, 160, 162, 165, 171, 186, 197, 215, 217, 226, 232, 233, 243

Liqueur, Irish cream, 165,197,212

Liqueur, maraschino, 40, 43, 54, 55, 57, 62, 74, 77, 84, 87, 89, 96, 100, 102, 119, 123, 131, 145, 148, 149, 157, 158, 164, 165, 172, 182, 187, 190, 202, 207, 211, 217, 224, 225, 226, 233, 234, 235, 240, 243, 244

Liqueur, melon, 135, 144, 158, 207

Liqueur, orange, 191

Liqueur, peach, 88, 168, 176

Liqueur, raspberry, 36, 64, 117, 132, 239

Liqueur, strawberry, 46, 105

Liqueur, vanilla, 53, 90

Loganberry juice, 101

Madeira, 42, 59, 62, 92, 151, 163, 168, 189, 192

Mango, 153

Manzanilla sherry (see *Sherry, manzanilla*)

Maple syrup, 67, 123, 165, 243

Maraschino cherry juice, 31, 35, 125

Maraschino liqueur (see *Liqueur, Maraschino*)

Mescal, 214

Milk, 57, 61, 64, 68, 69, 86, 98, 114, 127, 132, 139, 161, 163, 164, 168, 186, 210, 231, 241